Black America Series

Madison County Mississippi

BLACK AMERICA SERIES

MADISON COUNTY MISSISSIPPI

Jennifer E. Cheeks-Collins

ARCADIA PUBLISHING

ISBN 978-0-7385-1442-0

Published by Arcadia Publishing
Charleston, South Carolina

Printed in the United States of America

Library of Congress Catalog Card Number: 2002104392

For all general information contact Arcadia Publishing at:
Telephone 843-853-2070
Fax 843-853-0044
E-Mail sales@arcadiapublishing.com
For customer service and orders:
Toll-Free 1-888-313-2665

Visit us on the Internet at www.arcadiapublishing.com

Contents

ACKNOWLEDGMENTS

This publication is dedicated to the citizens of Madison County, past, present, and future. I could not have completed this book without the sincere generosity of these men and women, and I thank everyone who trusted me with their photos and believed in this project. Thank you for the encouragement and motivation you have given.

I give special thanks to Katie White and the Arcadia Publishing team. You and your team are to be commended for the avenue you provide for historic preservation.

Special thanks also goes to Jo Ann Gordon and staff at the Canton Convention and Visitors Bureau in Canton, Mississippi, and the Mississippi Department of Archives and History. This book is possible only because of the following people: Emma Barnes, Virgie Bartee, Eddie B. Berry, Stella Berry, Edward and Barbara Blackmon, Flonzie Goodloe Brown, Callie Bouldin, Bettie Cain, Maggie Cain, Thelma Cain, James and Alice Cheeks, Landres Cheeks, Clarice Coney, Tommie Garner, Mary L. Hart, Umble Hawkins, Louise Hayes, Polly S. Jacobs, L.V. Lipsey, Ruth Luckett, Modestine McCloud, Thelma Garner Myers, Alice Reed, James and Francis Sanders, Alice Scott, James Sims Jr., Cora Smith, Mrs. Bennie Smith, Carrie Smoot, Marie Stringfellow, Elenora Tate, Creasy Woodard, and the Velma Jackson High School.

God has put the following people in my life as positive influences and they give me encouragement: Joseph and Gail Basar, Tiana A. Budgewater, Atanyia Cheeks, Janet Cheeks, Lee and Joyce Collins, Sharon Collins, Annette Draine and family, Audwin and Angela Gray, Tatricia Bates Harris, Frederick Hart, Mary Hart, Ronnie Harvey, Yolanda Jackson, LaShonda E. Johnson, James and Thelma Myers, Jamila Myers, Keah Myers, and, last but not least, Shundra Summers. I greatly appreciate everything you all have done for me, individually and collectively. You all have given me an abundance of strength and courage. I thank you for your motivating words and most of all, your prayers.

To my parents—I thank you for the gift of life. Mom, you have gone above and beyond the call of duty in helping make this project come full circle. I could have never done this without you. Know that I admire you and you are an inspiration to me. You have set an excellent example, fit for all women to follow. Know that I am forever grateful for your love and trust. I love you!

Dad, you are never short for words and I really love that about you. I can see all the good that is in your heart. I thank you for the struggling in the 1960s—you didn't have to fight for my freedom and civil rights, but you did. Thank you for being James—I love you! Mom and Dad, I could have never completed this task with out your help. I dedicate this publication to you.

To my husband Keith—you are such an amazing person. I honor you for being a strong, loving, and giving husband. I sincerely thank you for always supporting me in things I believe in strongly. I cherish our love for one another, our relationship, and our family. I love you!

To my daughter, Kamryn Madison, I pray I can be a living example to you. May God forever guide your footsteps, comfort you, and live in your heart. You are such a blessing to our lives. Mommie and Daddy love you!

I send special prayers to heaven for everyone affected by the events of September 11, 2001. You will never be forgotten.

Lord, I thank you for all your greatness . . .

Jennifer E. Cheeks-Collins

INTRODUCTION

The land we know as Madison County holds a rich heritage of African-American history. Like most Southern states, Mississippi's African-American population consisted largely of slaves. The county was adorned with plantations worked primarily by slave labor. As the institution of slavery progressed in Madison County, the African-American population rapidly outnumbered the Caucasian population. African Americans—with few exceptions—were slaves in Madison County. People of color outnumbered other races, four to one. Once the institution of slavery was abolished, the African-American population remained steadfast.

After slavery, African Americans were faced with numerous obstacles. Most newly freed people of color were uneducated, had little or no resources, and some even found themselves homeless. Many ex-slaves chose not to leave their former owners' plantations, and they remained on as sharecroppers. Sharecropping became a very large and profitable business for white landowners and a very small number of black landowners. Often times, many families would live on a plantation and farm the land for the landowner. The sharecroppers or "tenants" were paid very little or even nothing because of debt owed to the landowner. Blacks who lived closer to the downtown areas faced poverty as well. Many lived in substandard housing and panhandled along the train tracks and in front of downtown stores because of lack of resources and revenue.

The lives of prosperous people of color were visible in the county. These people were rare, and they stood out vividly in the black community. Many people of color were determined to live a better quality of life. By the early 1930s, Madison County had black doctors, black dentists, and many black business owners.

Black citizens of Madison County became educated people, landowners, and various types of professionals. These achievements, still, came with many hardships. In the 1950s and 1960s Madison County experienced radical changes in the black community. People of color began to take a firm stand for racial equality and they demanded change through protests and marches. The Civil Rights era was one of the most empowering periods of change for blacks in Madison County. During those days, blacks fought hard for use of public facilities, better schools, equal voting rights, and fare wages. Change came through a handful of strong-willed Civil Rights workers in Madison County, and these men and women are to be commended for their tremendous efforts.

CORE (Congress of Racial Equality) and COFO (Council of Federated Organizations) chapters were started in Madison County in the 1960s. CORE and COFO, as well as other organizations like the National Association for the Advancement of Colored People (NAACP), gave blacks the much-needed support to help change the injustices of the era. Demonstrations, protests, boycotts, and marches made the 1960s memorable to both black and white citizens in Madison County. Many well-known leaders in the Civil Rights movement marched through Madison County, such as Dr. Martin Luther King Jr., Andrew Young, and Stokely Carmichael. Many white Northerners and some liberal-minded white Southerners spent summers in Madison County working for equal rights for minorities. The Civil Rights era will be forever embedded in the souls of blacks in Madison County. The pride and vivid memories of the era are clear to the hearts of Civil Rights pioneers who are still alive today. Many others have passed on, and we owe a significant debt of gratitude to them.

The 1970s and 1980s brought great hope to African Americans in Madison County. By this time the Civil Rights Bill was passed by Congress, giving blacks equal rights under the law. More

African Americans were taking part in higher education. Black businesses began to prosper in Madison County. Professional African Americans are now a part of the norm, and blacks can seen in most any profession in Madison County. Attorneys, doctors, educators, politicians, and many other noteworthy African-American professionals stand among social and economic classes that were once predominantly occupied by white citizens.

Black America: Madison County is intended to showcase and celebrate the lives of African American from all walks of life. Whether lawyers or homemakers, doctors or farmers, this book is meant to honor all African Americans and their contributions to Madison County, Mississippi.

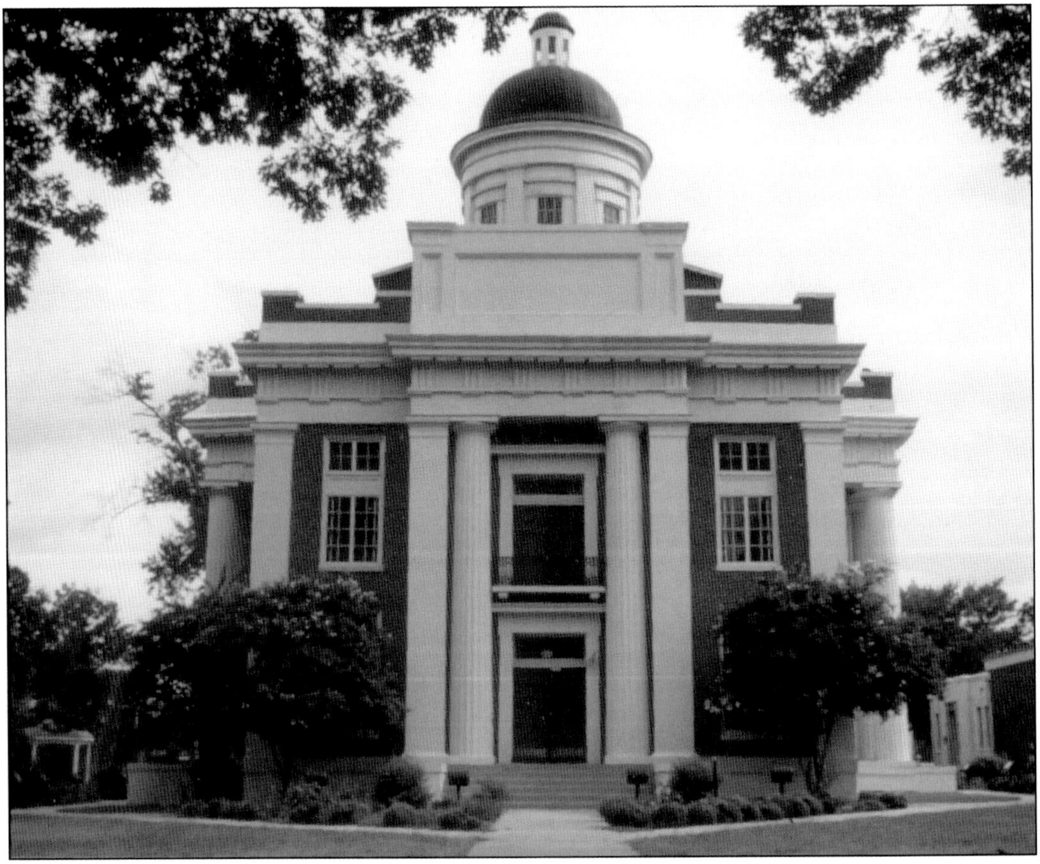

The Madison County Courthouse is located in historic downtown Canton. The courthouse was completed in 1857. This building is the third courthouse that was built in Madison County and is listed on the National Register of Historic Places. The structure above was built in the Greek Revival style, typical of most Southern courthouses built during that time. The courthouse maintains most of its original appearance, although changes have occurred within the courthouse to accommodate modern-day life.

One

Madison County Yesterday

"There is a way to look at the past. Don't hide from it. It will catch you if you don't repeat it."
Pearl Bailey, 1993

Life in Madison County in the past was typical of most Southern counties. African Americans were faced with slavery, sharecropping, segregation, and many other hardships. African Americans first came to Madison County in the early 1800s. Most were slaves in the county's early existence. Very few people of color were free. Life for African Americans immediately after the Civil War was not very different than before war, as they still faced many hardships. However, the churches organized in Madison County gave black residents a spiritual outlet to deal with their grief and oppression. Economically, African Americans were struggling during this period, but some people of color were resourceful in owning small business and farming their own land. There is much is to honor about Madison County in days long passed, and about the hard-working men and women who shaped the character of the black community.

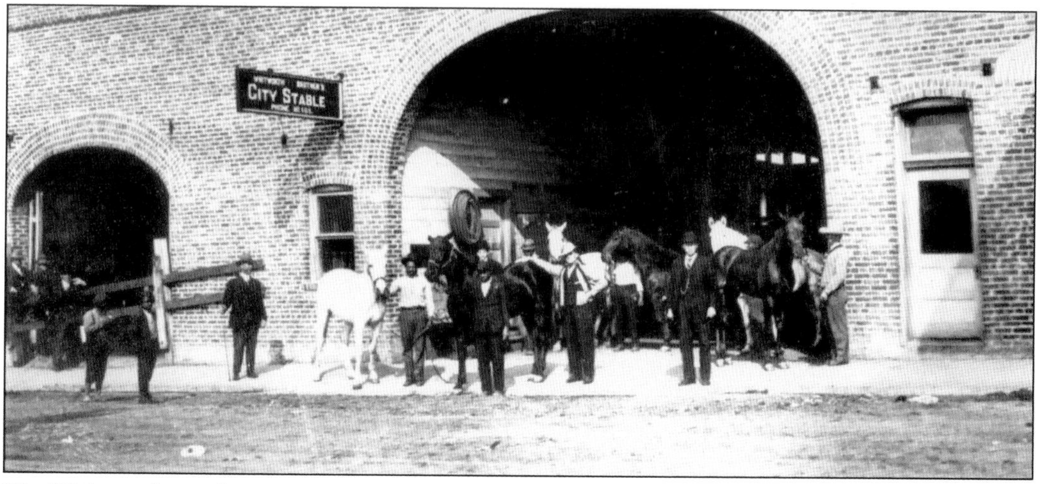

The Whitworth Brothers City Stable employed African-American men as stable hands. These men took great care of the horses; they knew the personality of each horse as if it were their own child. (Courtesy of the Mississippi Department of Archives and History.)

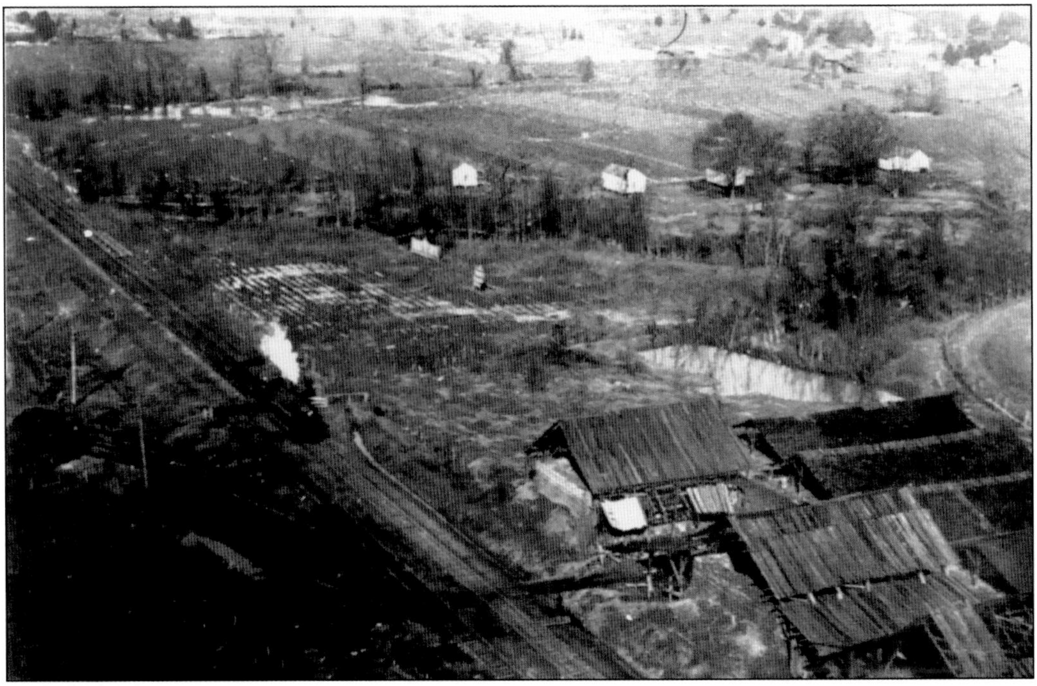

This bird's-eye view snapshot of Canton, Mississippi shows the countryside and rural areas in the outskirts of the city. This photo was taken south of Canton in the early 1900s. (Courtesy of the Mississippi Department of Archives and History.)

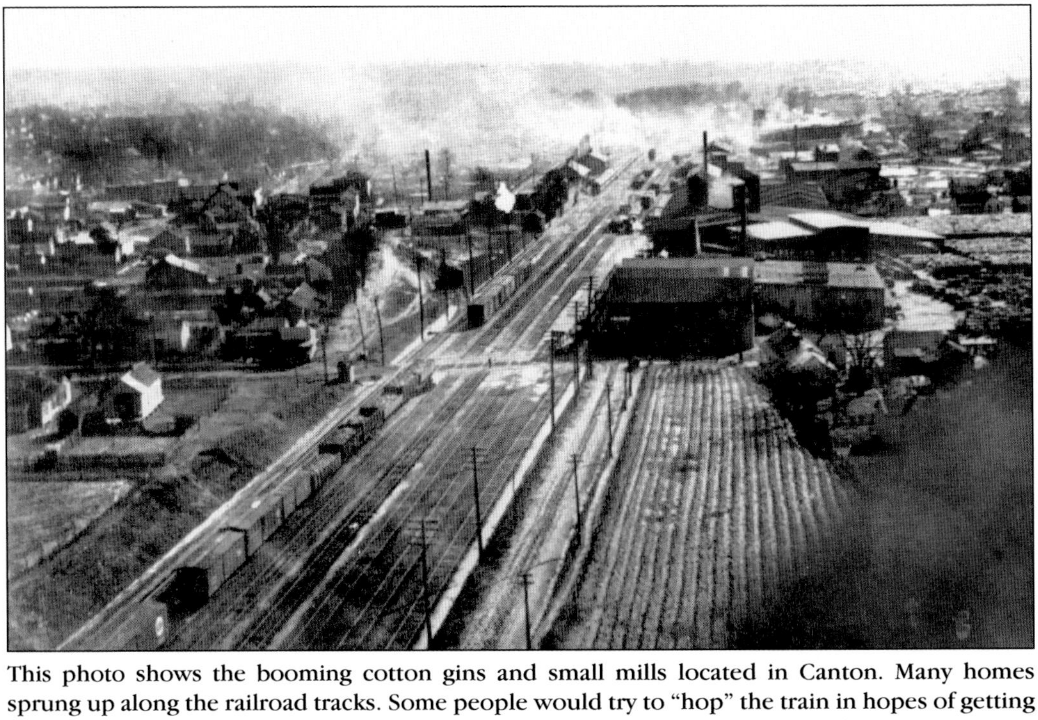

This photo shows the booming cotton gins and small mills located in Canton. Many homes sprung up along the railroad tracks. Some people would try to "hop" the train in hopes of getting a free ride northward. (Courtesy of the Mississippi Department of Archives and History.)

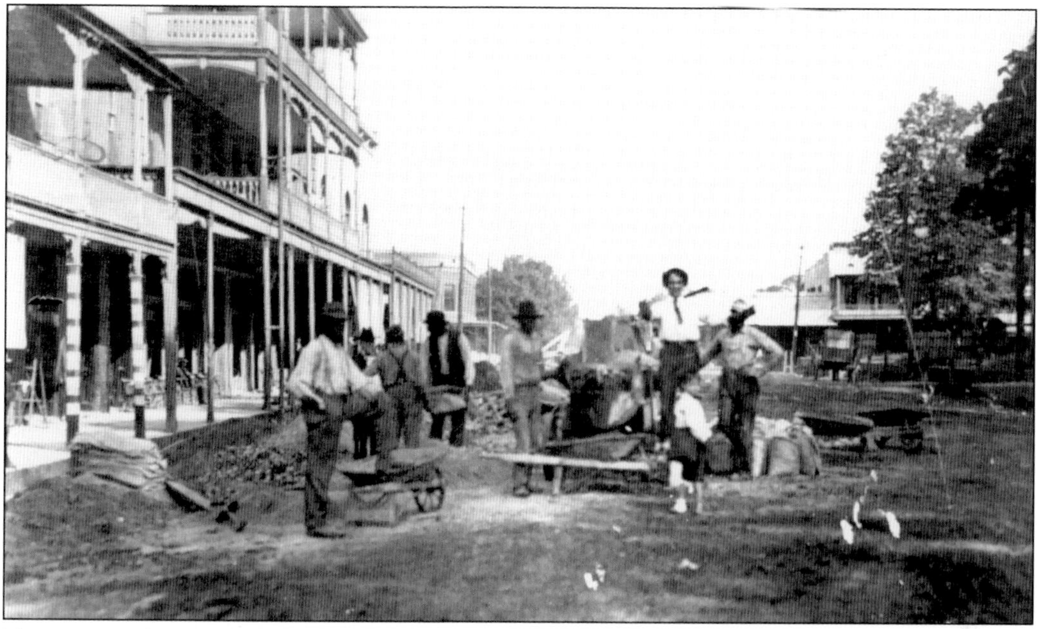

The men in this photo are seen paving Union Street on the west side of the courthouse square in Canton. This 1920s photo shows a rather young Canton in times of dirt roads, saloons, and horses and buggies. To the left of the men is what was then the very popular Trolio Hotel. (Courtesy of the Mississippi Department of Archives and History.)

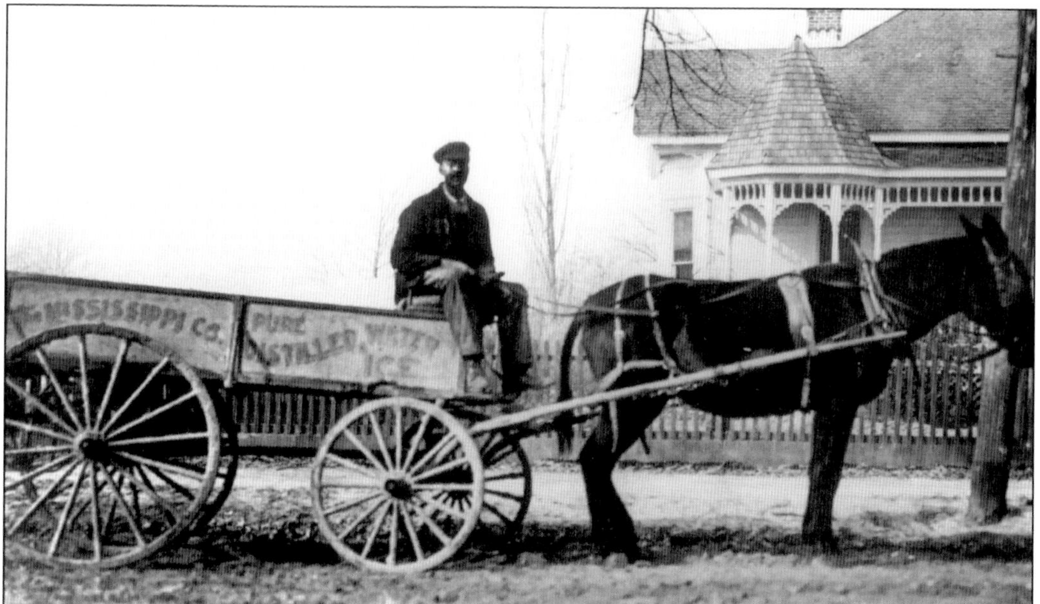

This unidentified gentleman delivered pure distilled water and ice to the citizens in Canton and the surrounding area for the Mississippi Ice Co. Most people did not have an electric icebox for freezing the household ice. Therefore, a delivery service was almost vital. This was considered a good job because, during these early years, most African Americans were sharecroppers or domestic workers. (Courtesy of the Mississippi Department of Archives and History.)

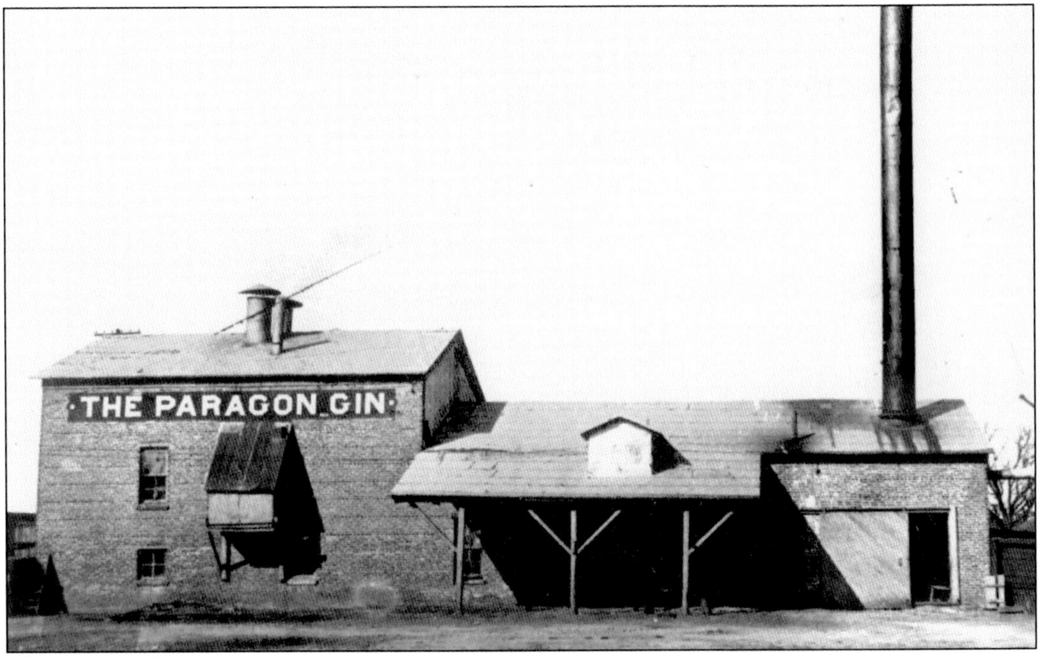

The Paragon Cotton Gin is pictured in the early 1900s. This was a booming and thriving gin in Canton. (Courtesy of the Mississippi Department of Archives and History.)

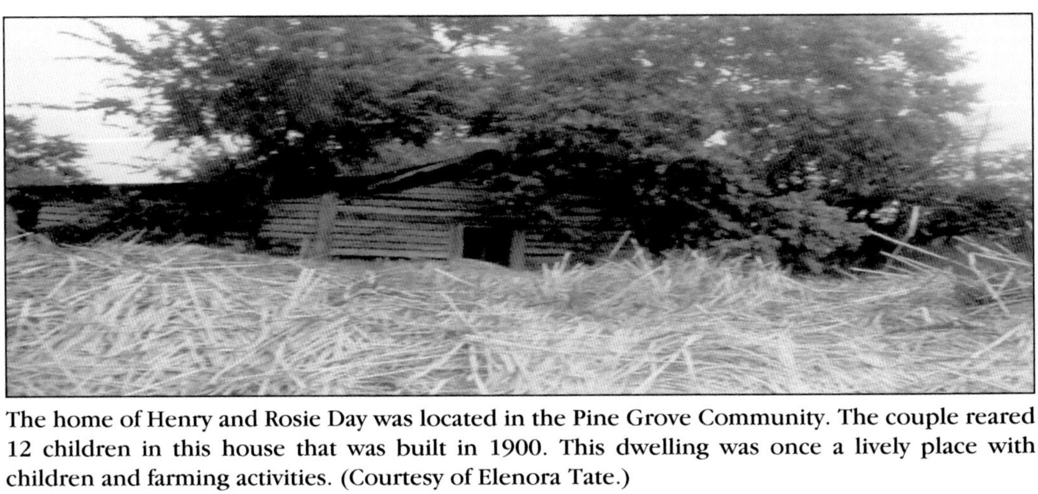

The home of Henry and Rosie Day was located in the Pine Grove Community. The couple reared 12 children in this house that was built in 1900. This dwelling was once a lively place with children and farming activities. (Courtesy of Elenora Tate.)

This ex-slave from Madison County was simply known as "Moma." She is seen here smiling, sitting in her old rocker, and holding her old stick. She is thought to be 93 in this photo from 1920. (Courtesy of Creasy Woodard.)

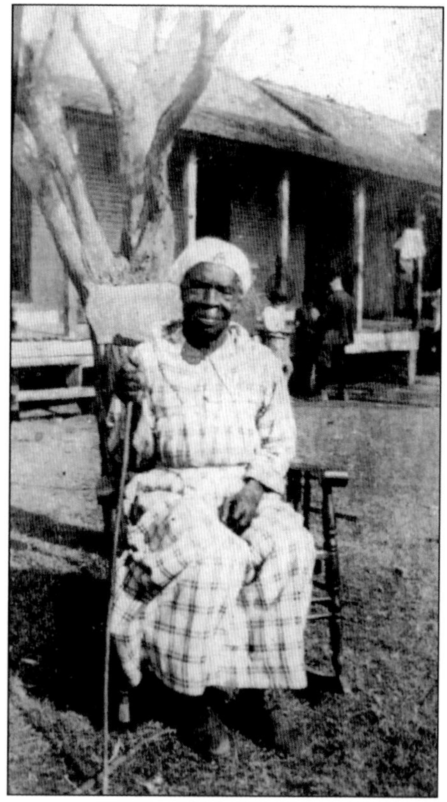

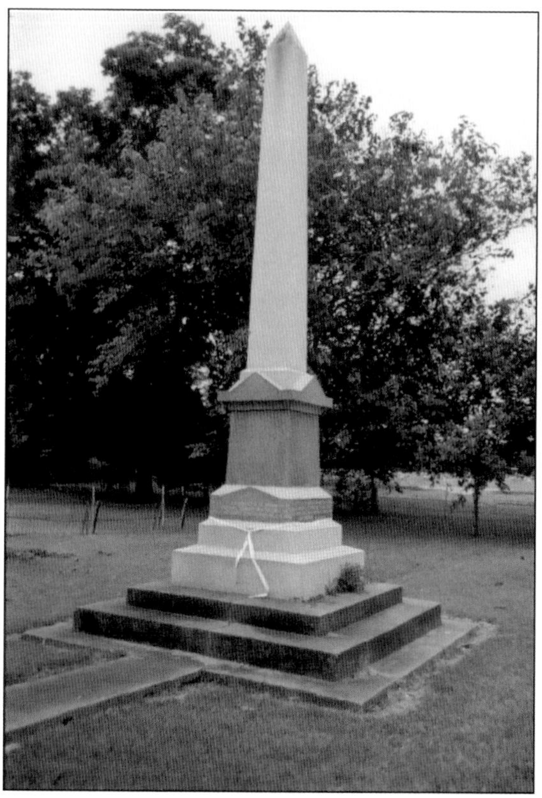

This monument was erected for slaves that went off to the Civil War with the Harvey Scouts from Madison. These slaves fought on the side of the Confederacy alongside their slave masters. They also served as servants on the battlefield. One loyal slave was individually recognized for his valor. The inscription on the monument reads, "A tribute to my faithful servant and friend, Willis Howcott, a colored boy of rare loyalty and faithfulness, whose memory I cherish with deep gratitude." (Courtesy of the Author.)

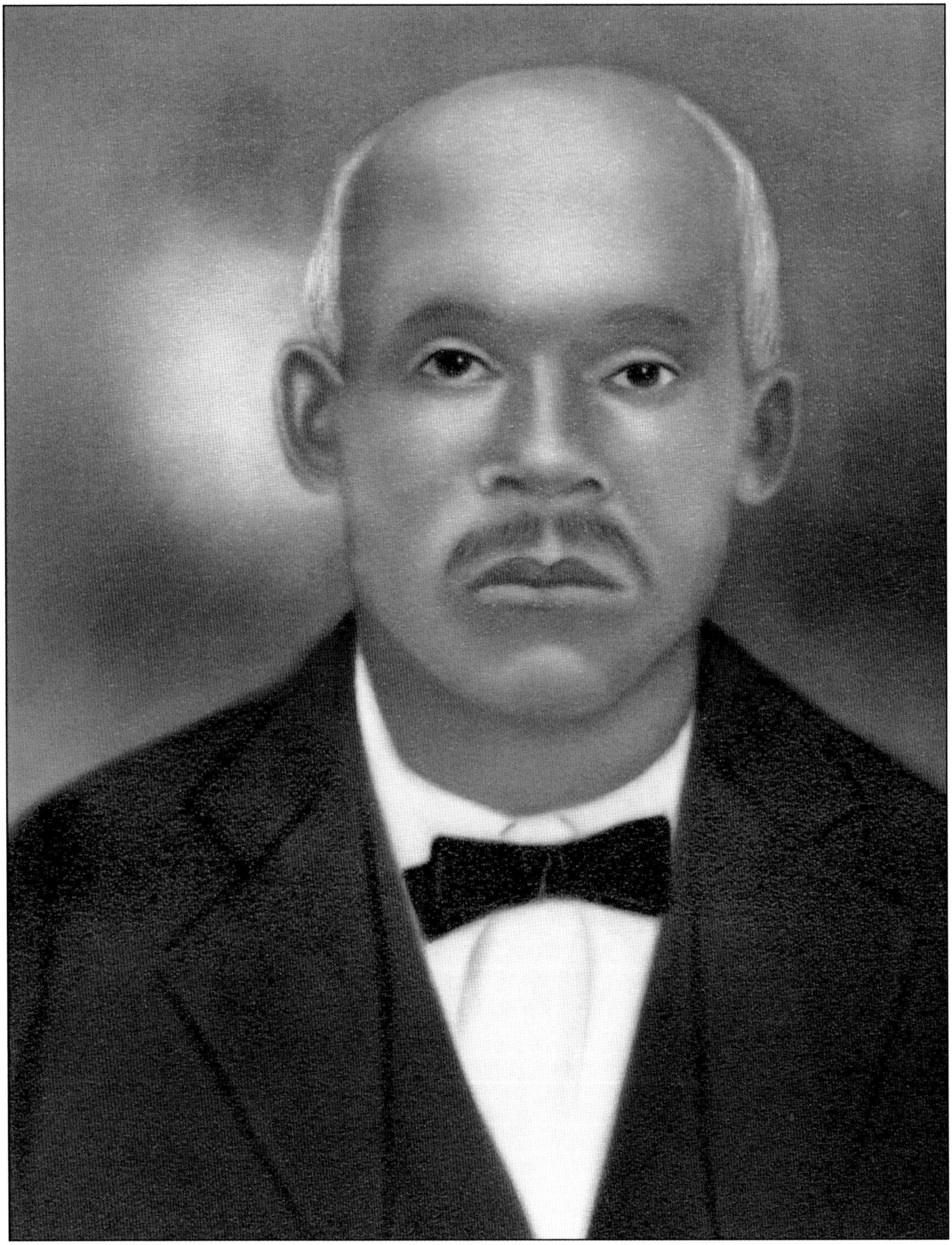

Joe Holbert of Madison County is the subject of this photograph. Holbert was the first African American to deliver mail in rural Madison County. Holbert normally delivered mail twice a week on horseback. This photo was taken in the late 1800s. (Courtesy of Ruth Luckett.)

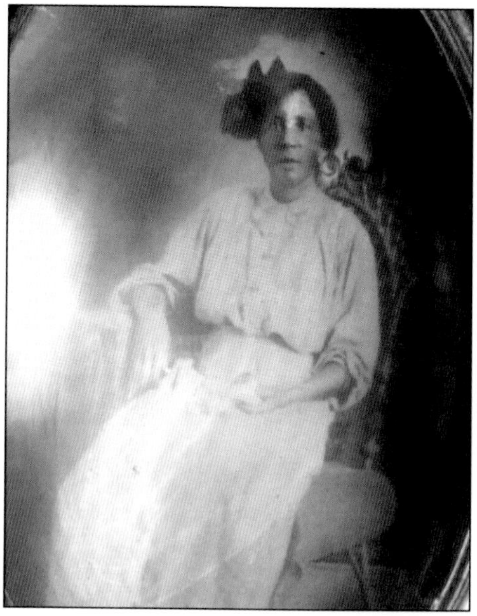

Ellen Day, born in 1910 in rural Madison County, poses for a 1930s photograph. Mrs. Day attended the Pleasant Gift Missionary Baptist Church. (Courtesy of Elenora Tate.)

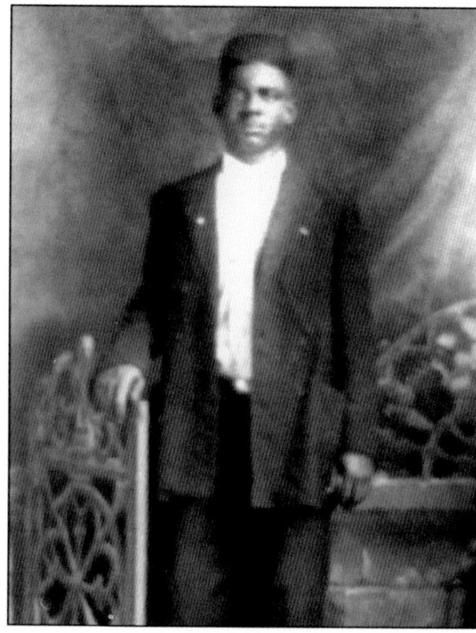

Clint Day stands with dignity for this early 1900s photo. Born and reared in Madison County, Day farmed for a living. He attended the Pleasant Gift Missionary Baptist Church. He lived in this county all his life. (Courtesy of Elenora Tate.)

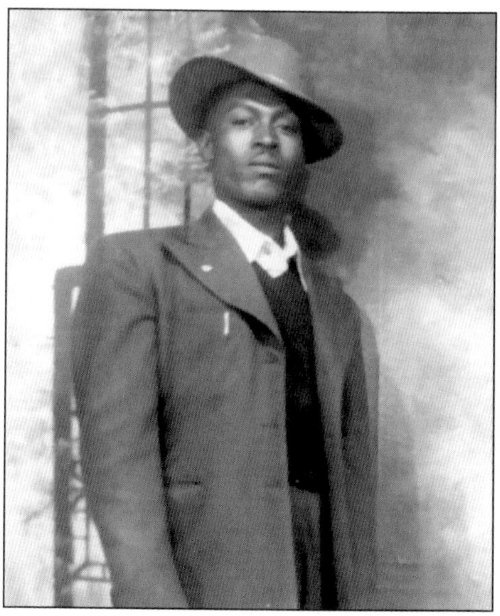

Earnest Cheeks poses proudly for this 1940s photo. He was born and reared in Madison County and well known in the community for his strong personality. (Courtesy of Alice Reed.)

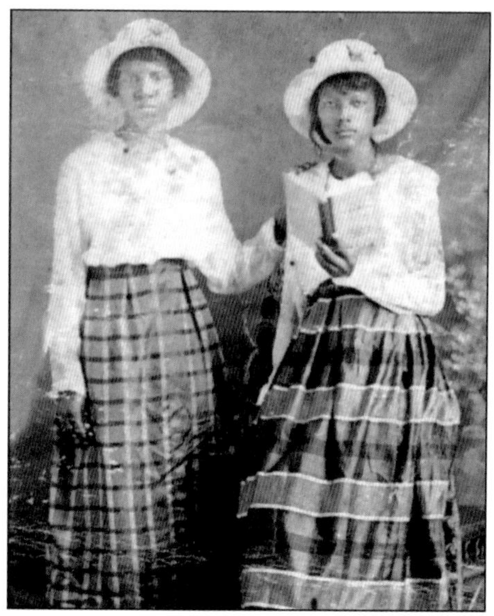

Pictured in this early 1920s photo are cousins Angie Miggins (left) and Lucille Cheeks (right). These two young ladies were both natives of Madison County, and they often posed in photographs together. (Courtesy of Alice Reed.)

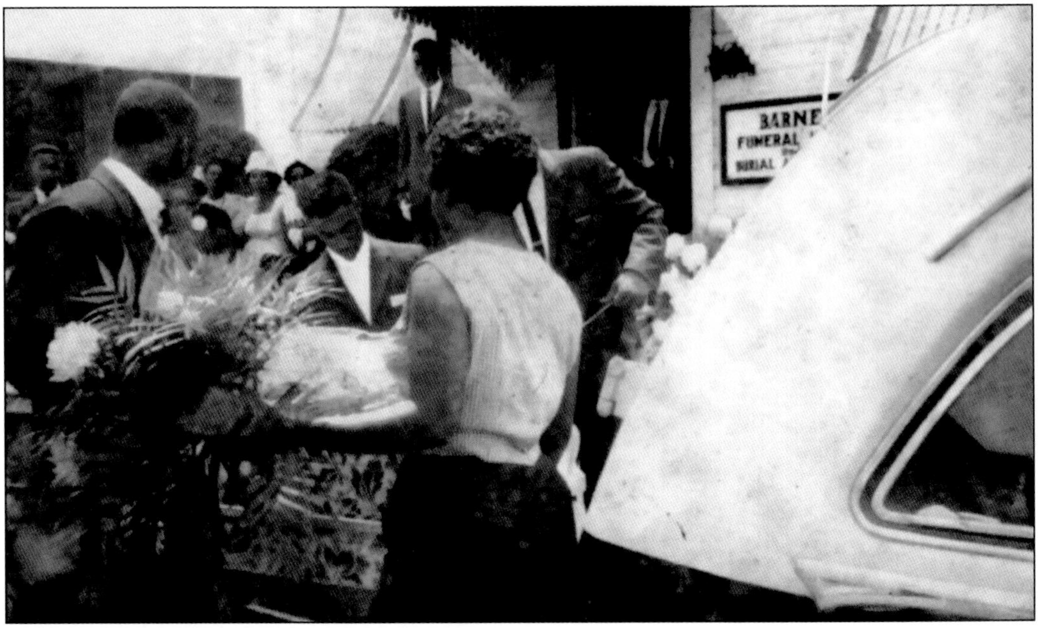

Barnes Funeral Home was an African-American funeral home in Madison County, located on Hickory Street in Canton. Employees at the funeral home are seen in this photo during in the 1960s. The funeral home served the black community in Madison County and neighboring counties. (Courtesy of Mrs. Emma Barnes.)

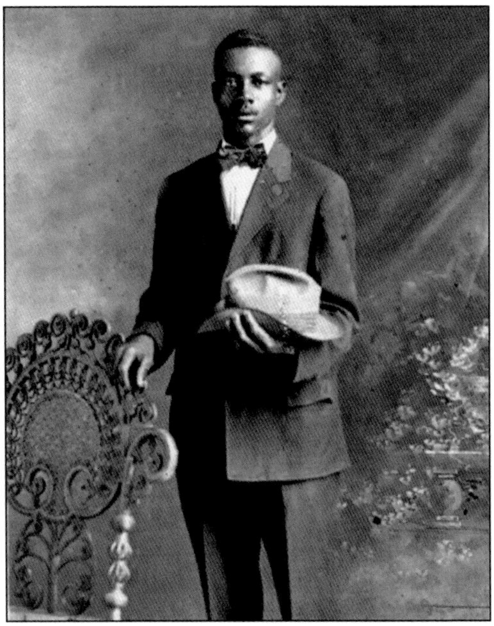

Nelson Hayes is seen this early 1900s photo. Notice the well-pressed suit and gentleman's hat he holds. He was reared in the Mount Hope Community, where he farmed for a living. (Courtesy of Creasy Woodard.)

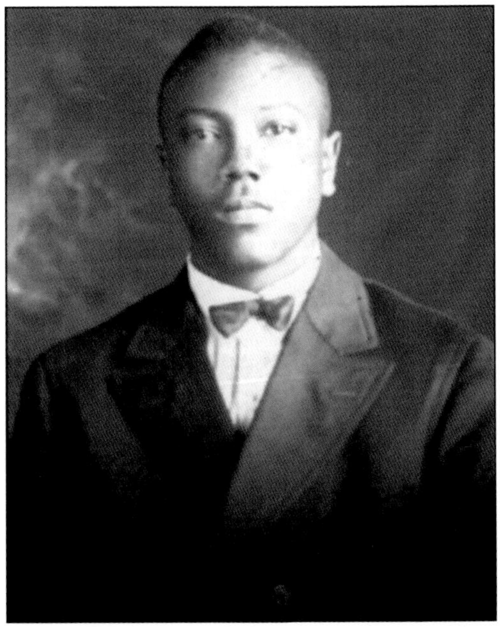

James Johnson is seen in this early 1900s photo. Johnson grew up in the Mount Hope community west of the city of Canton. He farmed in the same community for many years. (Courtesy of Creasy Woodard.)

Mr. and Mrs. Elijah Johnson are seen in this 1930s photo. Mr. Johnson worked as a farmer until he left Madison County at the age of 18. He then worked in the steel mills in Chicago, and lived to the age of 99. Mrs. Johnson was housewife and seamstress, but preceded her husband in death. (Courtesy of Creasy Woodard.)

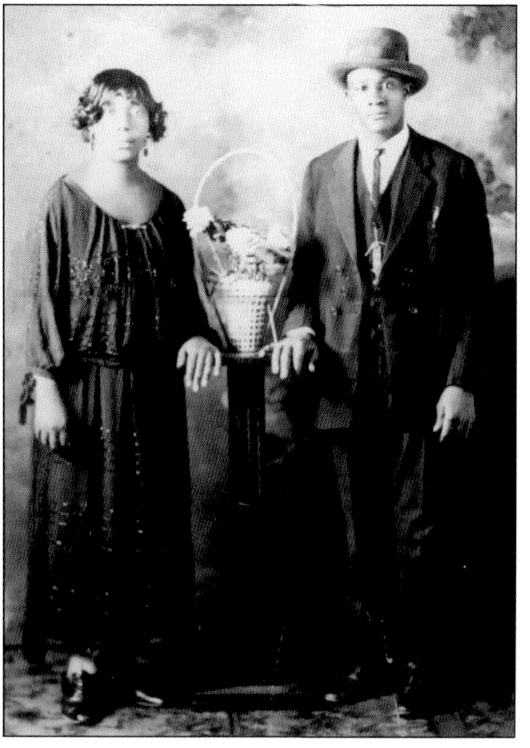

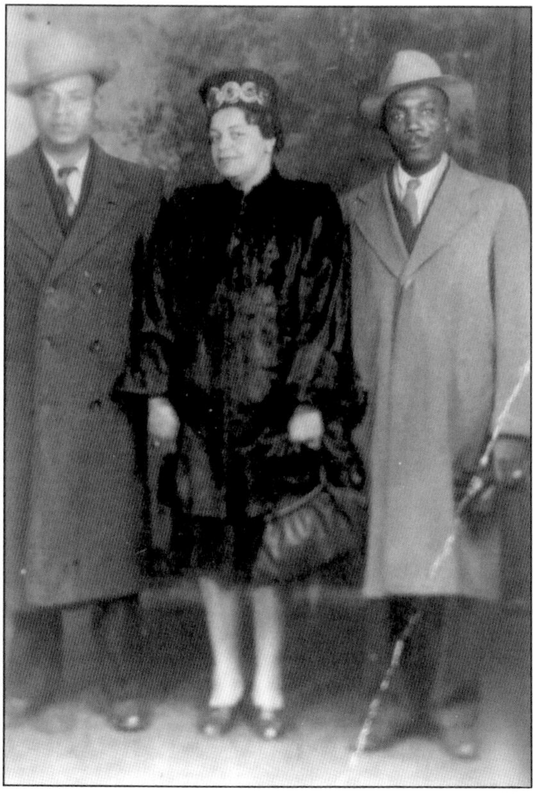

This 1959 photo shows Jimmy Cheeks, Hattie Cheeks Washington, and Albert Washington. Jimmy and Hattie are siblings. (Courtesy of Landres Cheeks.)

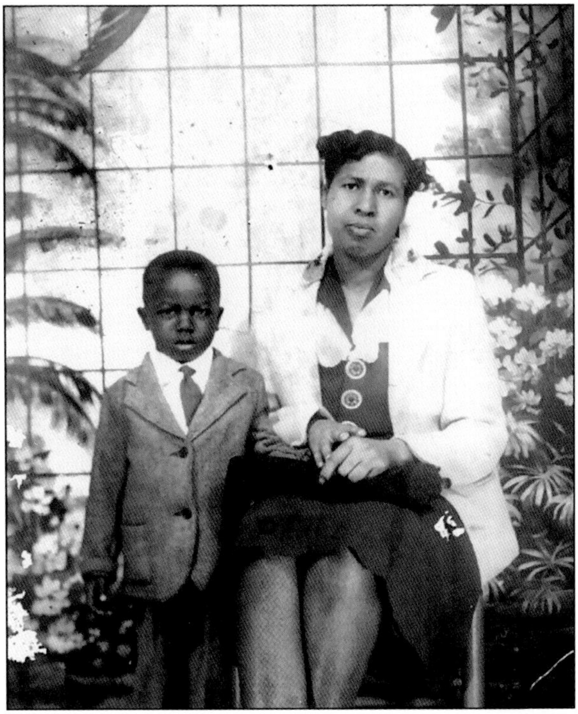

Carrie Smoot is seen with her son, Larry, in this 1946 photo. Smoot was active in the Civil Rights Movement in the 1960s. She worked hard as a mother, as well as an employee at Southern Furniture, the Tint Factory, and Johnson's Cleaners. She worked as a field hand driver during the sharecropping era in Madison County. Not many African-American women had this occupation in the 1950s and 1960s. (Courtesy of Carrie Smoot.)

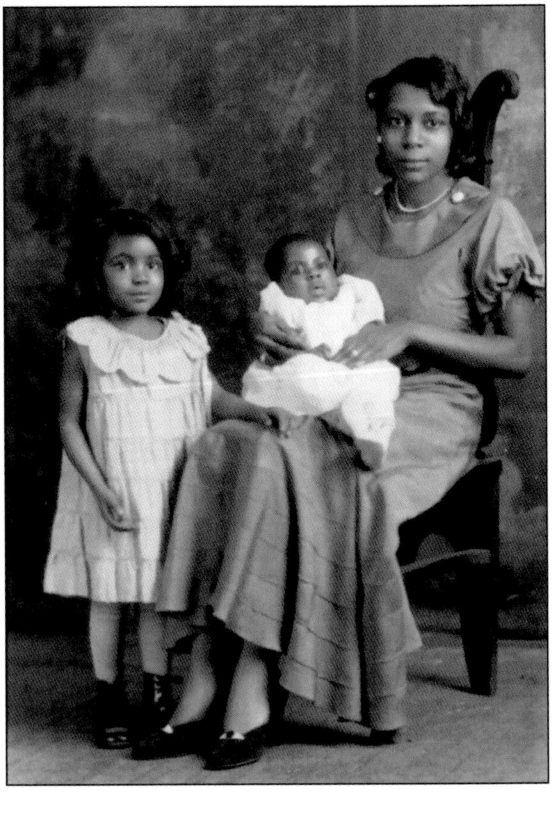

Georgia Lee Hayes and her two children, Mildred (standing) and Oscar (on her lap), are shown in this family photo in the early 1940s. She and her family later moved to Chicago. (Courtesy of Creasy Woodard.)

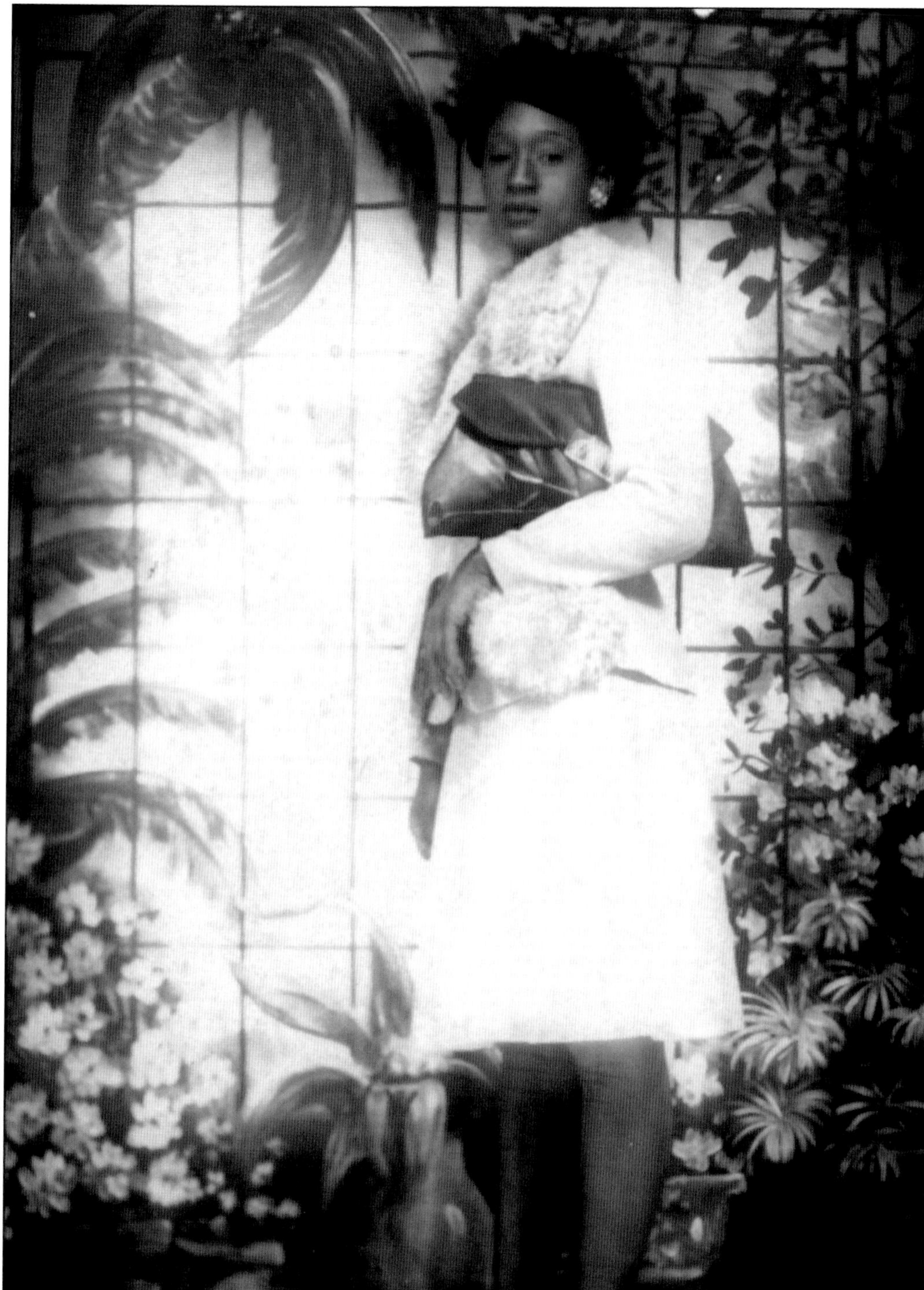

Juanita Green stood with grace as this 1940s photo was taken. Green lived in the Mount Hope community and she was educated at the Mount Hope School. She moved to New York shortly after this photo was taken. (Courtesy of Creasy Woodard.)

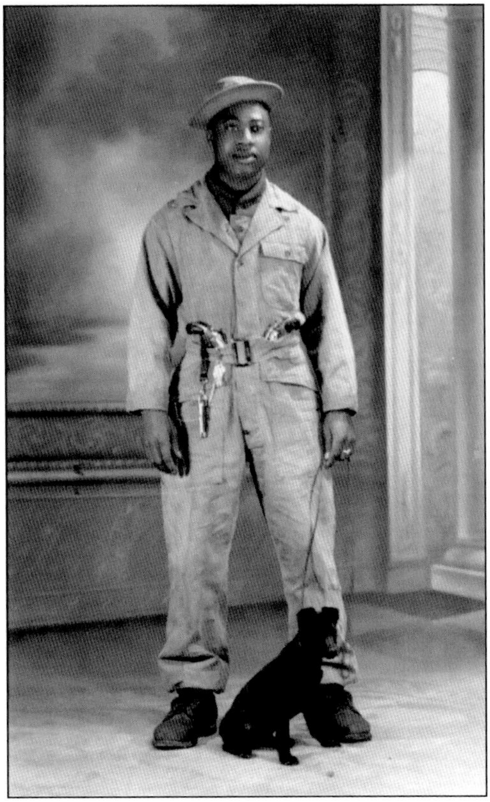

Dolphus Johnson is seen in this 1950s photo. He poses proudly with his two pistols and his puppy. Johnson lived in the Mount Hope community until he left Madison County as a teenager and headed for Chicago. (Courtesy of Creasy Woodard.)

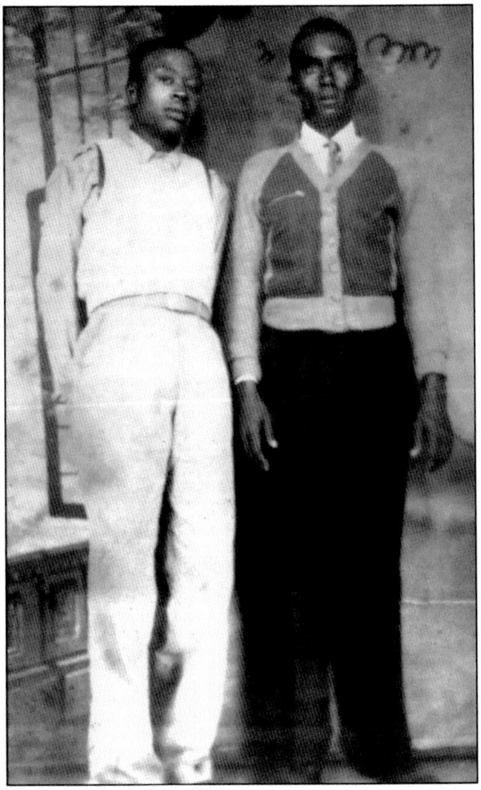

Coote Walker and Henry Day are seen in this 1930s photo. The brothers-in-law both farmed in eastern Madison County to support their families. They often spent time together, helping each other with various farming duties. (Courtesy of Elenora Tate.)

Carrie and Willie Smoot posed for this photo a year the after their December 12, 1934 wedding. Mr. Smoot passed away in the early 1970s. Mrs. Smoot currently resides in Canton at the age of 89. (Courtesy of Carrie Smoot.)

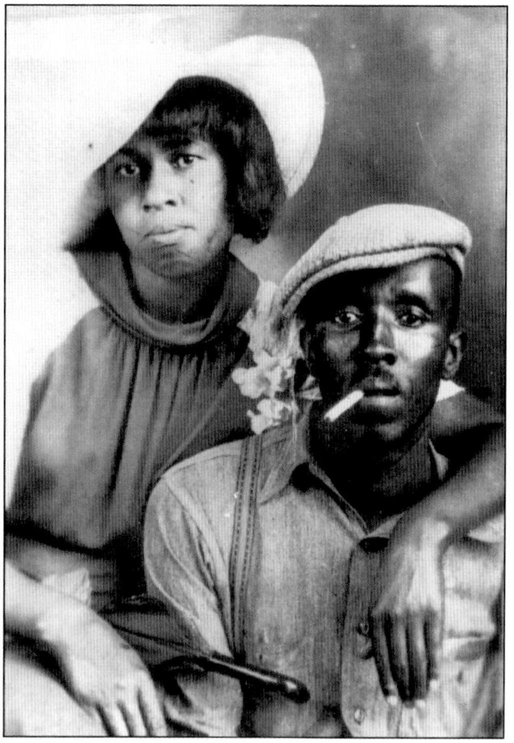

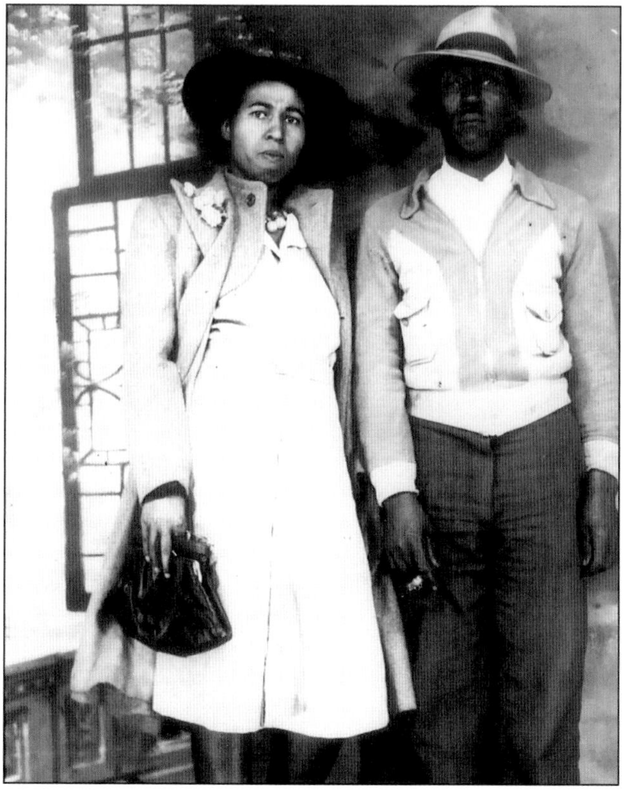

Another photo of Mr. and Mrs. Willie Smoot was taken in the 1940s. Willie Smoot was born on September 2, 1902, and Carrie Smoot was born on March 5, 1913—both in Madison County. Mr. Smoot farmed on Highway 43 in the Cedar Grove community. He was also a carpenter, musician, and singer. (Courtesy of Carrie Smoot.)

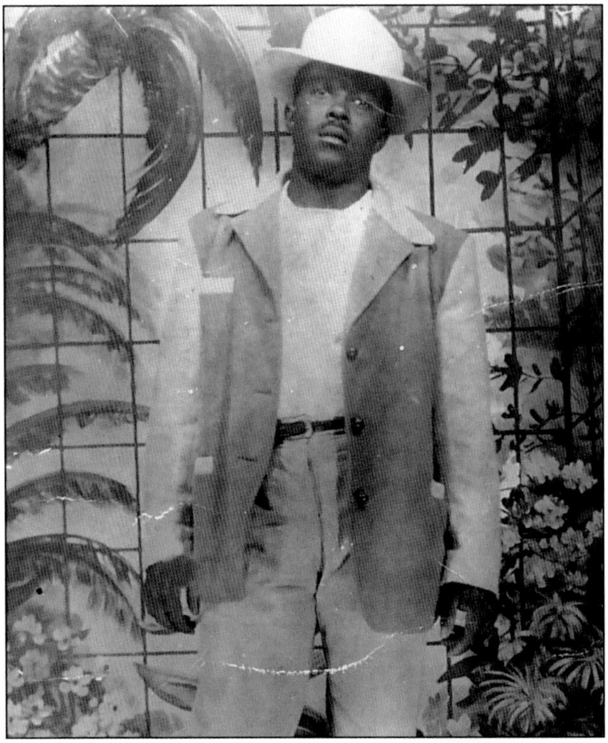

Richard Davis is seen in this 1948 photograph. Davis was born and reared in Madison County where he did various jobs to make a living. (Courtesy of Umble Hawkins.)

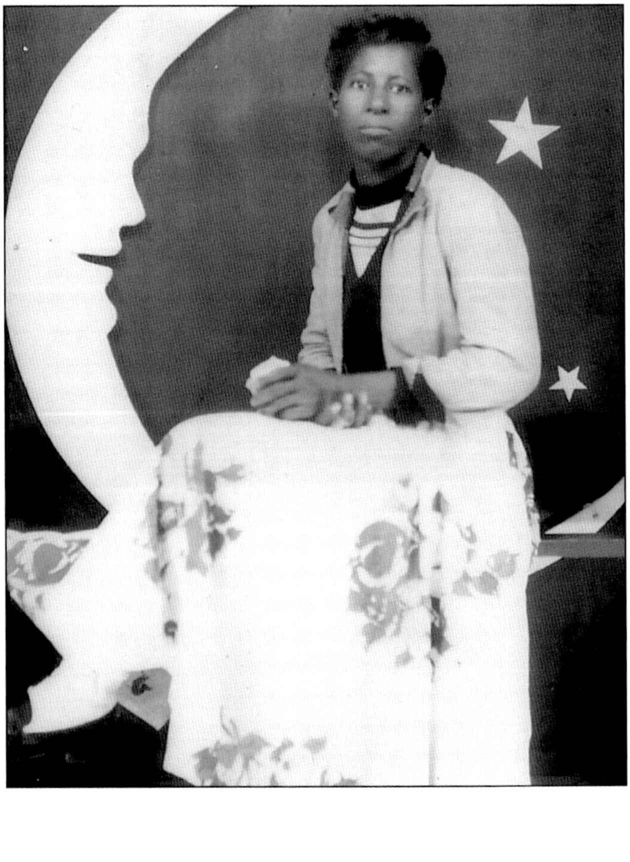

May Percilla Davis posed for this classic 1955 photograph. The background was common for the 1950s—many people took their place "on the moon" for a photograph. (Courtesy of Umble Hawkins.)

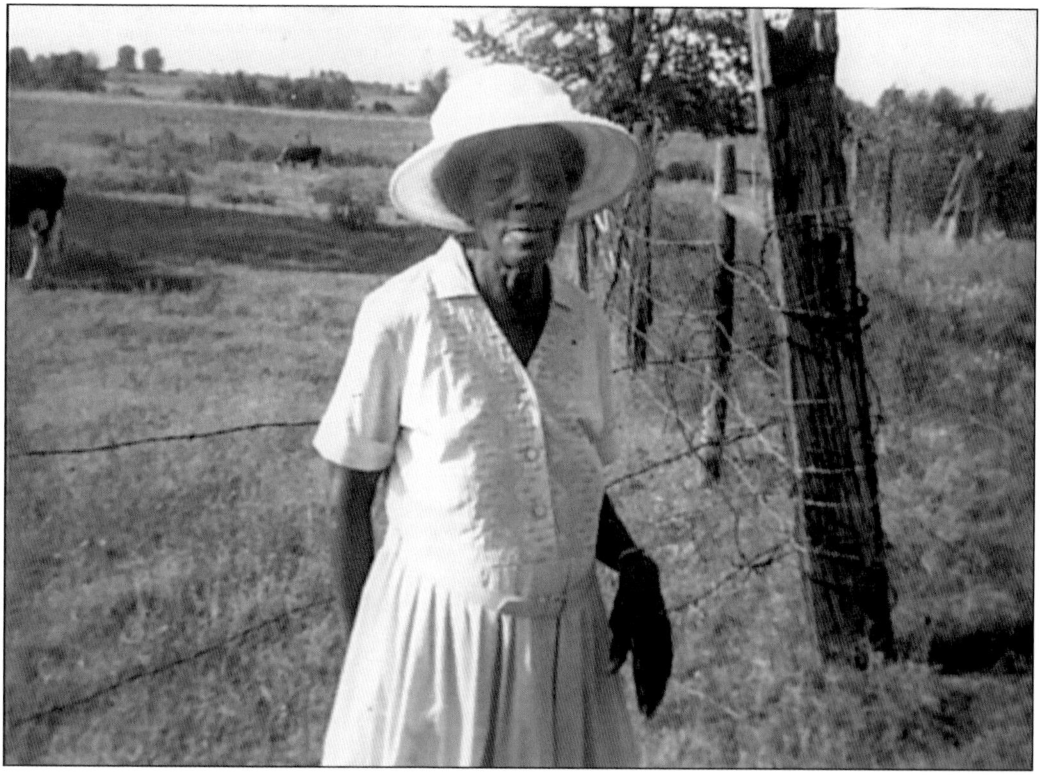

Pauline Harris, seen in 1965, was 100 years old when this photo was taken. Throughout her years in Madison County, she was a teacher at the Algona School, a farmer, and a homemaker. She posed for this photograph in front of her farm in rural Madison County. (Courtesy of Annie B. Berry.)

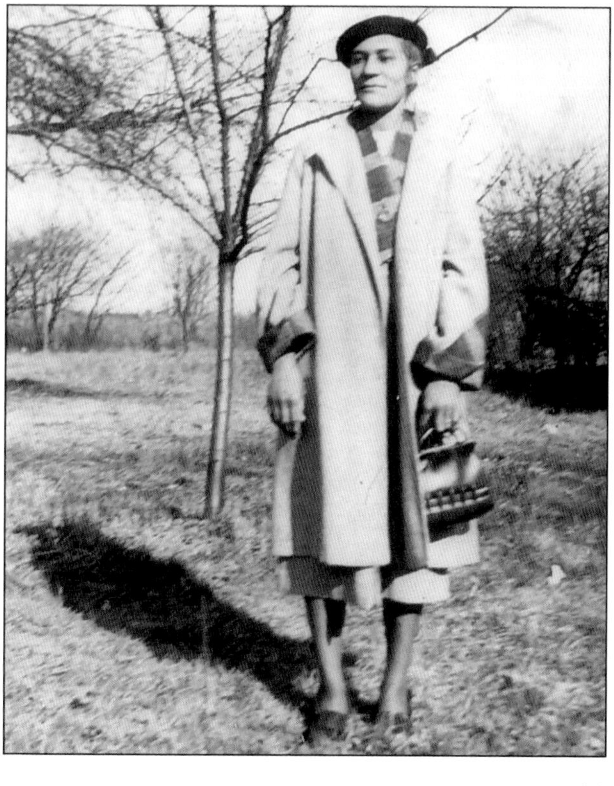

Gertrude Banks Merriweather was born in Madison County in 1902. She was a housewife after she married. (Courtesy of Thelma Cain.)

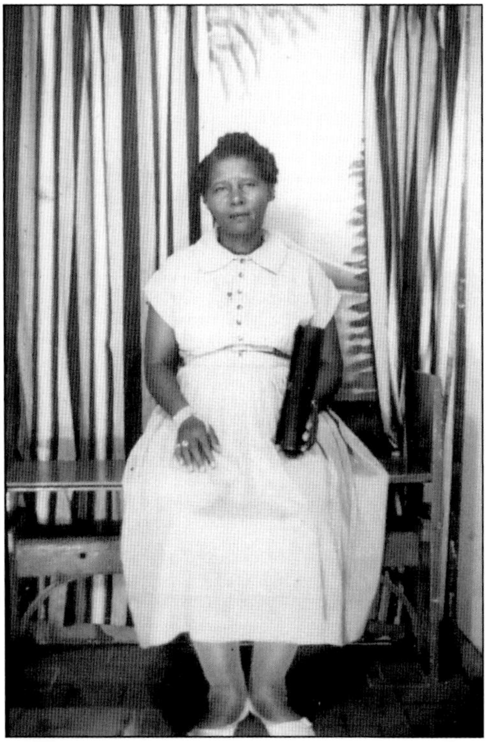

Armeter Walker is seen in this 1930s photograph. Walker was born in Madison County. She farmed the fields to provide for her five children. Later in her life, she moved to Chicago. (Courtesy of Elenora Tate.)

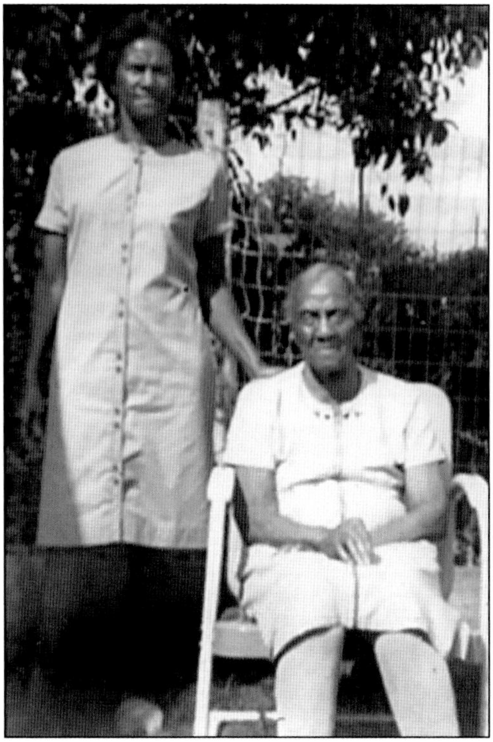

Mattie Banks (standing) and Ledora Sims (sitting) are pictured in 1950. Mother and daughter were both born and reared in Madison County and farmed for a living. They later moved to Hinds County. (Courtesy of James and Francis Sanders.)

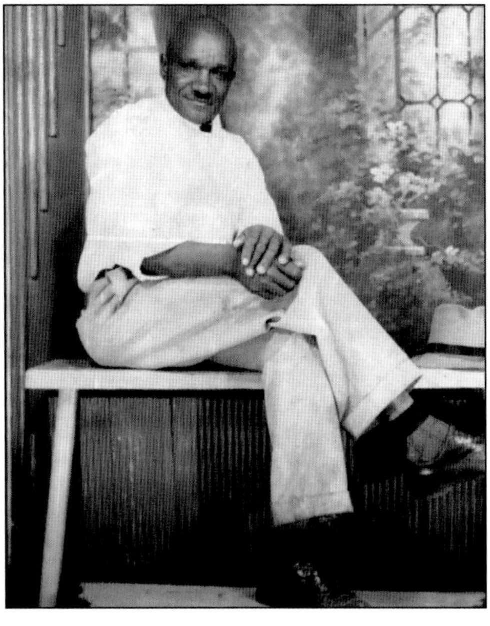

Dillard Horn poses with his hat at his side for this photo. He raised and farmed corn, cotton, and other goods for a living. (Courtesy of Creasy Woodard.)

Two

Places of Praise and Worship

"Our creator is the same and never changes despite the names given Him by people here and in all parts of the world. Even if we gave Him no name at all, He would still be there, within us, waiting to give us good on this earth."

George Washington Carver, 1911

Most African-American communities were centered around the church. Shortly after the Civil War, large numbers of African Americans took advantage of their newly gained freedom and worshiped together freely. Most churches started under bush arbors until stable structures could be built. Few churches could afford to buy their land, but some church members could and did purchase the land. The church is clearly the foundation of the community, serving as a safe haven, a center for education, and a meeting place. Madison County has many more historically black churches that, due to space constraints and picture availability, are not included in this chapter.

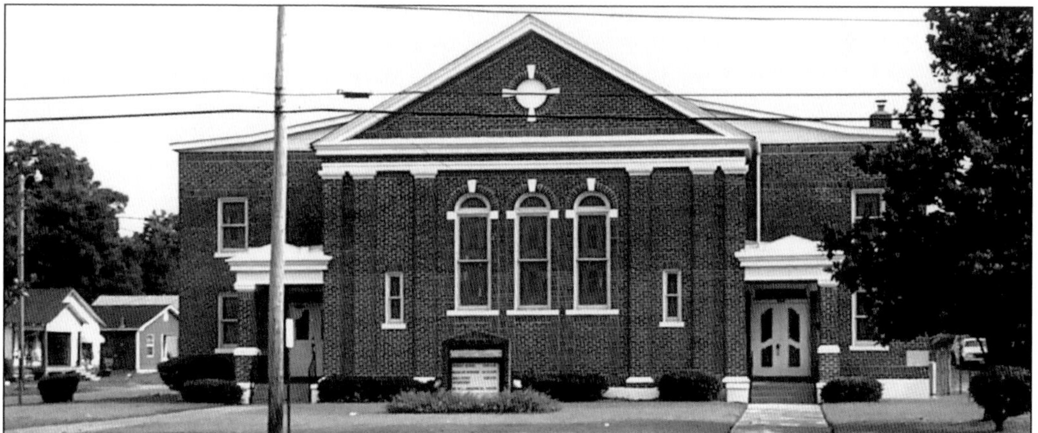

Mt. Zion Missionary Baptist Church was founded in 1865 by a white preacher, Rev. T.J. Drane. This building was erected in 1929. This church played a vital role in the Civil Rights movement in the 1960s, opening its doors to the people of Madison County who fought for Civil Rights. The church hosted Dr. Martin Luther King Jr., as well as other well-known black leaders. (Courtesy of the Author.)

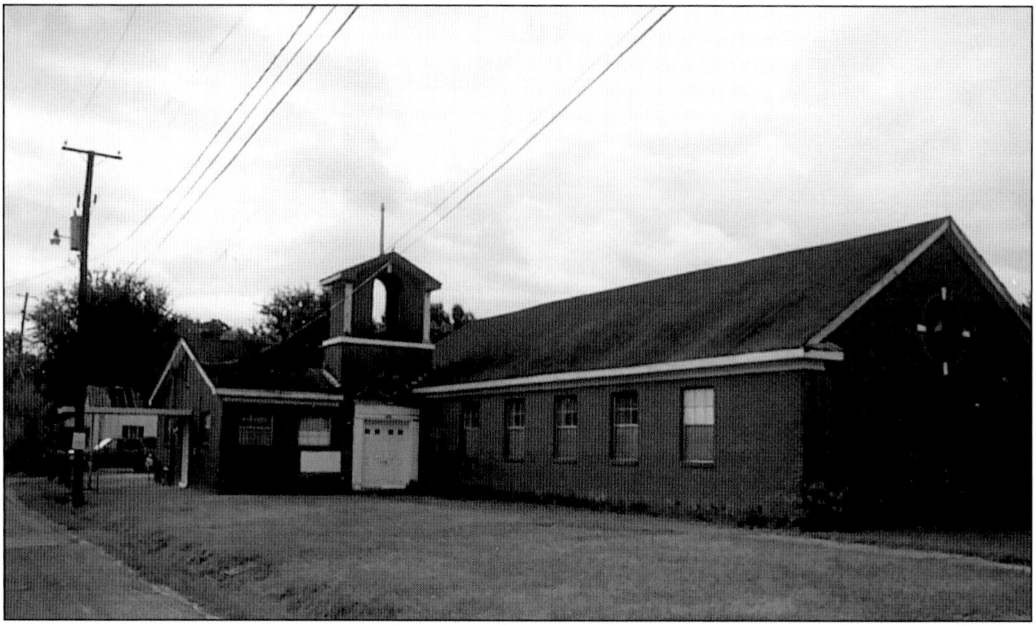

Asbury United Methodist Church is thought to be the oldest African-American church organized in Madison County. A slave named Clarinda Garrett Jackson organized this church in 1824. She and other slaves had church services in a bush arbor until the Civil War ended. The members built several church buildings after the Civil War. This building was constructed in 1924 on Cameron Street in Canton. The church played an active role in the Civil Rights movement. Meetings and rallies were held at this church often. (Courtesy of the Author.)

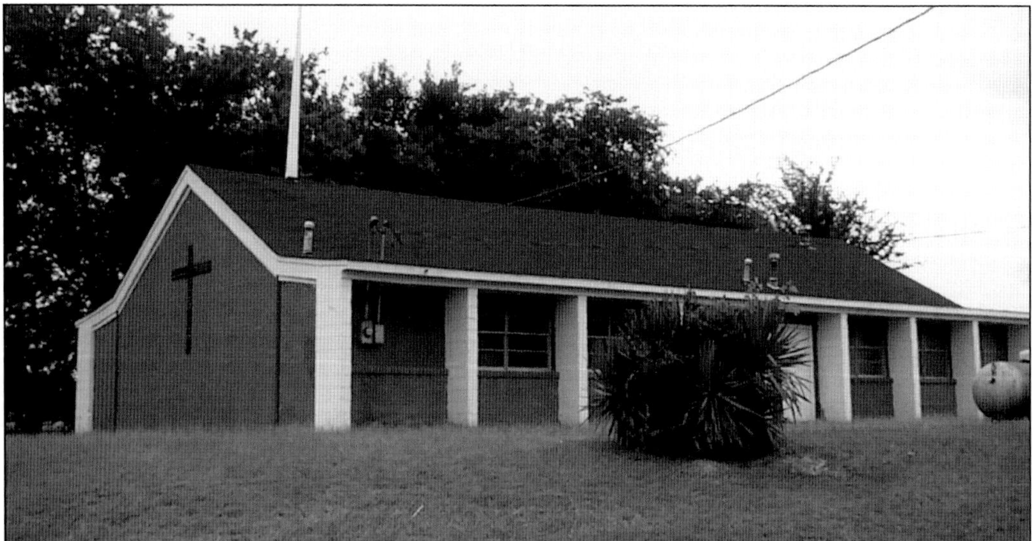

Cedar Grove Baptist Church, located east of Canton on Highway 43, was organized in 1887. This church fell victim to the violence that was a part of the Civil Rights movement. The day after a Civil Rights meeting was held there, the church mysteriously caught fire and burned. The congregation did rebuild, and they continue to worship in the building. (Courtesy of the Author.)

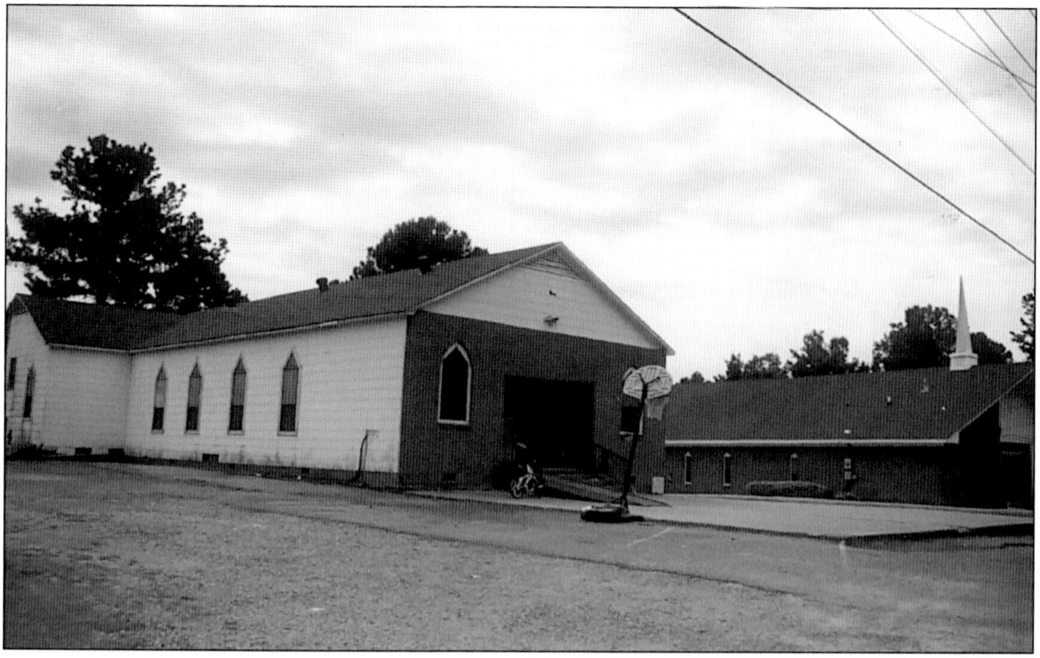

Ridley Hill Missionary Baptist Church was founded in 1872 by Rev. C.H. McDonald. The old church is on the left and the new modern-day structure is on the right. Ex-slaves in rural Madison organized the church. (Courtesy of the Author.)

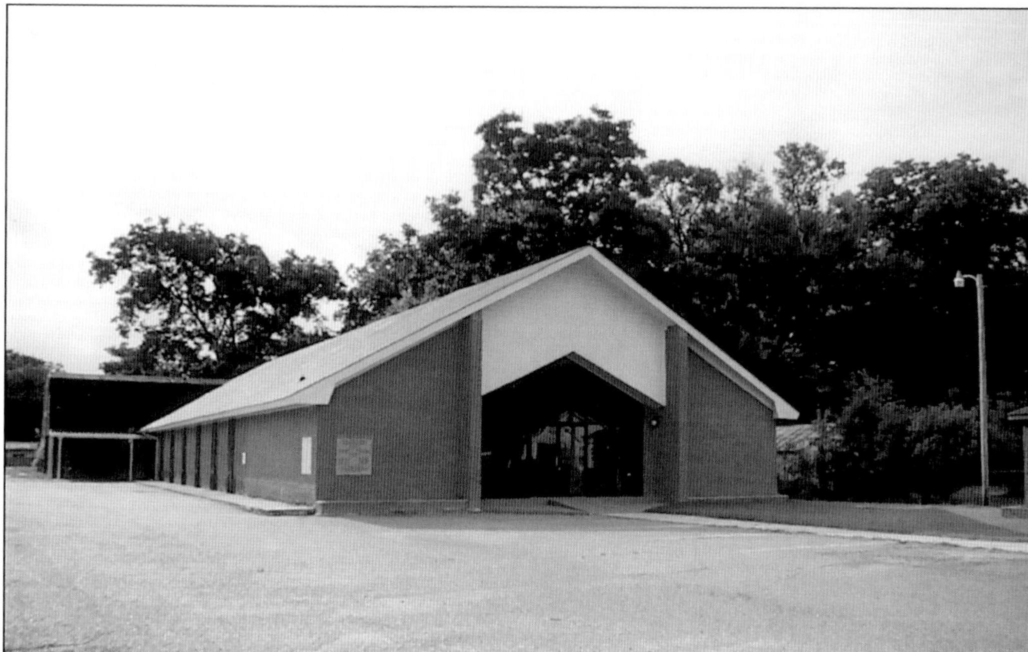

Saint Paul African Methodist Episcopal Zion Church was founded in 1871 by the Rev. G.W. Sims. Located in Canton, the church has served the African-American community in this city since its existence. (Courtesy of the Author.)

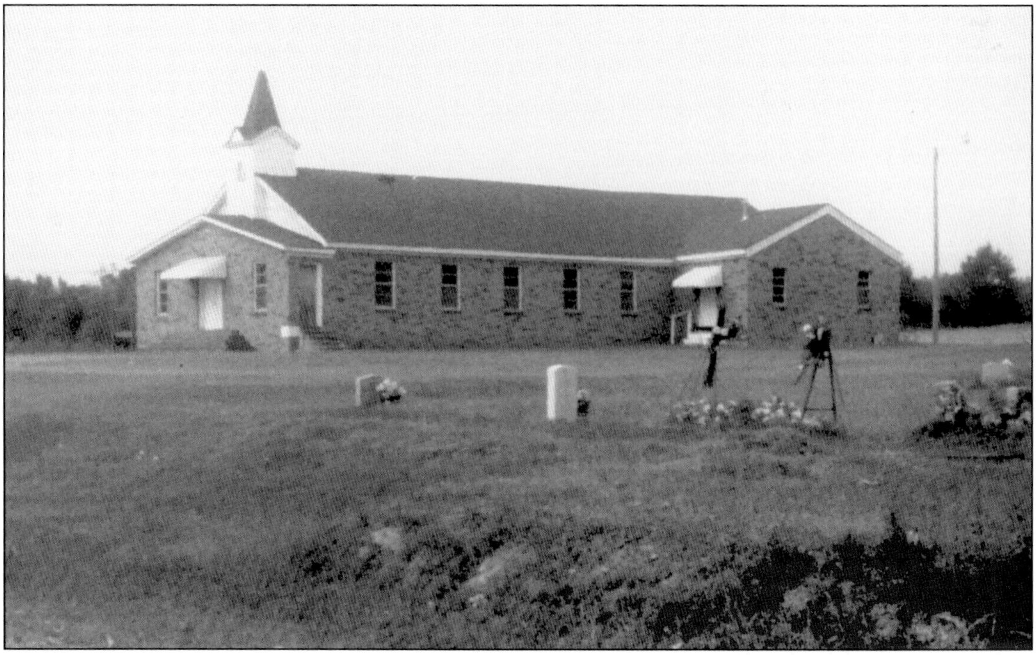

Pictured is the Harvey Chapel Missionary Baptist Church. This is the third building that the congregation built. The church was organized in 1885 in Canton on land donated by plantation owner George Harvey. (Courtesy of L.V. Lipsey.)

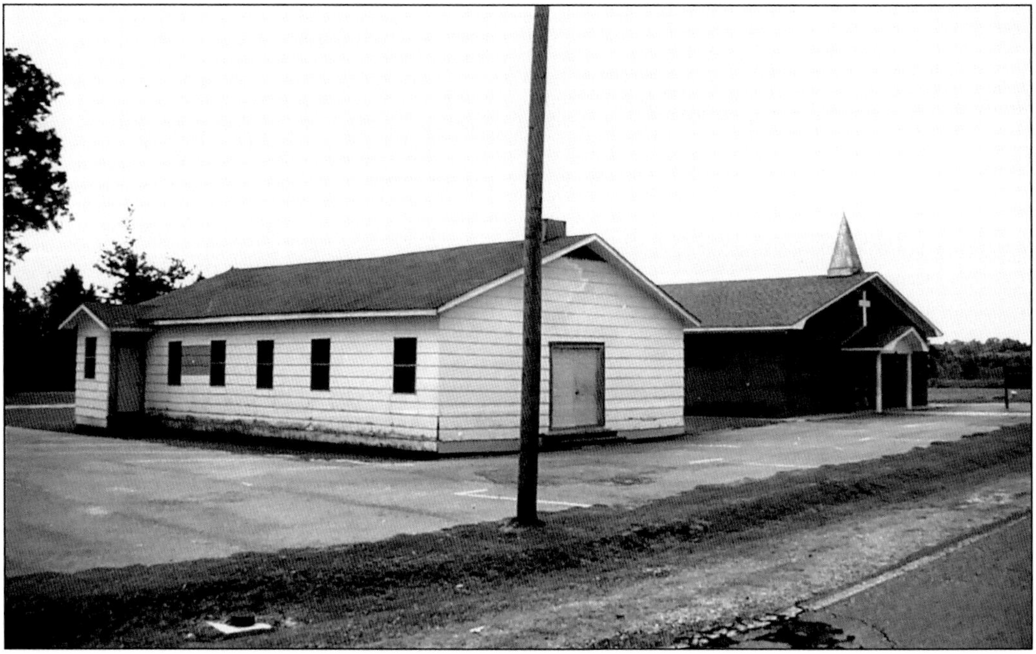

Saint James Missionary Baptist Church was organized in 1910. Members first met for church services in a Masonic Hall. A landowner by the name of Mr. James, for the purpose of building a church, later donated land. An older church structure is seen to the left and a new brick structure is seen to the right in this photograph. (Courtesy of the Author.)

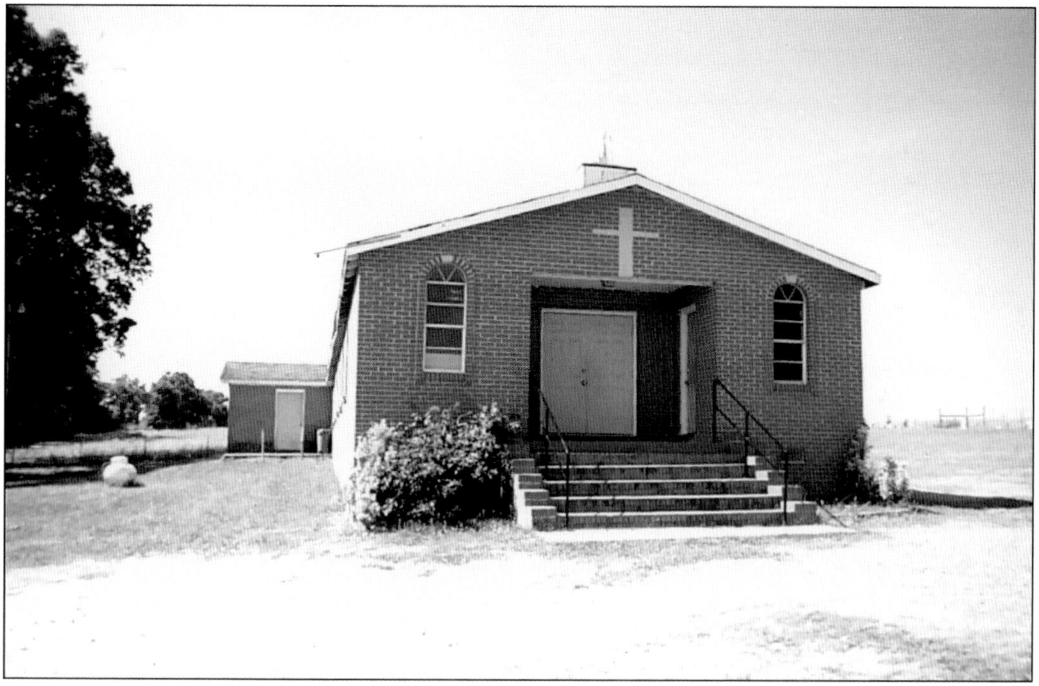

Union Hill Missionary Baptist Church is located in Flora and was founded in 1931. First located on Hill Place, the church was later built on Highway 22 (seen here). (Courtesy of the Author.)

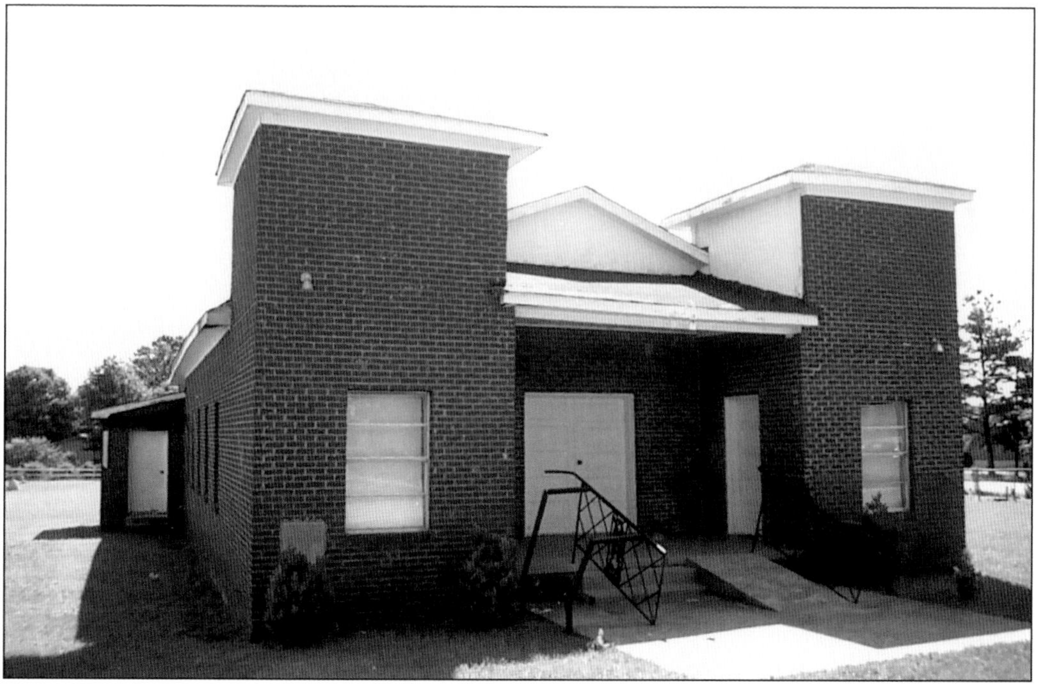

Woodman Hill Missionary Baptist Church was organized in 1883 by ex-slaves on Old Kerney Park Road in Flora. This is the original building but there have been several renovations. The United States Army donated the land for this church. (Courtesy of the Author.)

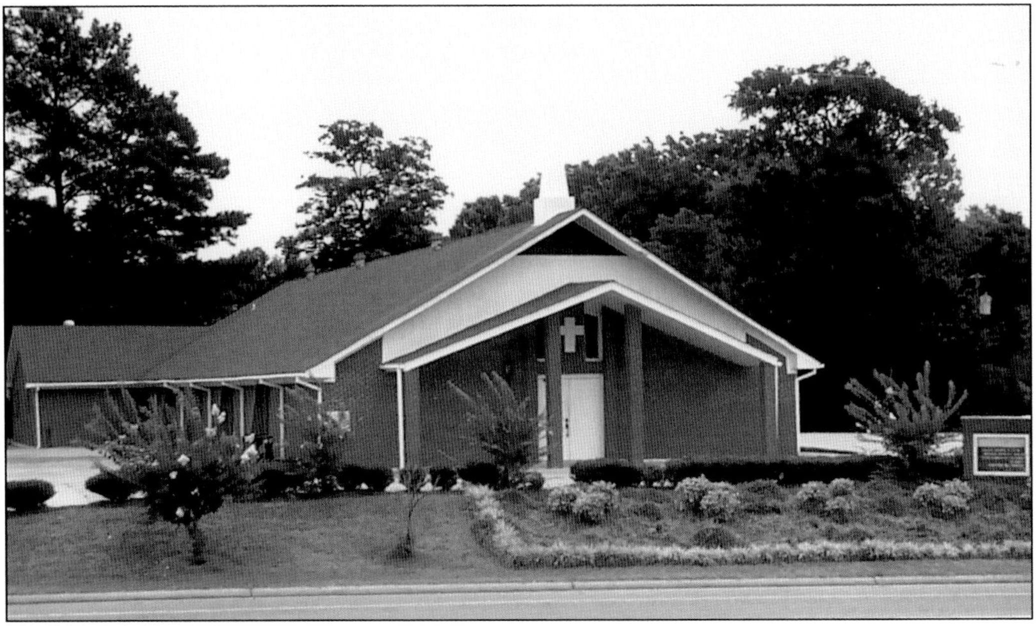

Mount Able Missionary Baptist Church was founded in 1900 in Canton. The church is located upon a hill on Highway 43. This is the latest structure that the members of the congregation have erected. (Courtesy of the Author.)

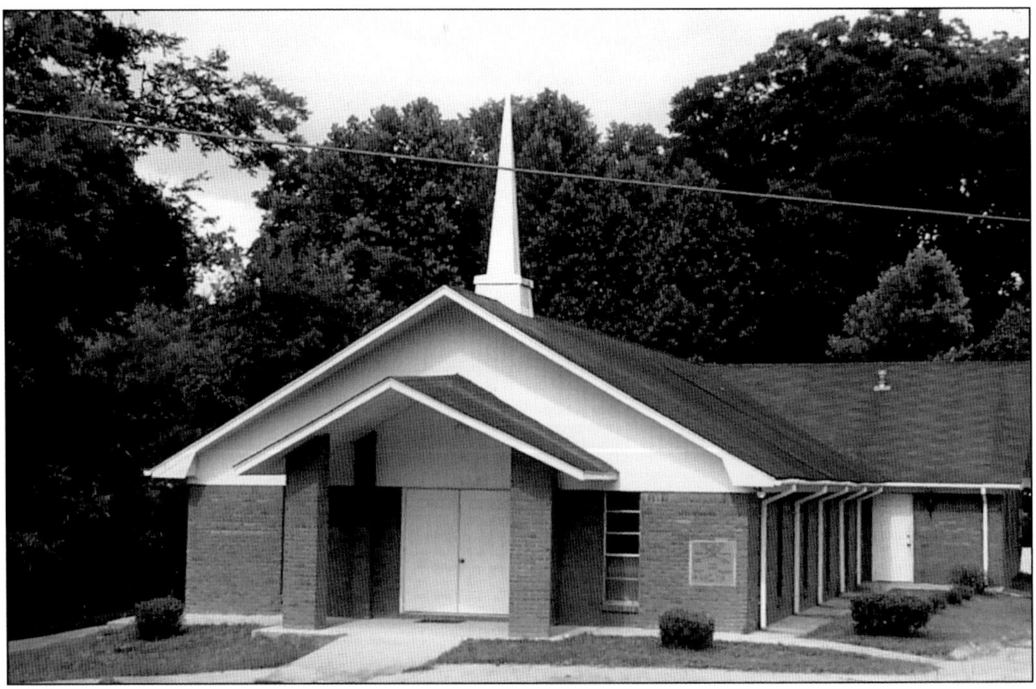

Members of the Southern Hill Missionary Baptist Church, founded in 1923, originally met in a house. The house later burned and members found themselves without a place to worship. Rev. John Wesley Johnson donated the land for a church structure. The church is currently in the same location as the first building. (Courtesy of the Author.)

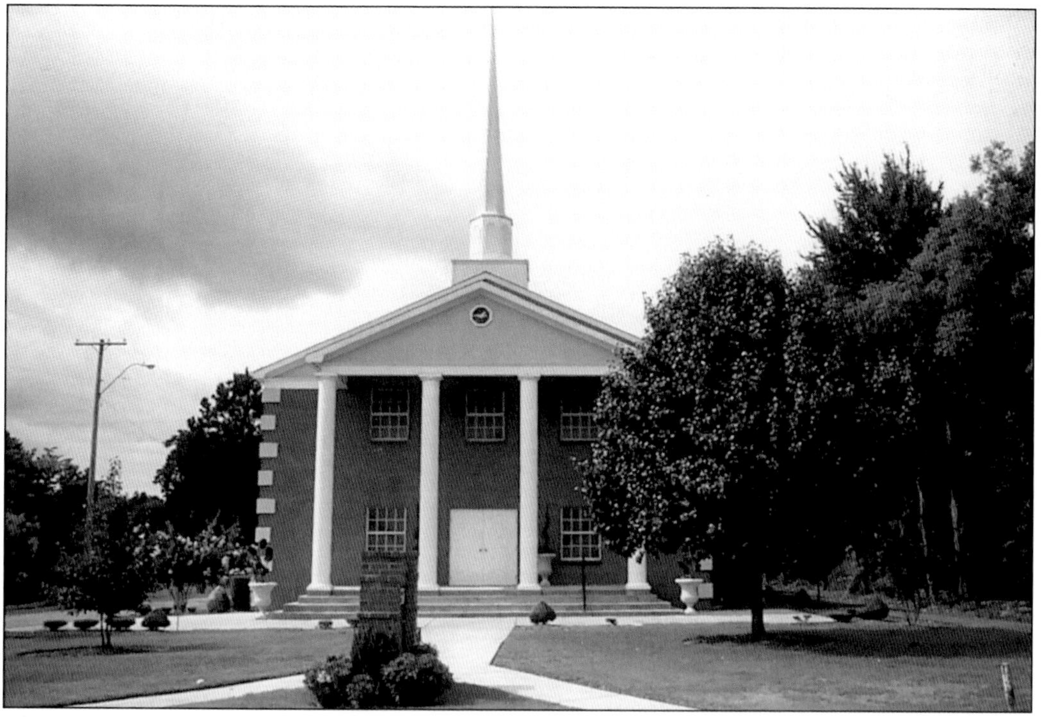

Liberty Missionary Baptist Church was established when members from the South Liberty Church built their first church in the early 1900s. Some members left the church and built what they named New Liberty Missionary Baptist Church on South West in Canton. The members of this church later dropped the "New" and the church is known today as Liberty Baptist Church. It is currently located on West Fulton Street in Canton. (Courtesy of the Author.)

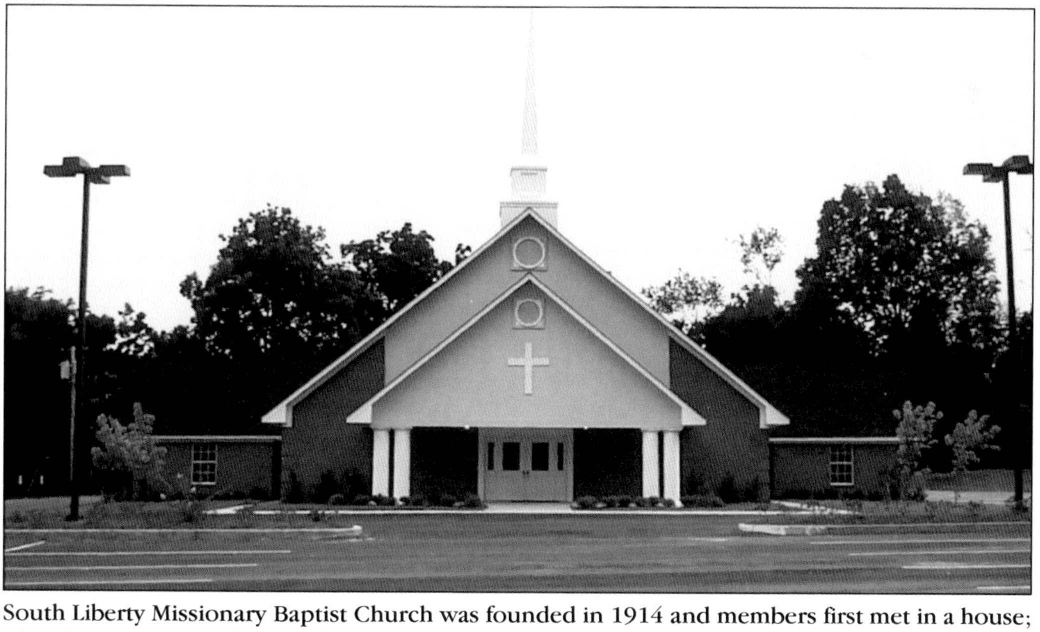

South Liberty Missionary Baptist Church was founded in 1914 and members first met in a house; a brick structure was later built. The new structure is seen here. (Courtesy of the Author.)

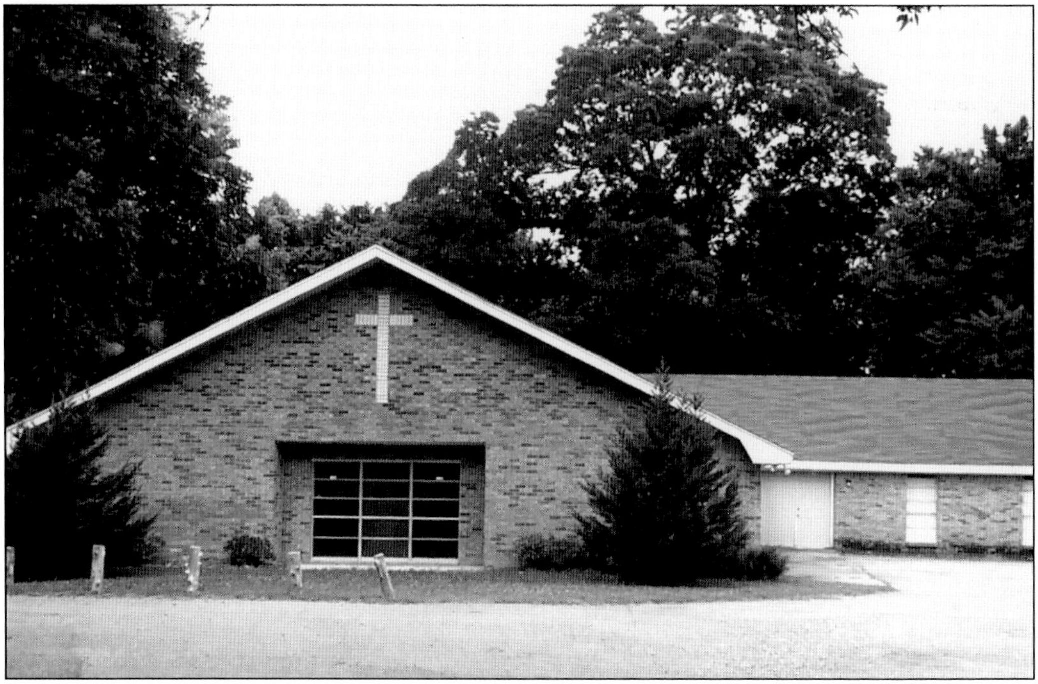

Livingston Baptist Church was organized in 1856 by local African Americans. The church is located east of Flora. Its members bought the land for this church, which has served the African-American community in Madison County since its existence. (Courtesy of the Author.)

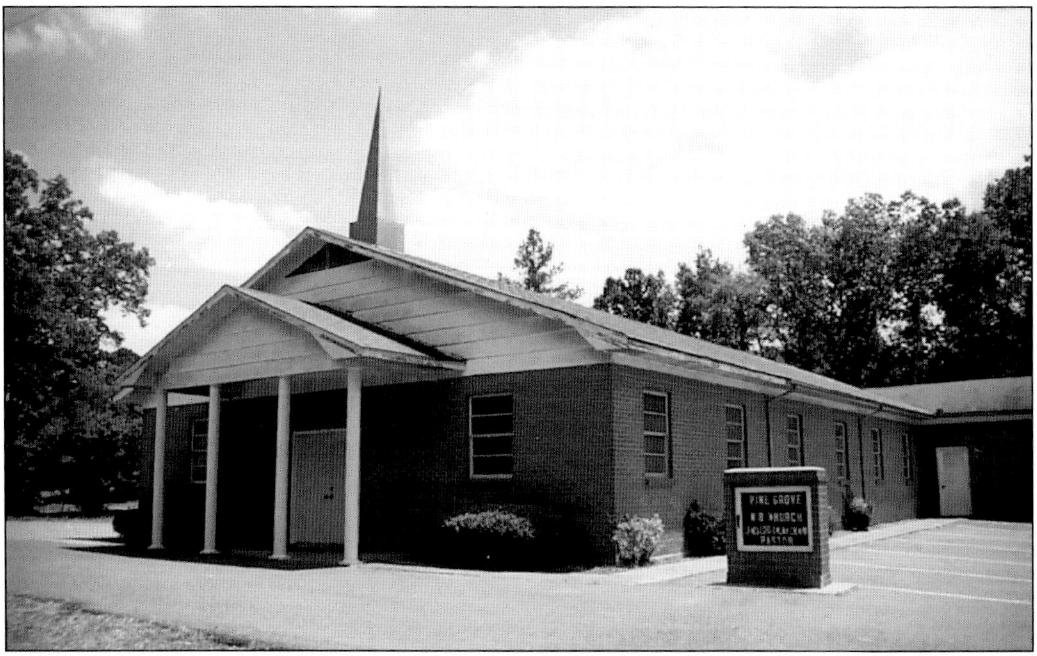

Pine Grove Missionary Baptist Church is located in Sharon. This church was organized in 1860. The first name of the church was Hickory Grove. Later the church moved to its present-day location and was renamed Pine Grove Missionary Baptist Church (Courtesy of the Author.)

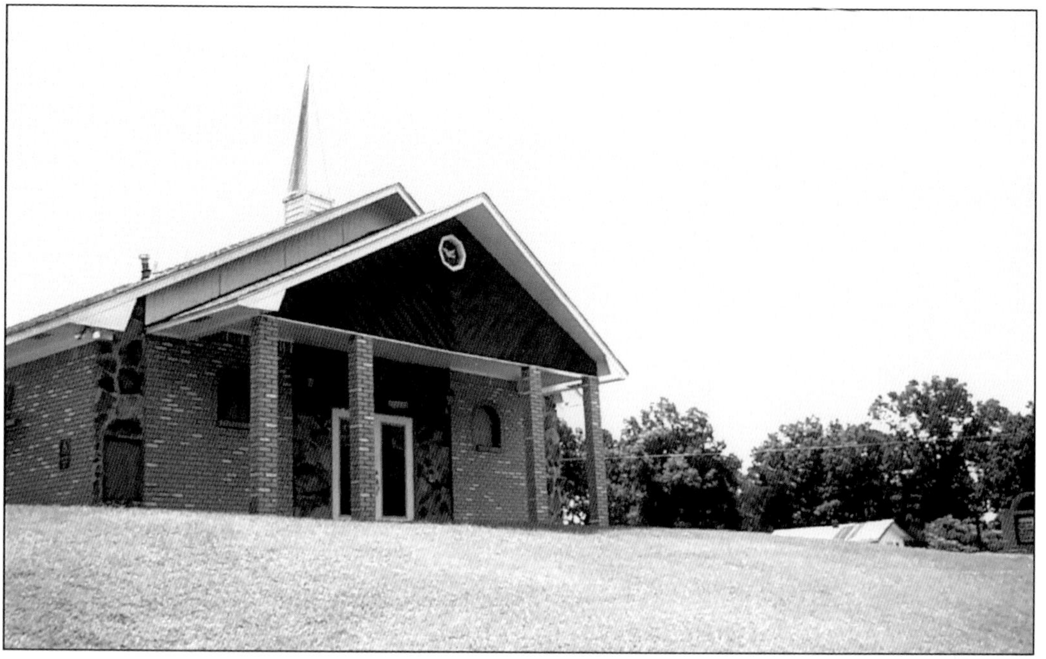

Middleton Grove AME Church was located on Way Road north of Canton. An African-American by the name of John Middleton donated the land in 1882 for the purpose of a church. The church was later built in 1886 in the same location. (Courtesy of the Author.)

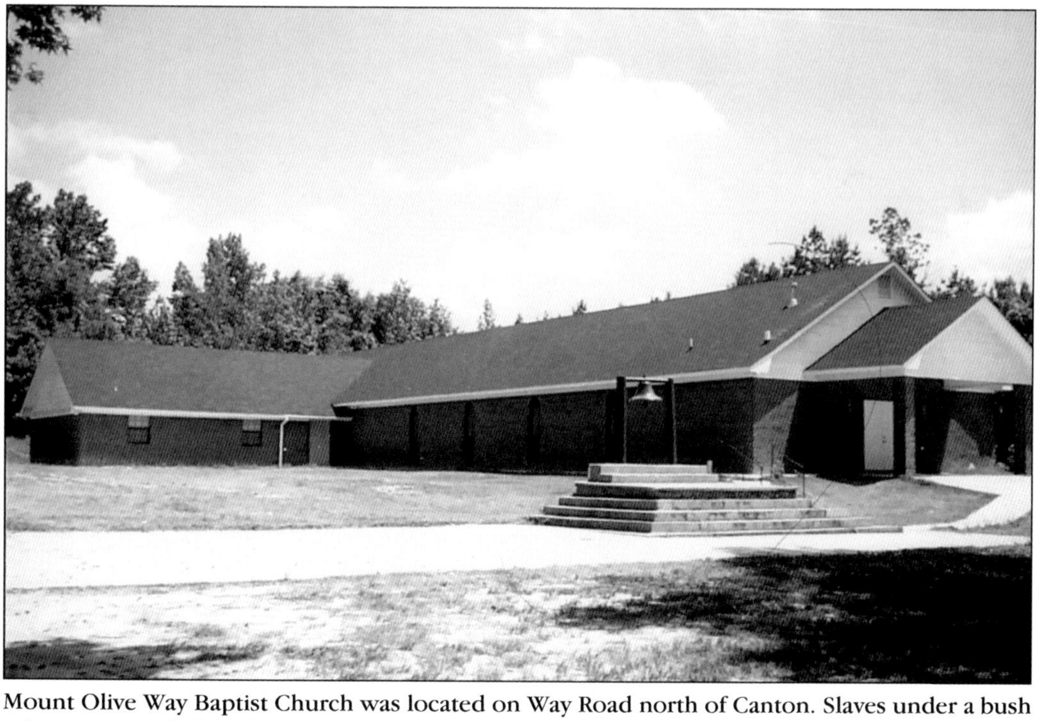

Mount Olive Way Baptist Church was located on Way Road north of Canton. Slaves under a bush arbor organized this church in 1850. A white landowner donated land for the slaves to have worship service. The church is currently in the same location. (Courtesy of the Author.)

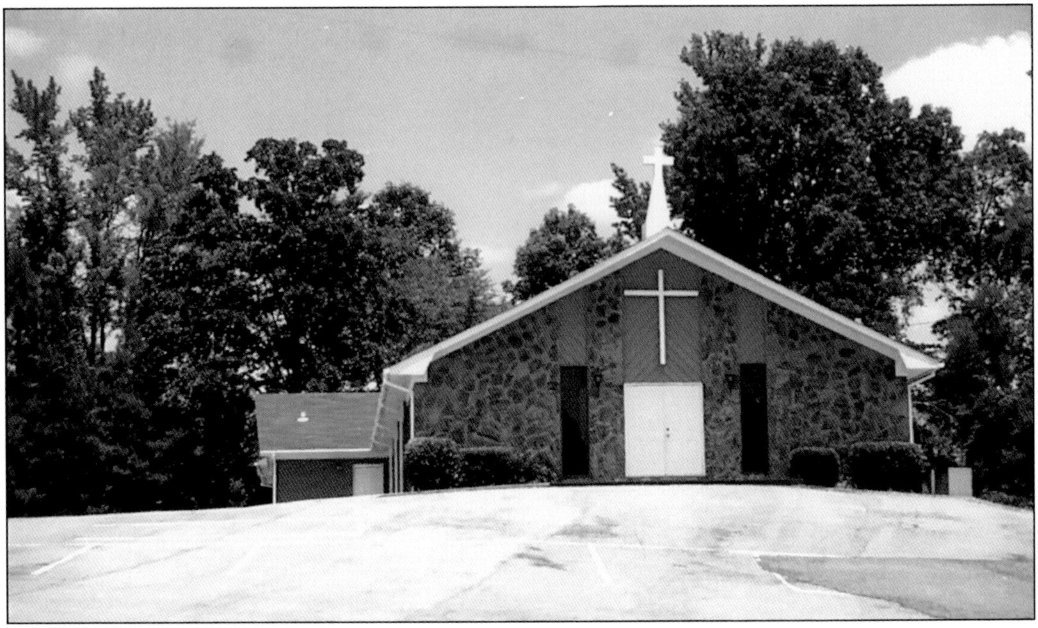

Greater Murphy AME Church was located in Camden. This church was organized in the late 1800s on donated land. A school was also located on the property. The school is now located across the road from the church. (Courtesy of the Author.)

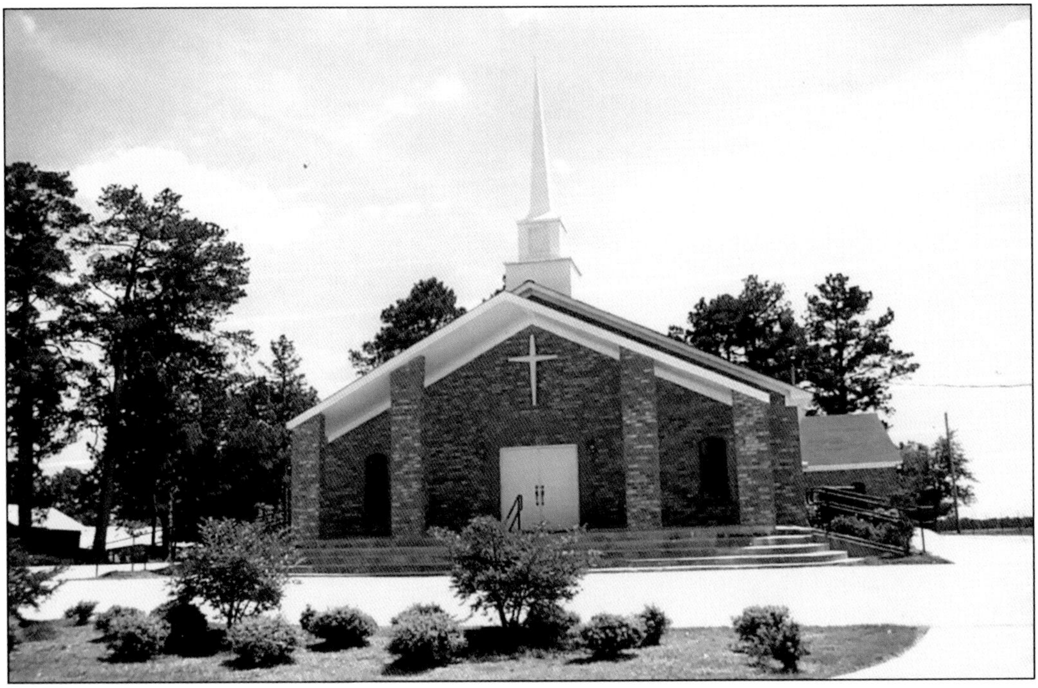

Mary Grove Baptist Church was founded in 1877 by former slaves. Jim Owens donated land in a field for the congregation to have worship services. In 1901, the congregation moved to Rankin Road. A storm severely damaged the church in 1953 and the members rebuilt. The latest church, seen in this photograph, was built in 1997. (Courtesy of the Author.)

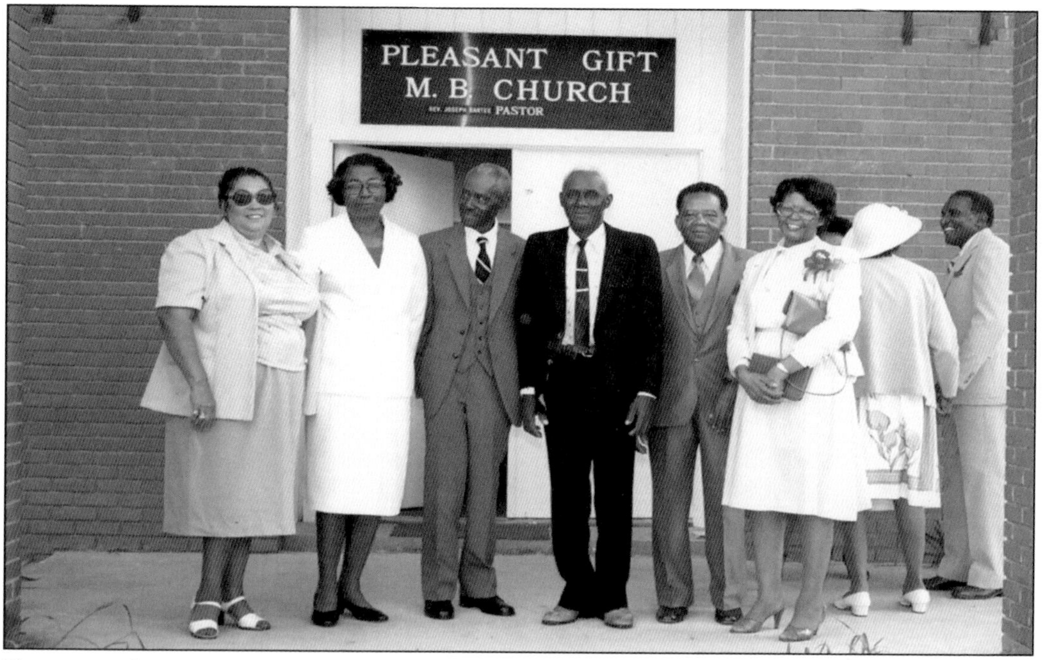

Pleasant Gift Missionary was founded in 1850. The Pitchfords family donated the patch of land located between Farmhaven and Sharon in east Madison County. Included in this image, from left to right, are unidentified, Cora Day, Jonathan Day, Henry Day, Robert Seals, and the rest are unidentified.

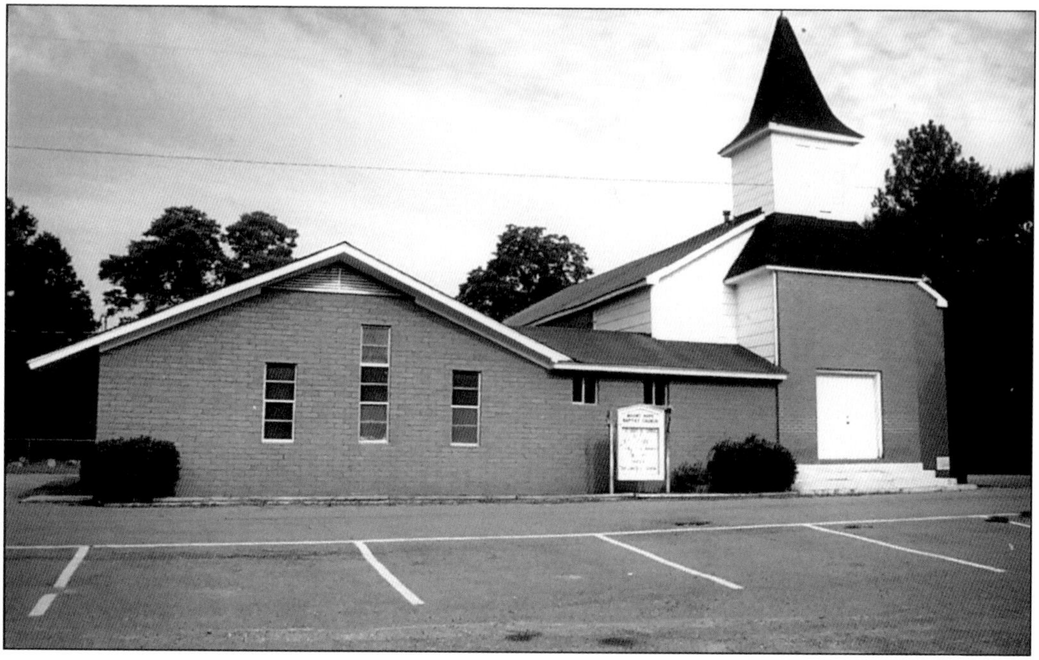

Mount Hope Missionary Baptist Church was organized in 1869 west of Canton. Landowner Penquite Cameron donated land to tenants who lived on his plantation. Members held services under a bush arbor until they built their first wooden structure. (Courtesy of the Author.)

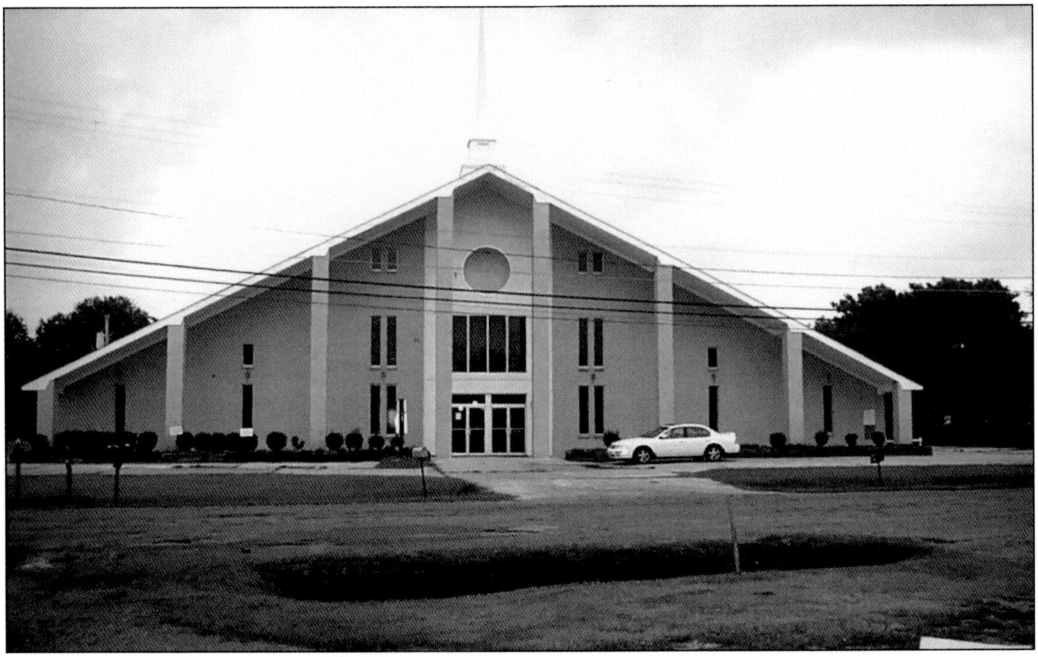

Greater Mount Levi Full Gospel Church was first named Mount Richards Baptist Church and was located west of Canton. The church moved to Fulton Street in Canton in 1955. In 1972, Levi Goolsby gave additional land for the church members to build a sanctuary. The members built a church in 1974; the structure seen in this photograph is the latest building. (Courtesy of the Author.)

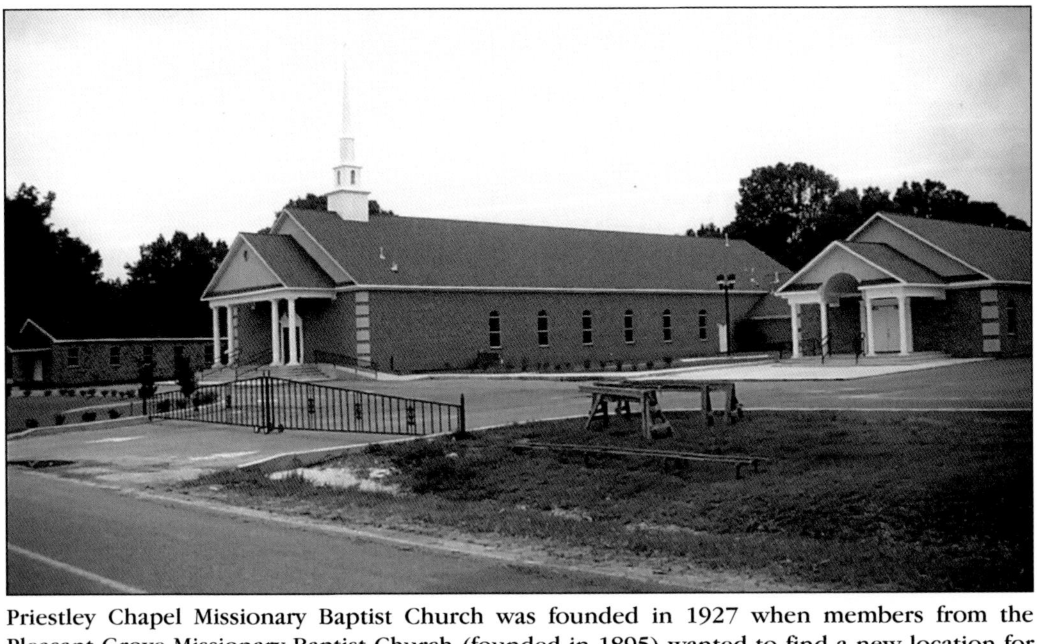

Priestley Chapel Missionary Baptist Church was founded in 1927 when members from the Pleasant Grove Missionary Baptist Church (founded in 1895) wanted to find a new location for the church. In 1927, church trustee Ed Merriweather and Reverend Robertson left Pleasant Grove and started what is now Priestley Chapel Missionary Baptist Church.

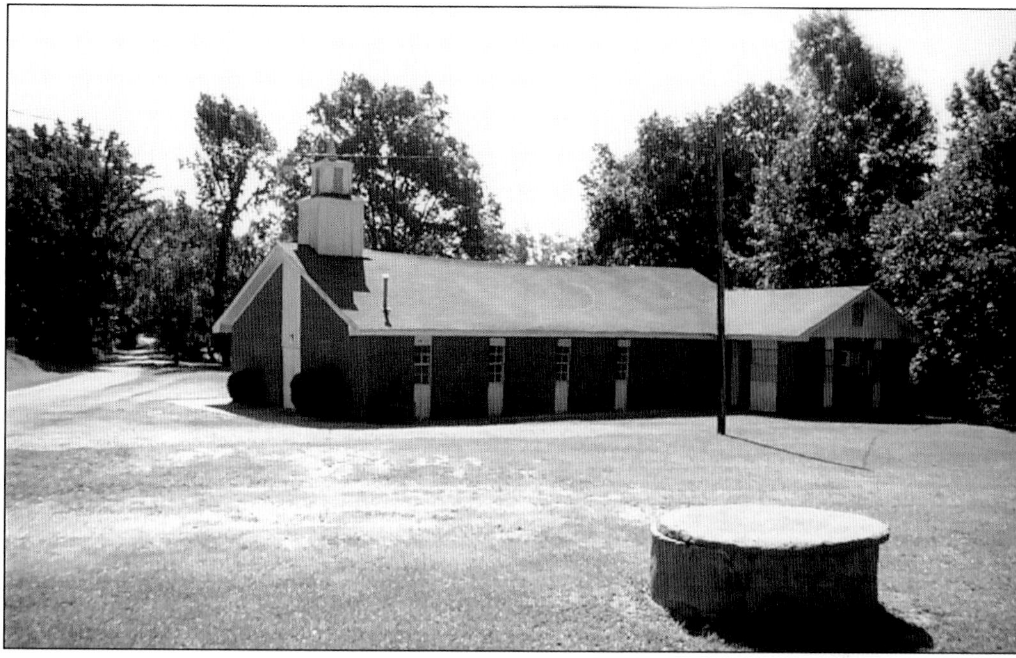

Mount Ollie Way Missionary Baptist Church was founded in the 1850s. Slaves first met under a bush arbor for church services and later land was donated to the slaves for a church. The church congregation continues to worship in the same location. (Courtesy of the Author.)

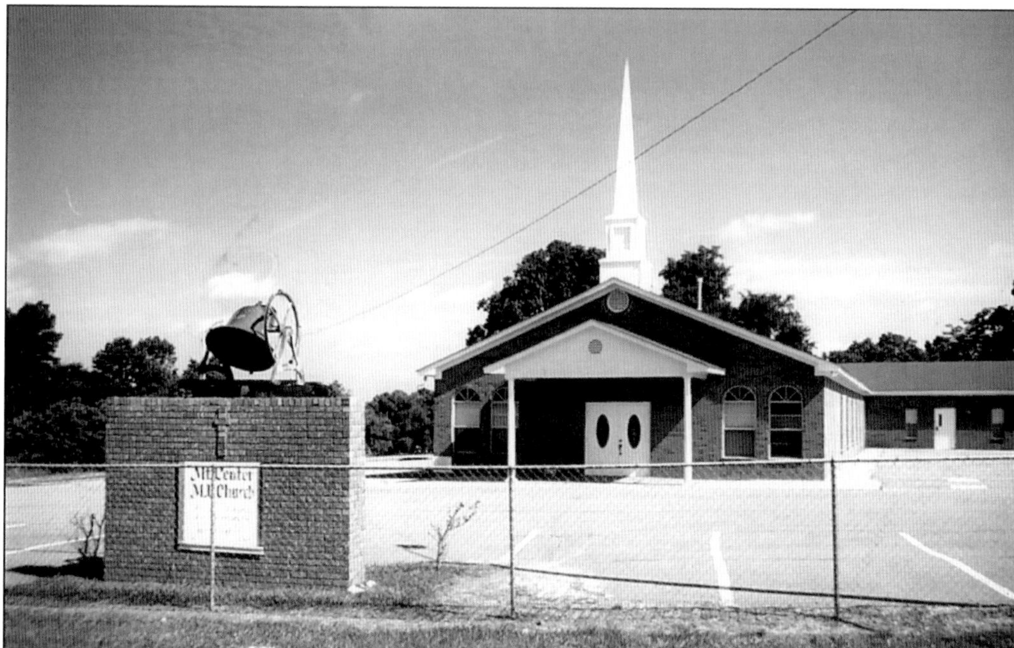

Mount Center Missionary Baptist Church, located in Pocahontas, was started under a bush arbor in the late 1800s. Members of the church purchased the land from Bell Cheetam. (Courtesy of the Author.)

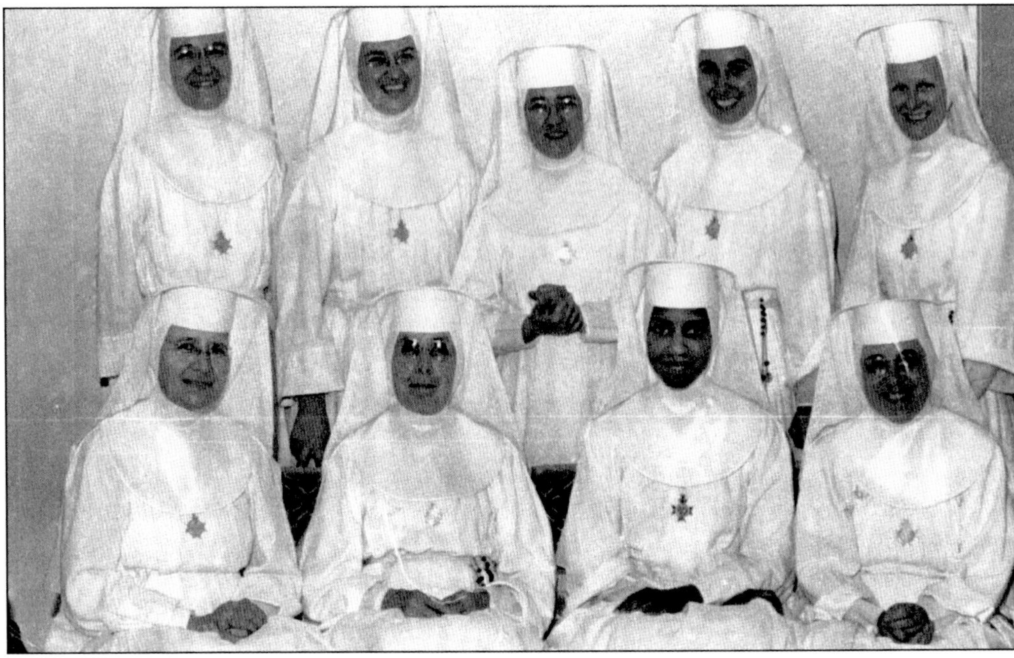

Teachers and nuns at the Holy Child Jesus Catholic Church and School in Canton are seen in this 1966 photo. The private school educated African-American children in the Canton area. Pictured from left to right are (first row) Enrico ?, Mary Walters, Sarah ?, Willie Mae Fisher, and Edna ?; (second row) Beatenia ?, Josena ?, Thea Bowman, and Anglelinda ?. Sister Thea Bowman was the daughter of a physician and a schoolteacher; she was born in Canton and educated at the Holy Child Jesus Catholic School. Sister Bowman became one of the leading advocates of African-American Rights and their inclusion in the Catholic faith. She was known nationally for her work in Catholicism and the African-American community (Courtesy of Ruth Luckett.)

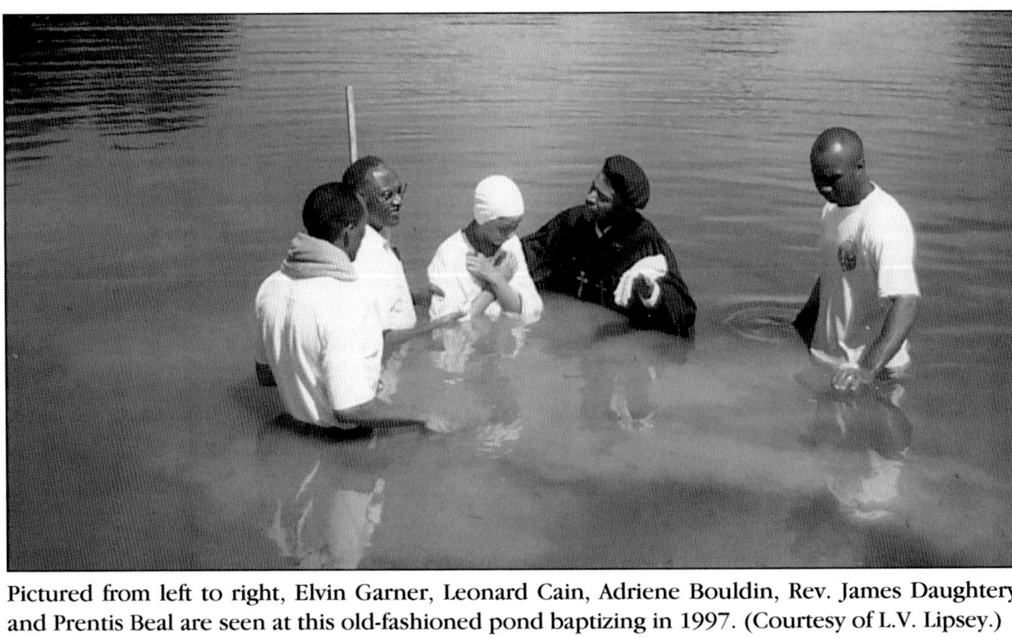

Pictured from left to right, Elvin Garner, Leonard Cain, Adriene Bouldin, Rev. James Daughtery, and Prentis Beal are seen at this old-fashioned pond baptizing in 1997. (Courtesy of L.V. Lipsey.)

Three

SCHOOL DAYS

"A little learning, indeed, may be a dangerous thing, but the want of learning is a calamity to any people."

Frederick Douglass, 1894

Education is an important part of life for African Americans in Madison County. In the early years of education, some black children could only go to school six to nine months out of the year because of farming duties. Children who lived in the city, as well as the rural areas, were subjected to substandard schools. Schools were segregated—and the black schools were often in desperate need of constant repair. Teachers and staff in these schools stood firm to educate African-American children against all odds. Many successful leaders and prominent professionals are products of predominantly black schools in Madison County. From magnet schools to top sports programming, education in Madison County is better than ever for all races.

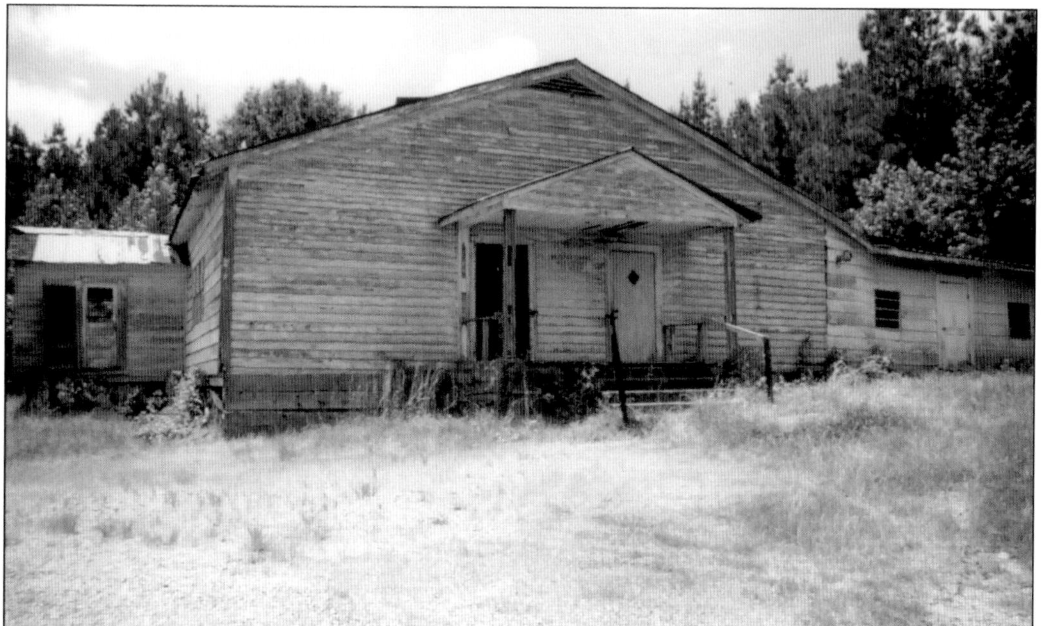

Murphey Chapel Headstart Center in Camden educated young African-American children in the community. (Courtesy of the Author.)

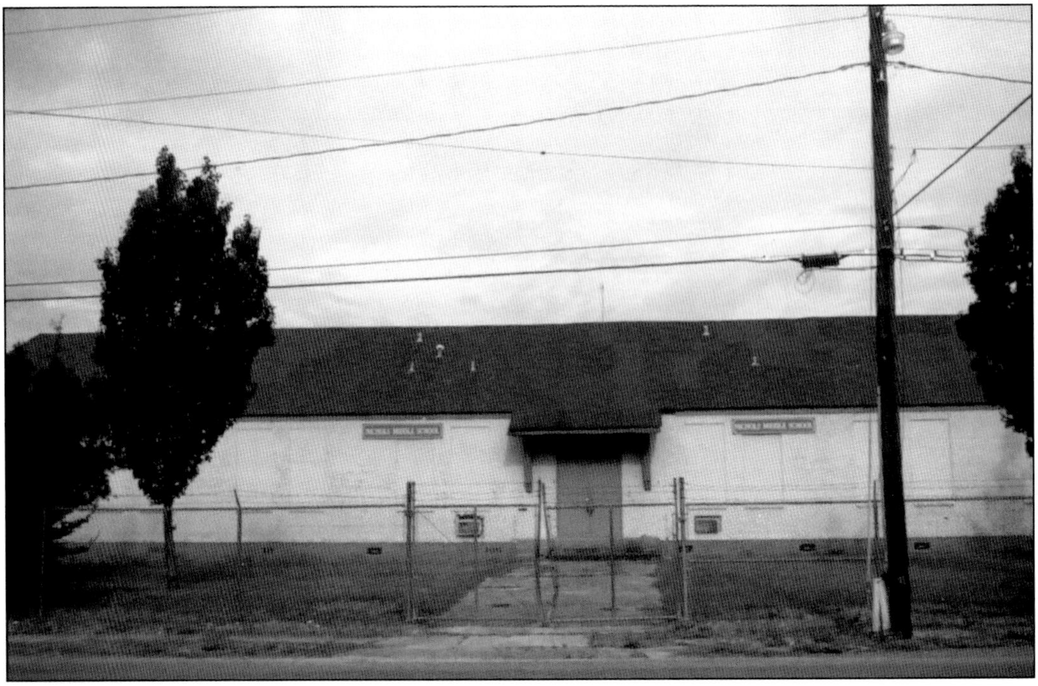

This was the old Cameron Street School were African-American students in Canton went to high school. After Rogers High School was built for the African-American students, this facility became Nichols Middle School. (Courtesy of the Author.)

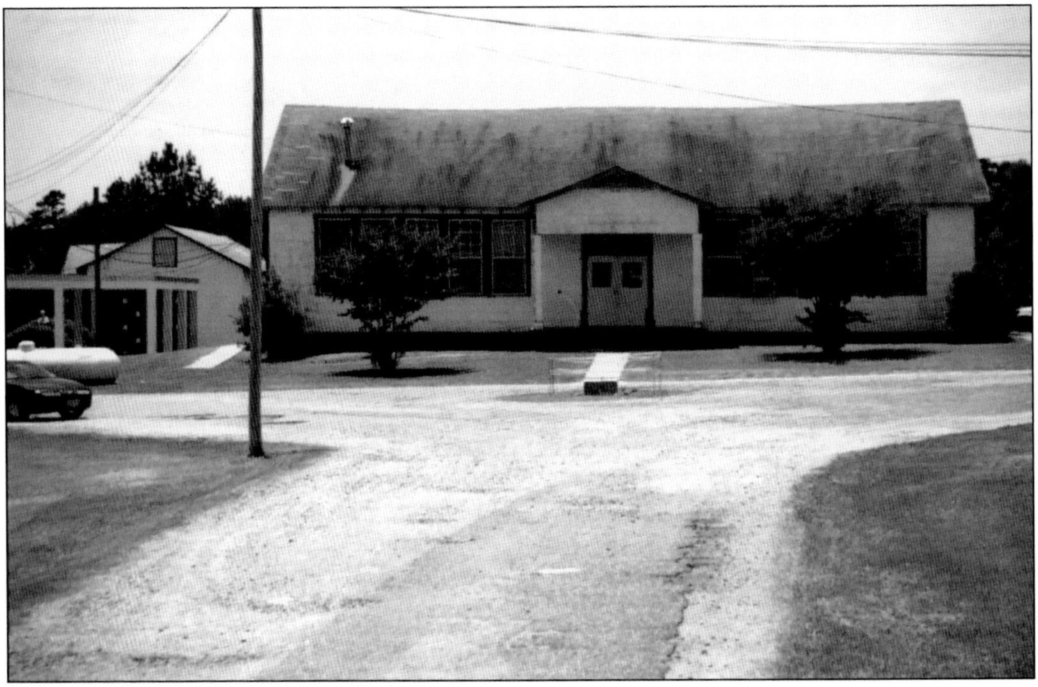

Sacred Heart Catholic School in Camden was established in 1944. This was a private institution that educated young African-American children in Madison County. (Courtesy of the Author.)

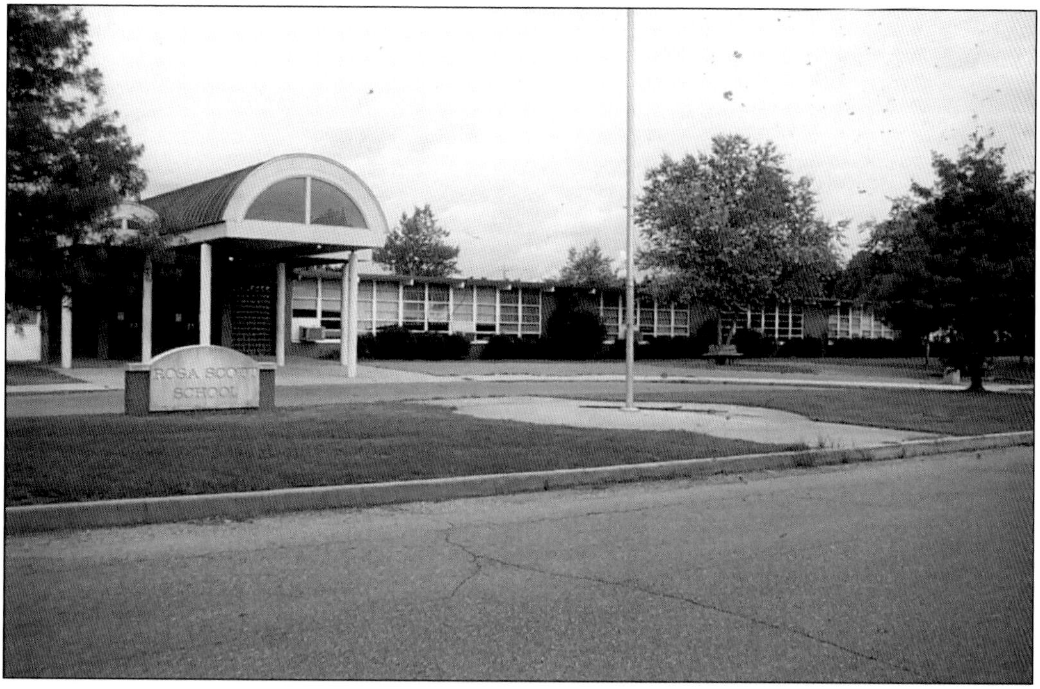

Rosa Scott School in the city of Madison is seen in this photograph. The school was named after Rosa Allie Scott, who was an advocate for Civil and Human Rights. She raised funds for the building of this school in the 1930s. She is buried on the school grounds. (Courtesy of the Author.)

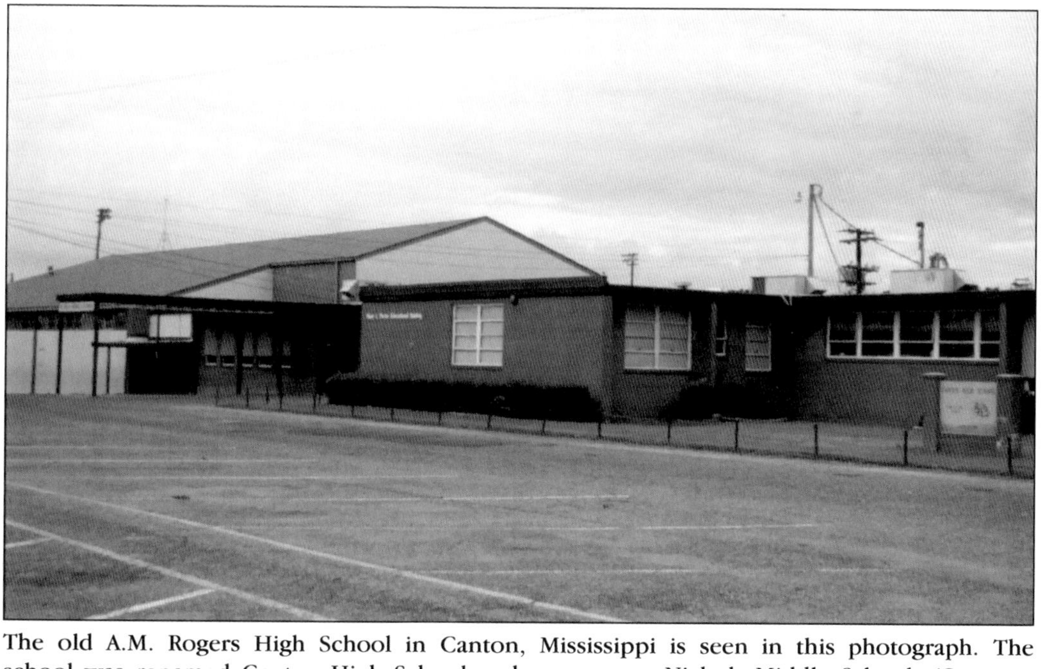

The old A.M. Rogers High School in Canton, Mississippi is seen in this photograph. The school was renamed Canton High School and now serves Nichols Middle School. (Courtesy of the Author.)

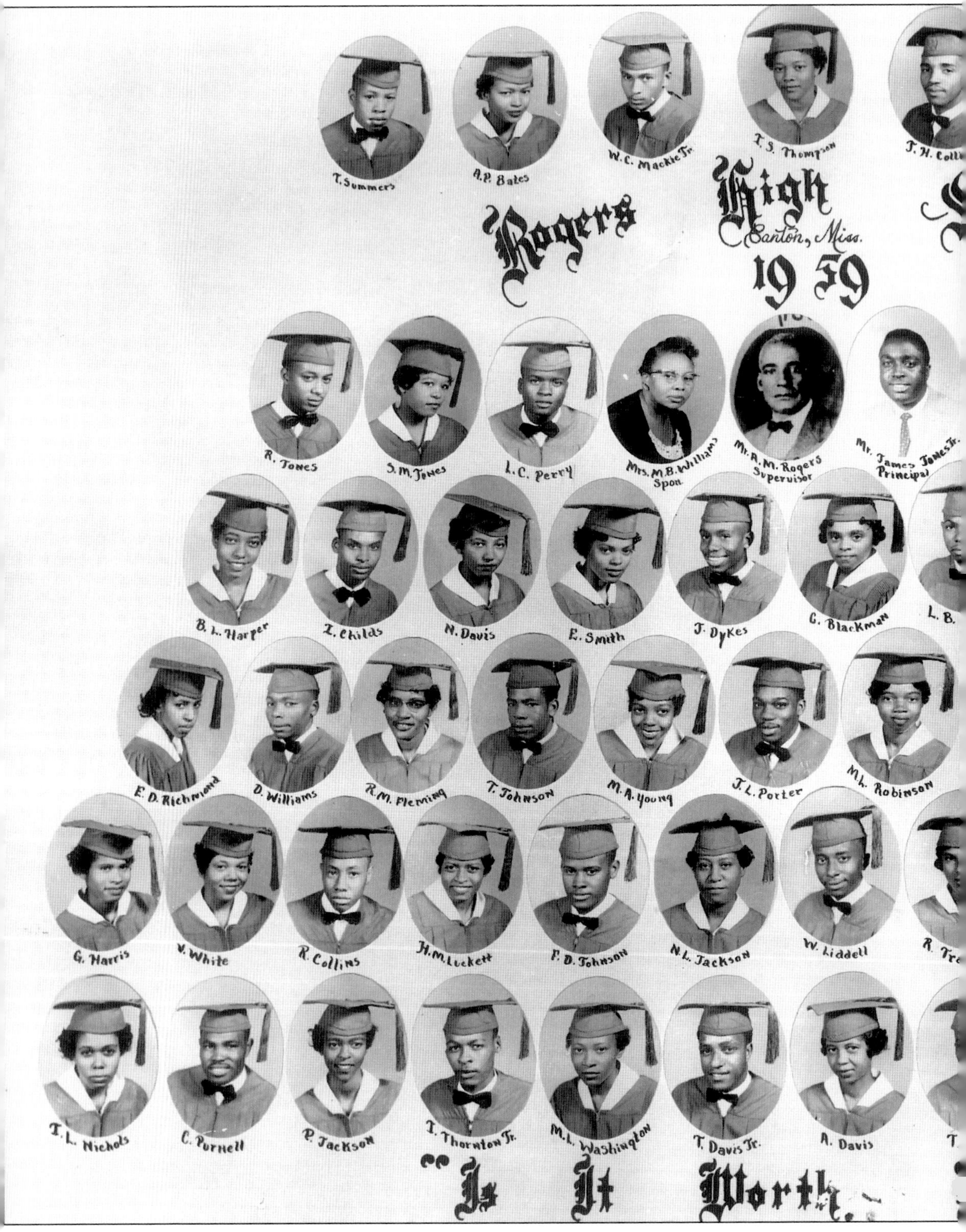
T. Summers
A.P. Bates
W.C. Mackie Jr.
T.S. Thompson
Rogers High
Canton, Miss.
1959
R. Jones
S.M. Jones
L.C. Perry
Mrs. M.B. Williams Spon.
Mr. A.M. Rogers Supervisor
Mr. James Jones Jr. Principal
B.L. Harper
I. Childs
N. Davis
E. Smith
J. Dykes
C. Blackman
E.D. Richmond
D. Williams
R.M. Fleming
T. Johnson
M.A. Young
J.L. Porter
M.L. Robinson
G. Harris
V. White
R. Collins
H.M. Luckett
F.D. Johnson
N.L. Jackson
W. Liddell
T.L. Nichols
C. Purnell
P. Jackson
I. Thornton Jr.
M.L. Washington
T. Davis Jr.
A. Davis
"Is It Worth

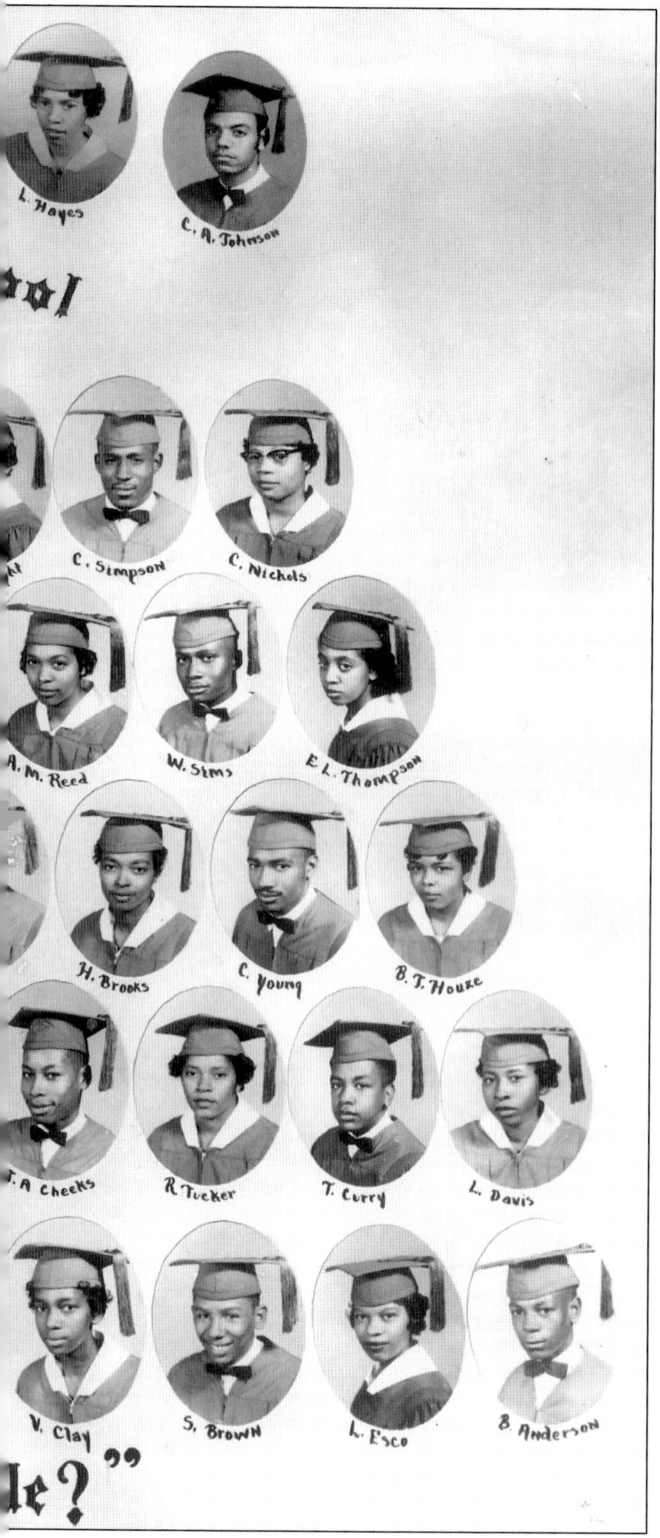

The Rogers High School Class of 1959 senior graduating class is shown here. (Courtesy of Louise Hayes.)

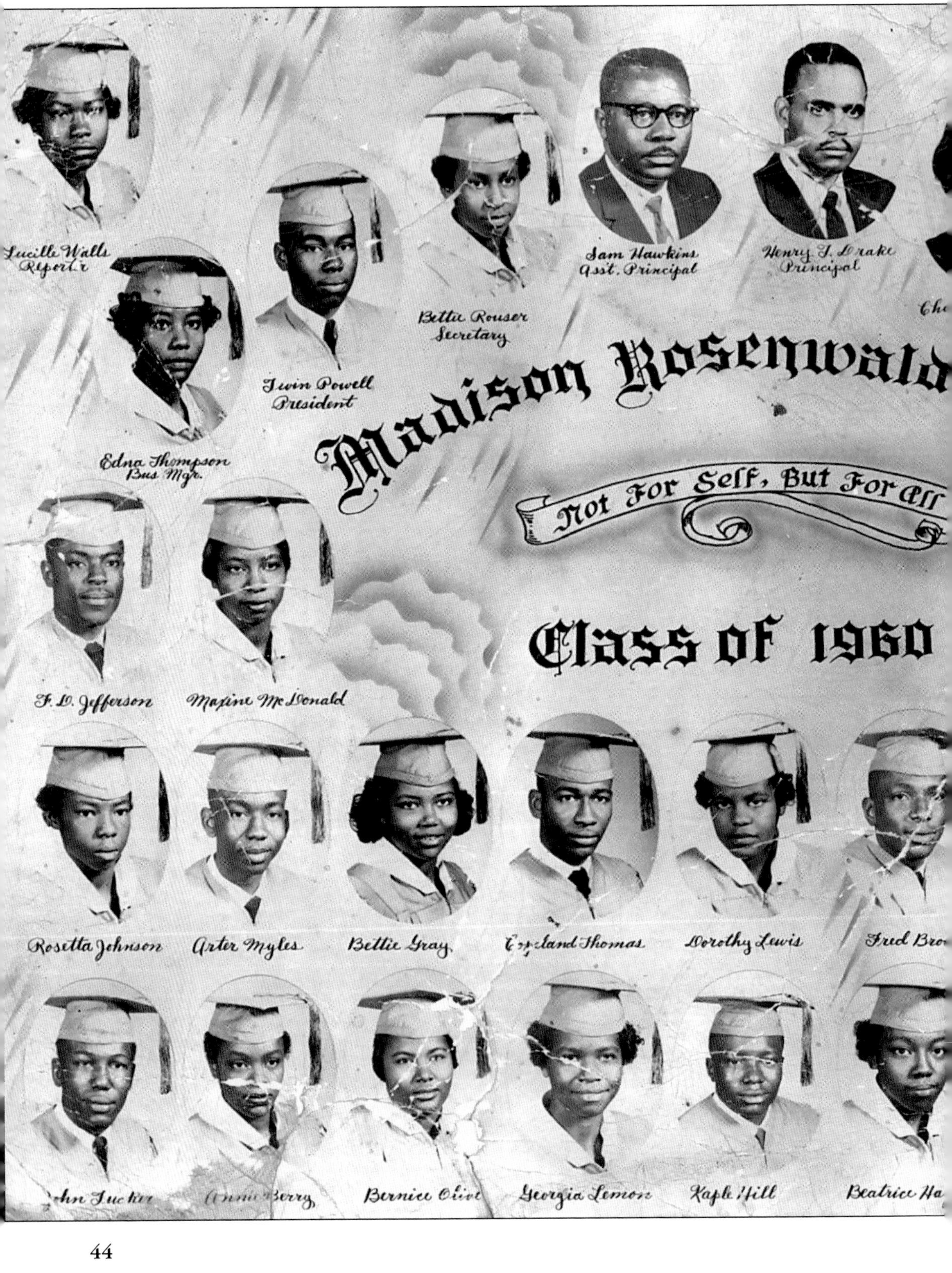

Lucille Walls
Reporter
Edna Thompson
Bus Mgr.
Irvin Powell
President
Bettie Rouser
Secretary
Sam Hawkins
Asst. Principal
Henry T. Drake
Principal
Madison Rosenwald
Not For Self, But For All
Class of 1960
F. D. Jefferson
Maxine McDonald
Rosetta Johnson
Arter Myles
Bettie Gray
Copeland Thomas
Dorothy Lewis
Annie Berry
Bernice Olive
Georgia Lemon
Kaple Hill

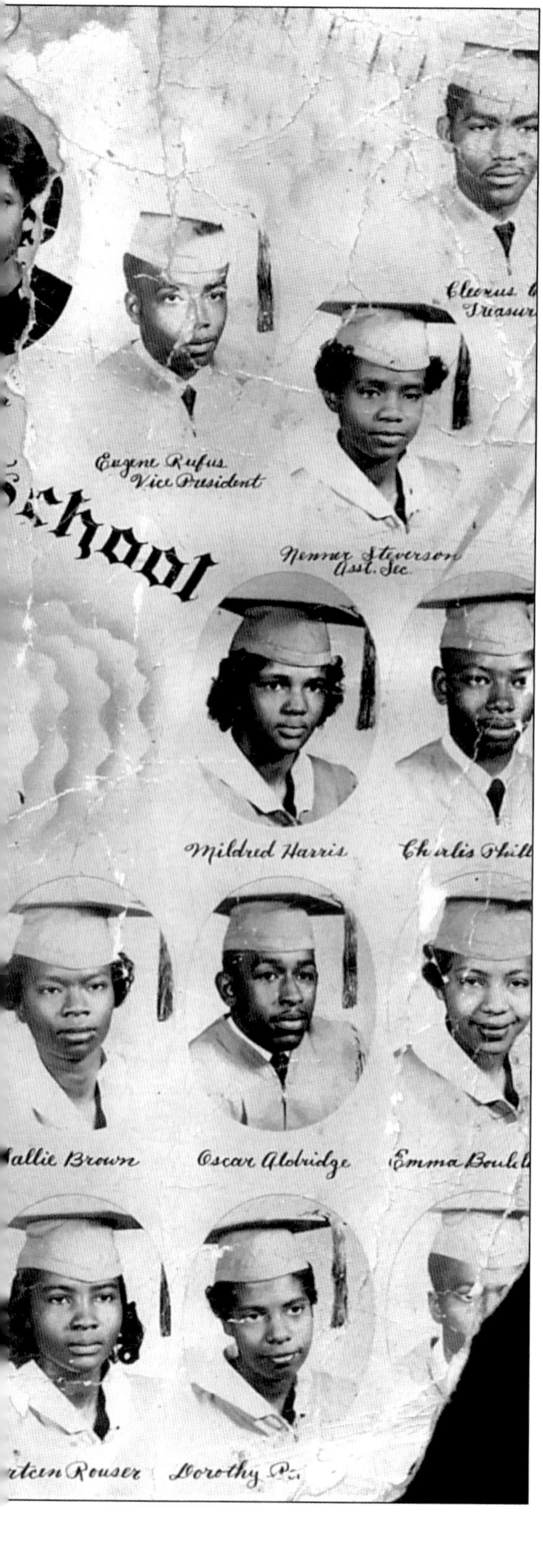

The Madison Rosenwald School Class of 1960 senior graduating class is shown here. (Courtesy of Annie B. Berry.)

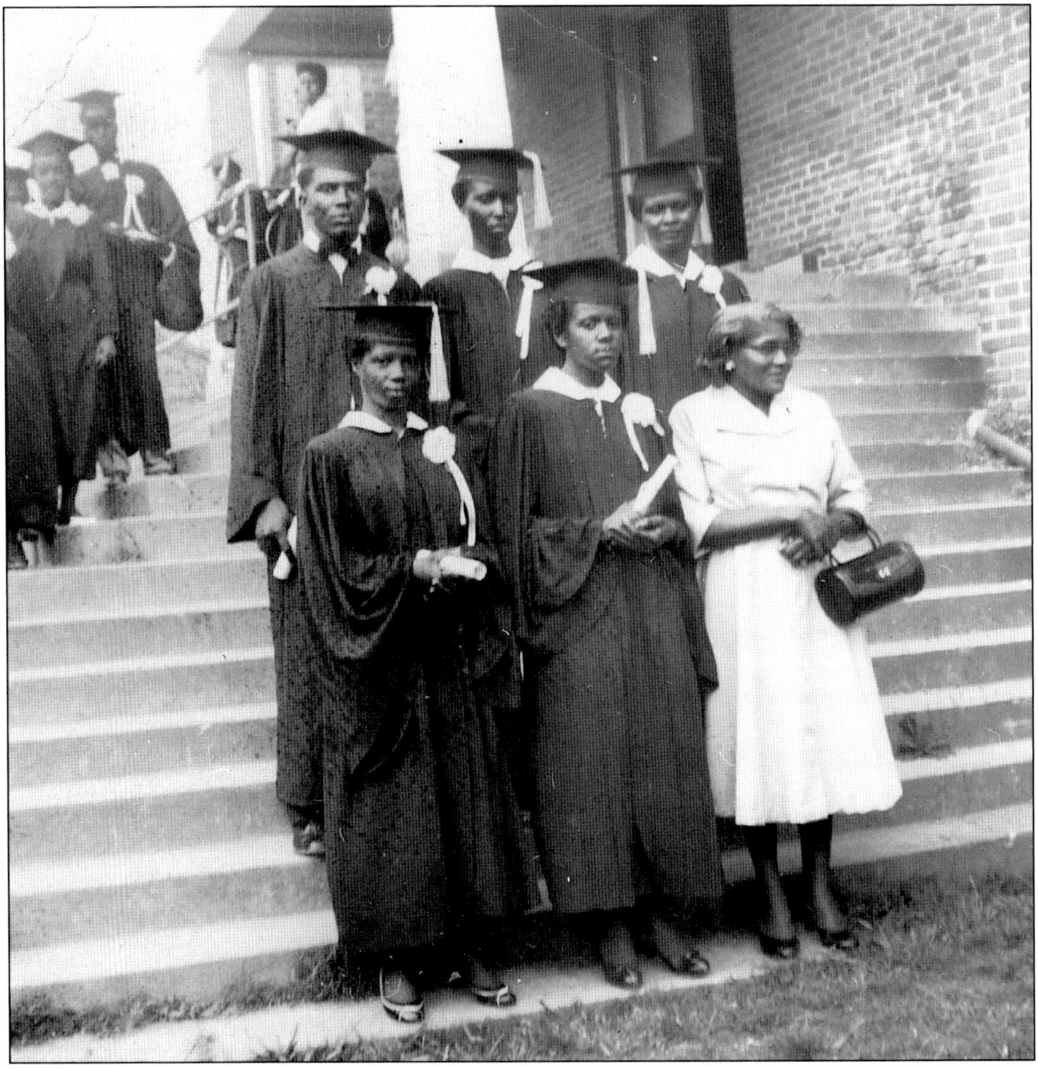

Pictured here is the 1955 Graduating class from the Madison County Training School. The photo was taken after the graduation in 1955. This school was established by Solomon High and educated black children in rural Madison County west of Canton. (Courtesy of Virgie Bartee.)

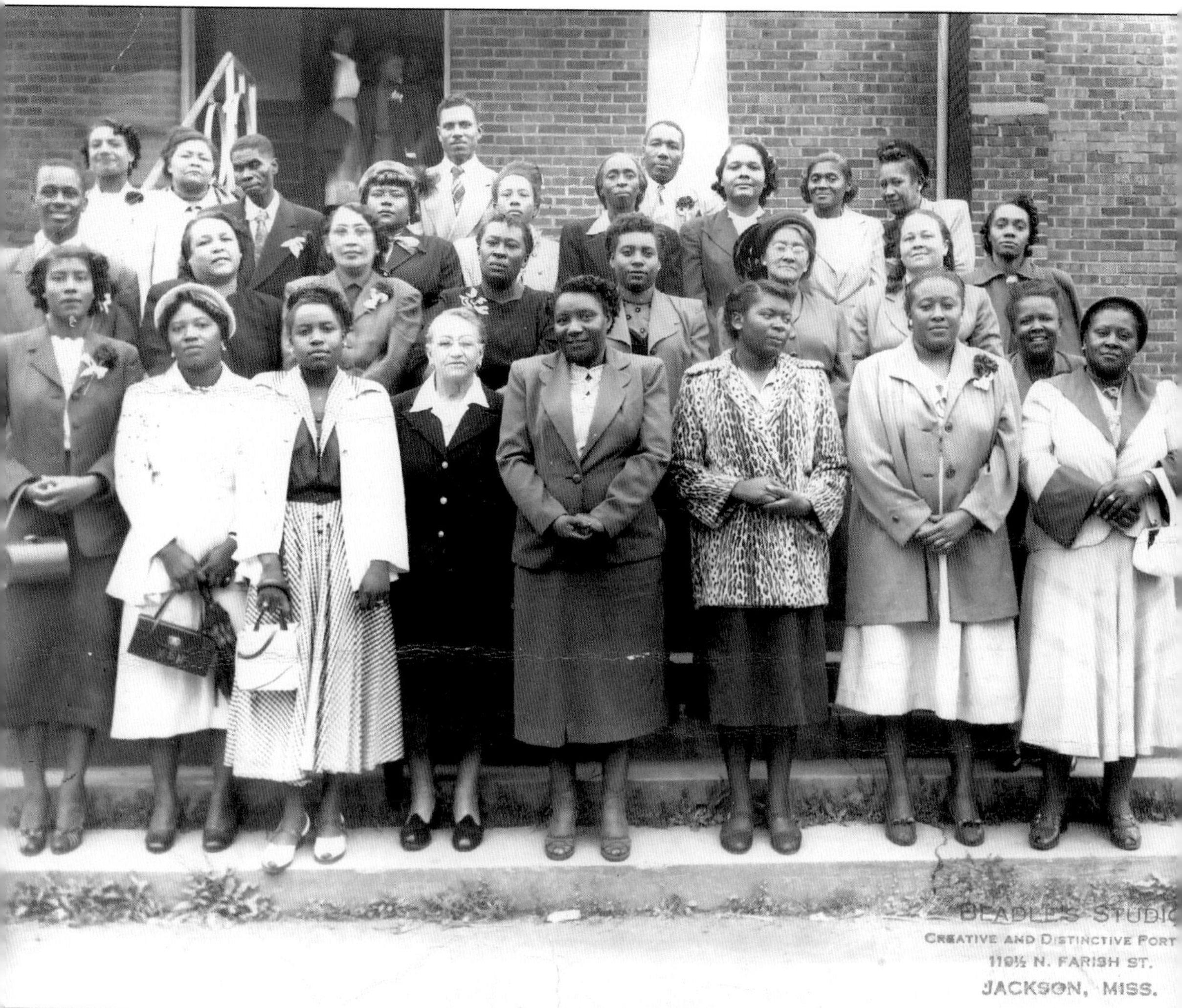

Pictured here (and seen on the front cover of the book) are the teachers from the 1957–1958 school year at the Madison County Rural Schools. Working in substandard conditions, they taught young black children in rural Madison County starting with the elementary grades through high school grades. "Shop" was an important class for young boys who attended this school because it enabled them to learn a trade and work more efficiently on the farm. (Courtesy of Virgie Bartee.)

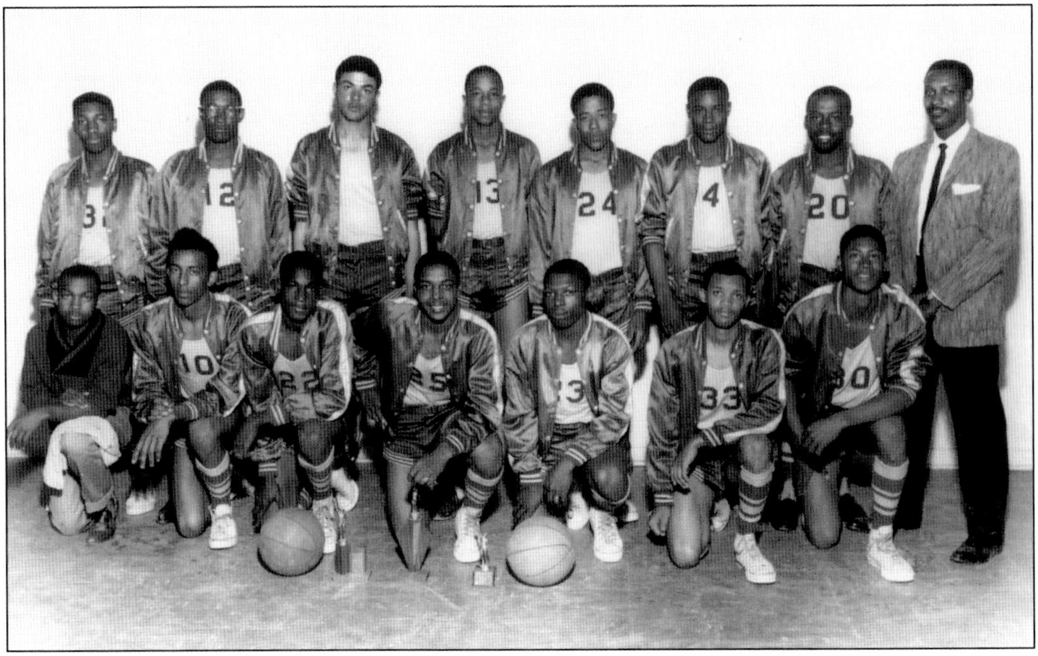

The Velma Jackson High School Boys Varsity Basketball team is shown here. Boys' basketball was a very competitive sport in Madison County. The young men display three trophies they won. (Courtesy of the Velma Jackson High School.)

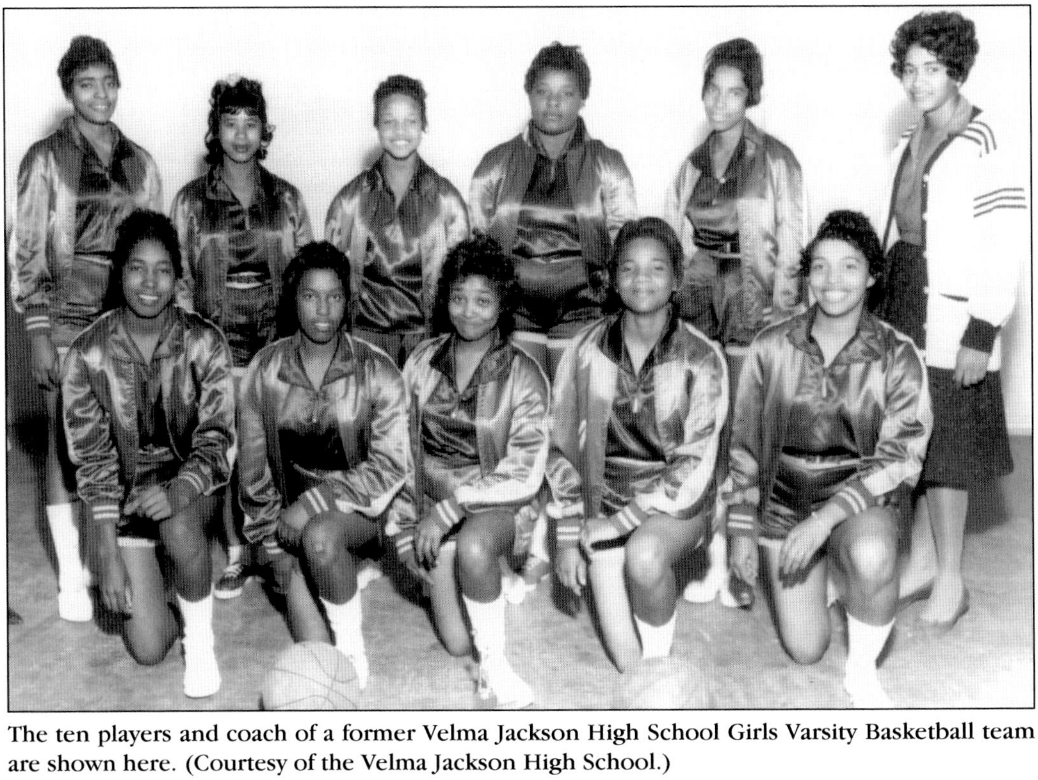

The ten players and coach of a former Velma Jackson High School Girls Varsity Basketball team are shown here. (Courtesy of the Velma Jackson High School.)

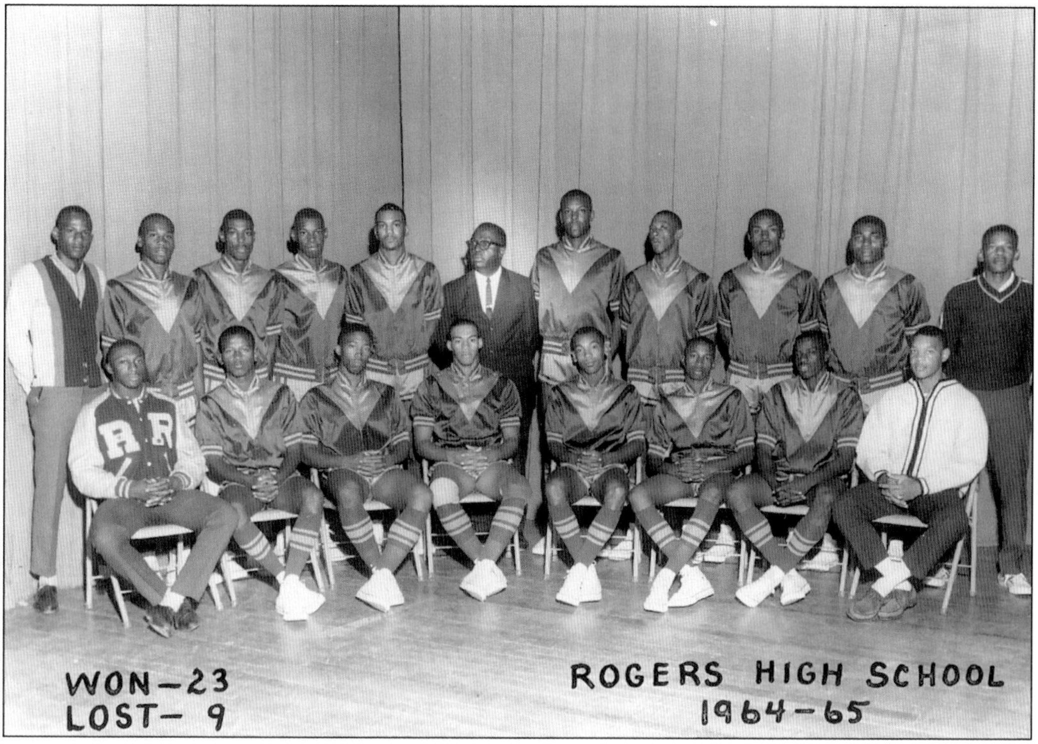

The 1964–1965 Rogers High School Basketball team was coached by school principal James Jones Jr. The school was known countywide for its talented and winning basketball teams. (Courtesy of Virgie Bartee.)

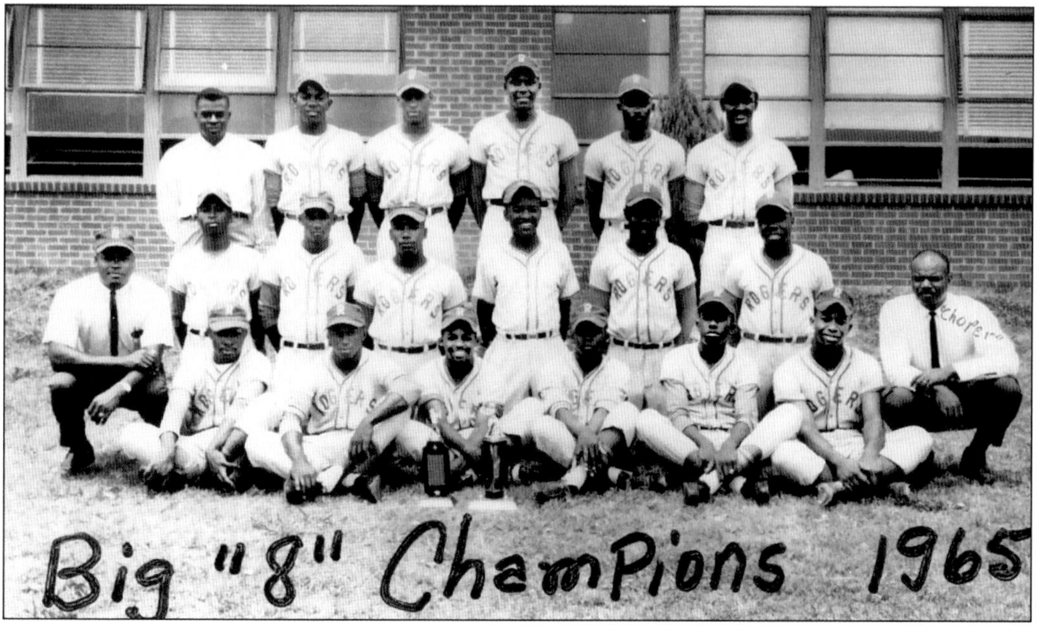

The Rogers High School baseball team took home the honors of the Big "8" Championship in 1965 and boasted some of the best athletes in the city of Canton. (Courtesy of Virgie Bartee.)

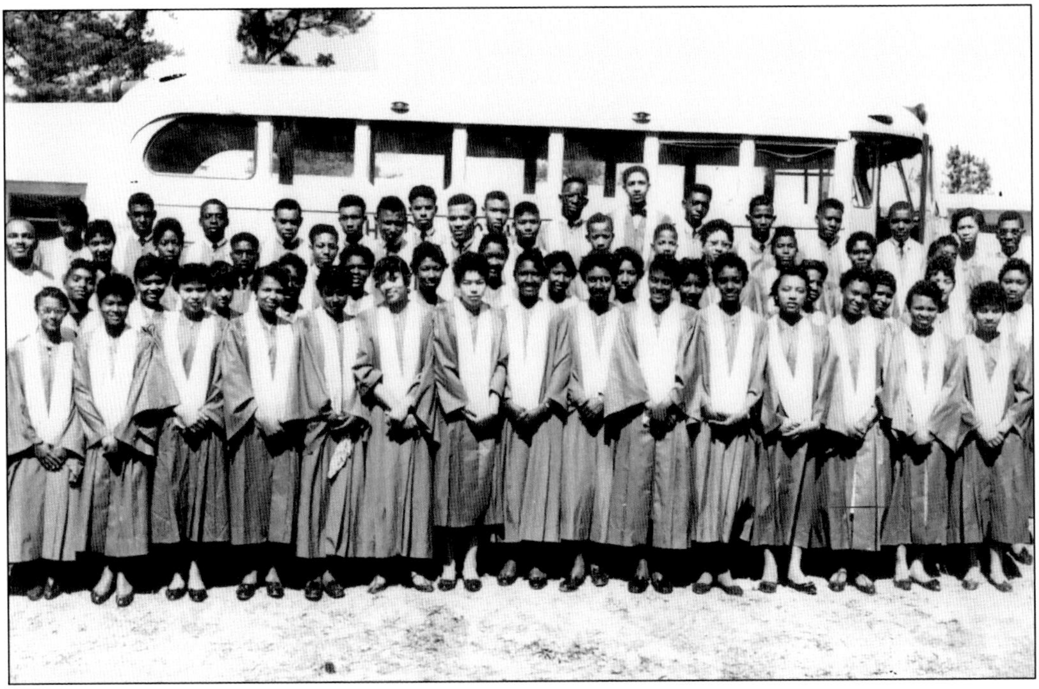

The Velma Jackson High School choir performed gospel music throughout the county, traveling on the school bus pictured in the background. Seen here are 58 choir members. Singing in the school choir was a notable and respectable extra-curricular activity. (Courtesy of the Velma Jackson High School.)

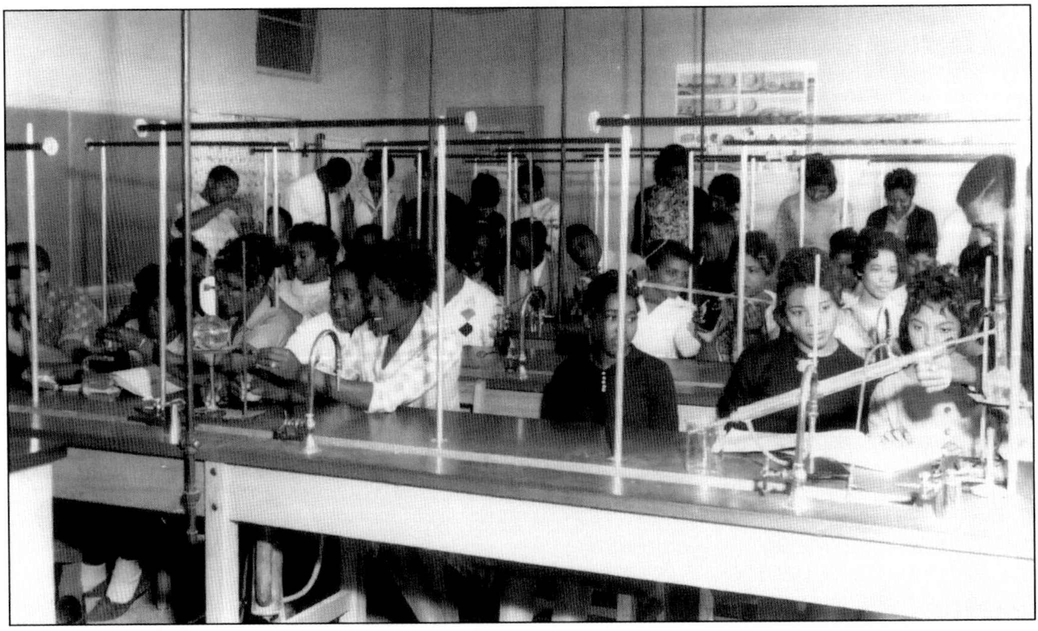

Students at the Velma Jackson High School experiment in their new chemistry lab. The lab allowed students to carry out hands-on chemistry projects. Many rural African-American schools did not have this luxury. (Courtesy of the Velma Jackson High School.)

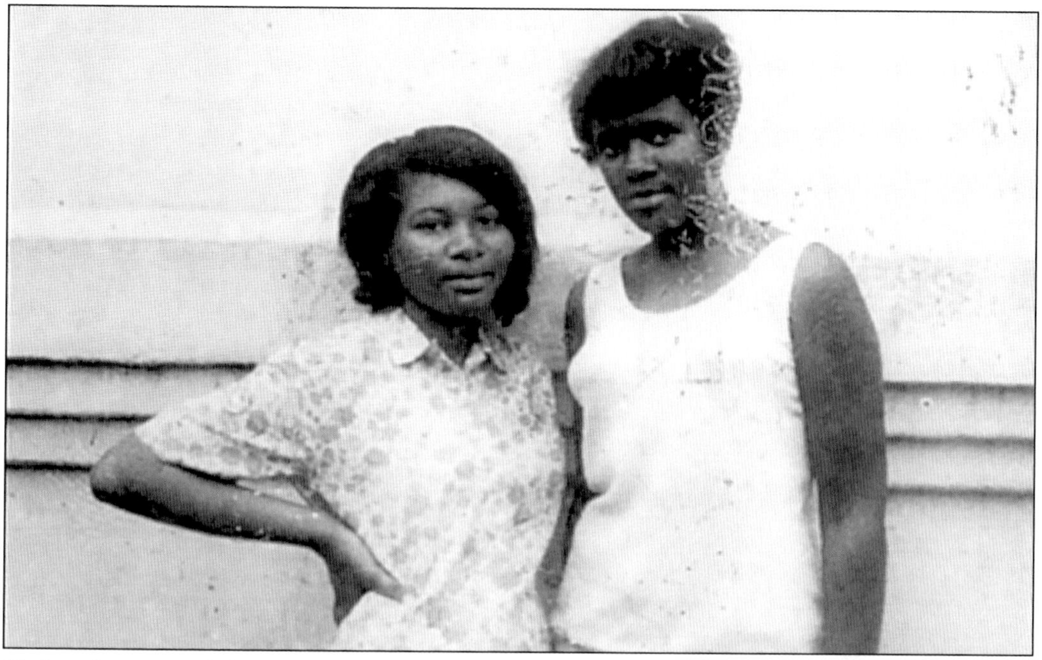

Thelma Garner and Ernestine McLaurin pose for this photo at Rogers High School in 1968. Both of these young ladies grew up together in the "Tin Top" community west of Canton. (Courtesy of Thelma Garner Myers.)

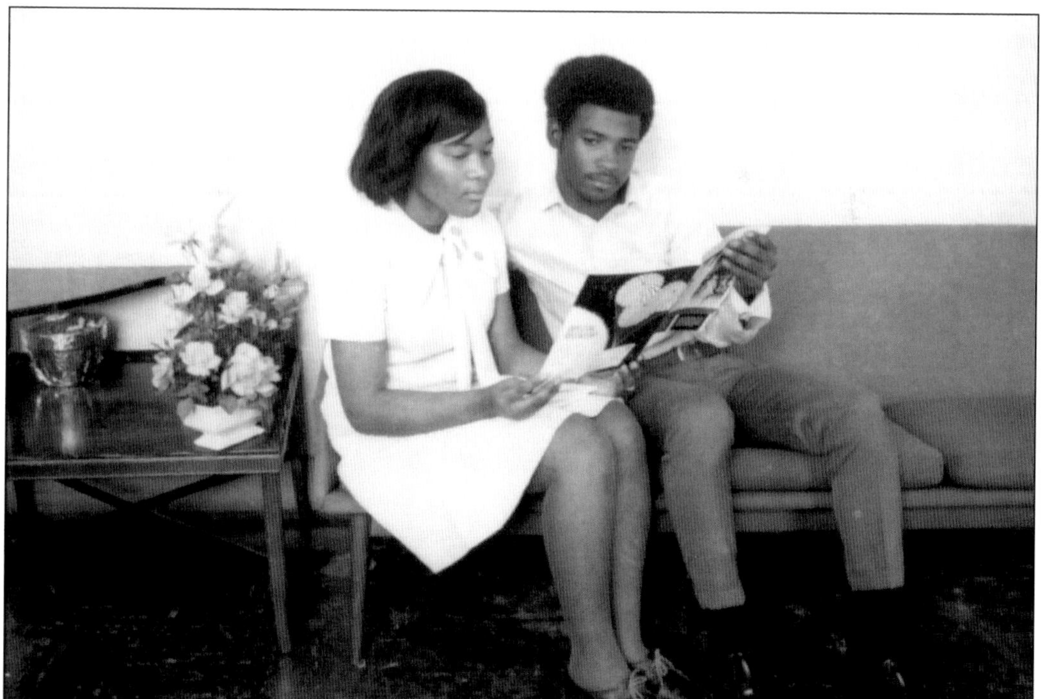

Thelma Garner and Charles Ruffin were voted "Most Quiet" of their 1970 Canton High School graduating class. This photo was featured in their yearbook. (Courtesy of Thelma Garner Myers.)

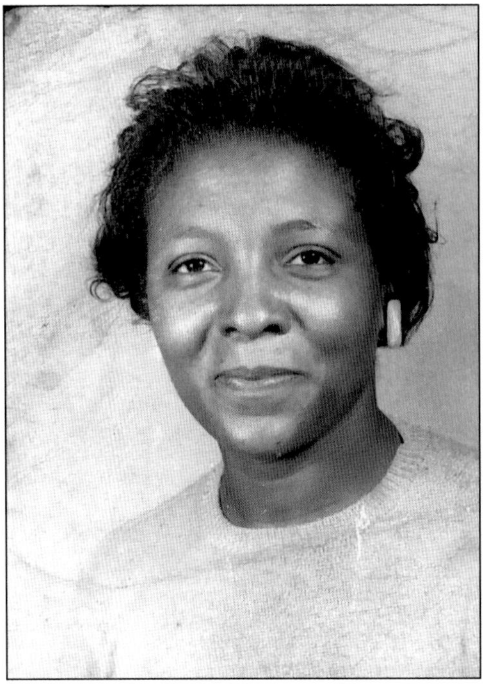

Pictured here is Lauren Banks, who was a school bus driver in rural Madison County in the 1960s. (Courtesy of Annie B. Berry.)

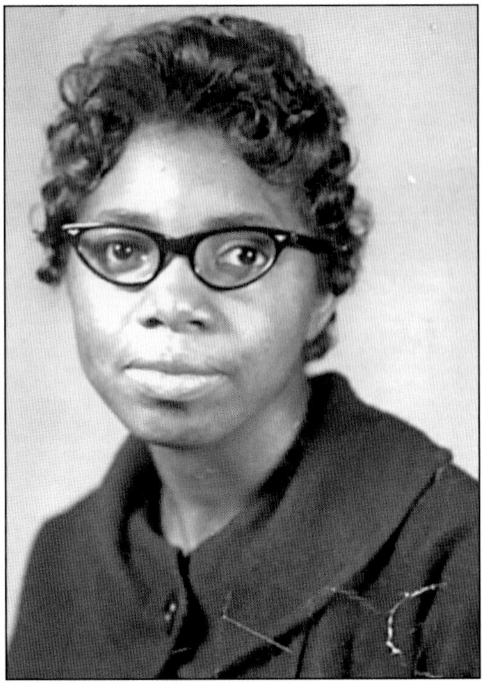

This is Katie McMurtey's 1963 school photo. She received her education from Madison County Public Schools. (Courtesy of James and Francis Sanders.)

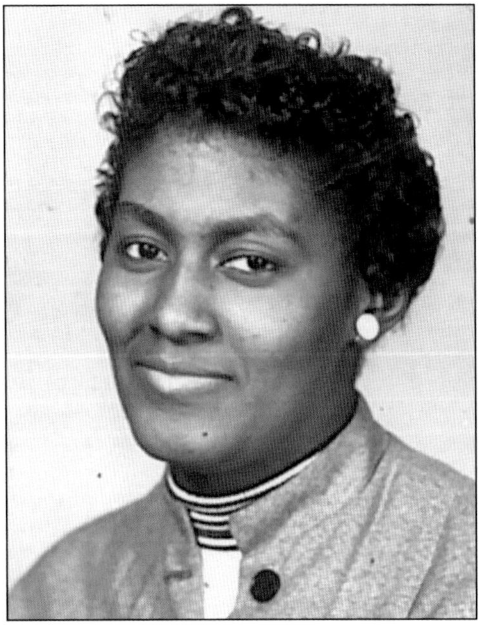

Mrs. Taylor, pictured in this 1959, was a teacher at the Madison County Training School. (Courtesy of Virgie Bartee.)

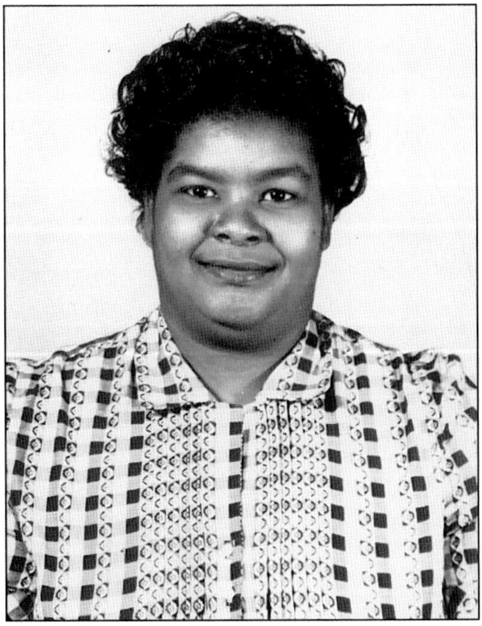

Lillian Ford was a teacher at the Madison County Training School. (Courtesy of Virgie Bartee.)

This is Elois Daughtey's 1957 school photo from the Madison County Training School. (Courtesy of Virgie Bartee.)

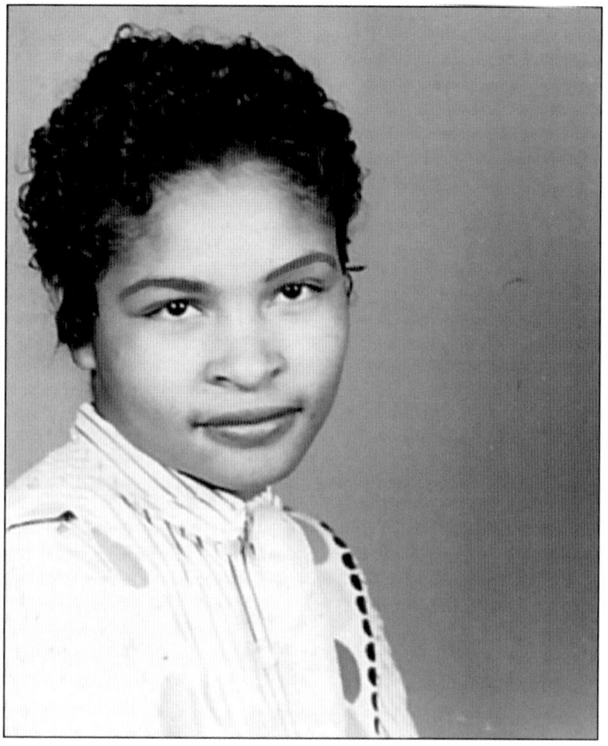

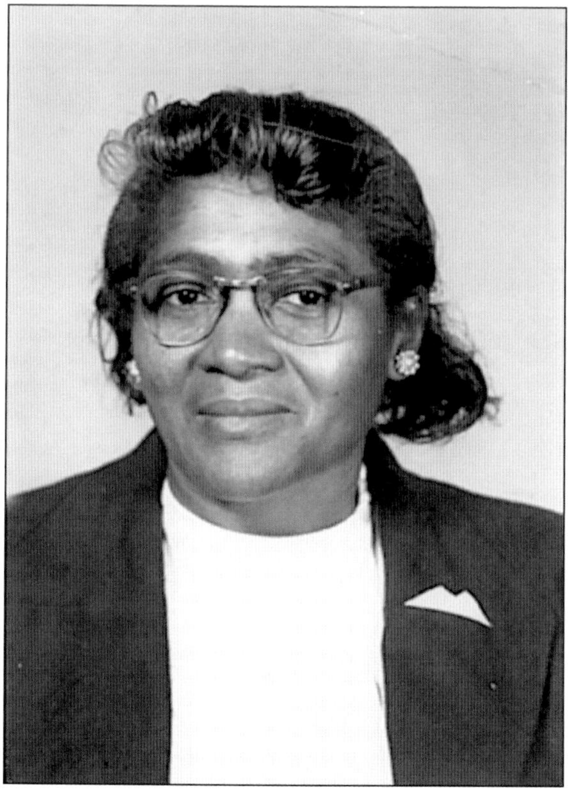

Pictured here is Virgie Bartee in 1959. She was the principal of the Madison County Training School. (Courtesy of Virgie Bartee.)

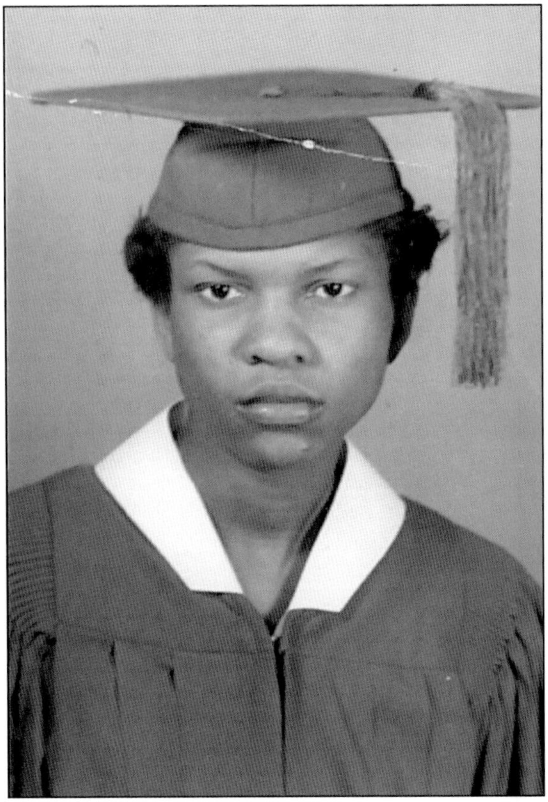

Maggie Cain graduated from Cameron Street High School in 1956. (Courtesy of Maggie Cain.)

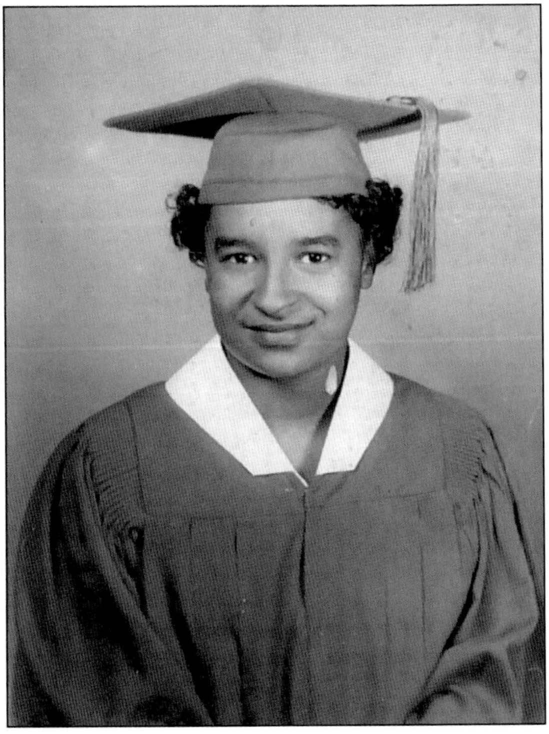

Emma Lou Watkins is seen in her cap-and-gown photograph. Watkins graduated from the Cameron Street High School in Canton. (Courtesy of James and Francis Sanders.)

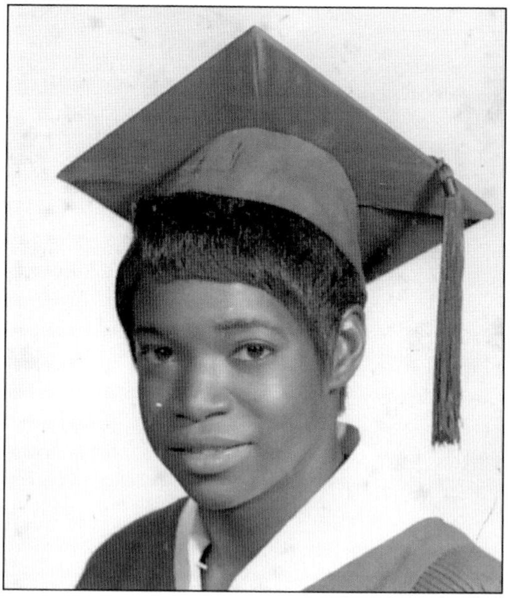

Varie Porter is seen in a 1969 graduation photo from Rogers High School. (Courtesy of Umble Hawkins.)

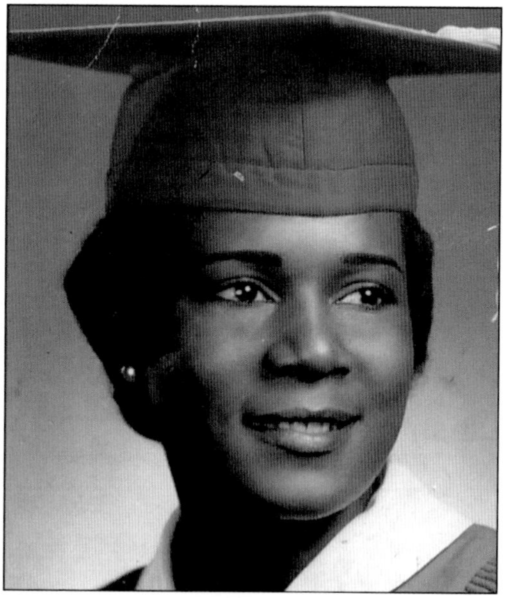

Sadie Davis graduated from Madison Rosenwald High School in 1960. (Courtesy of Umble Hawkins.)

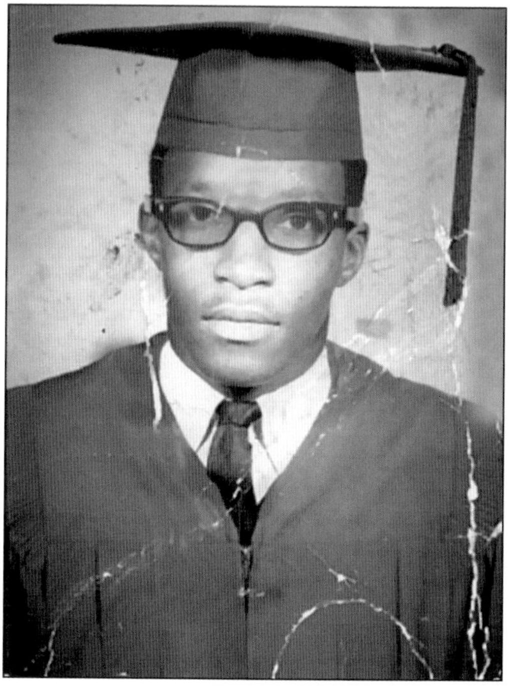

Albert Porter was a 1965 Rogers High School graduate. (Courtesy of Umble Hawkins.)

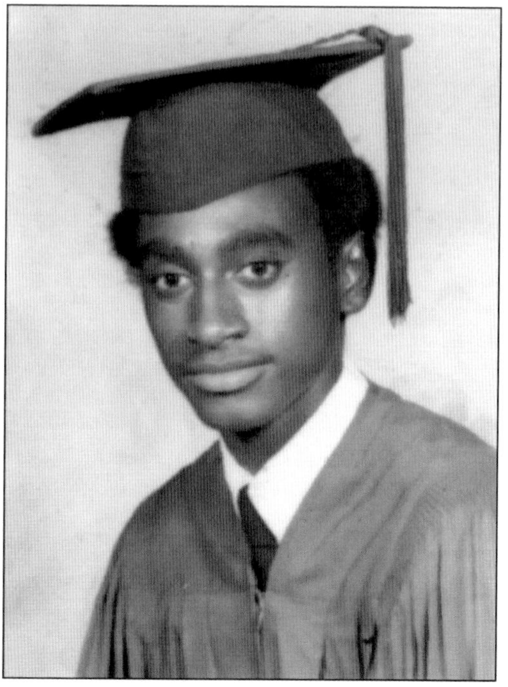

Walter Lee Beale graduated from Rogers High School in 1970. (Courtesy of Thelma Garner Myers.)

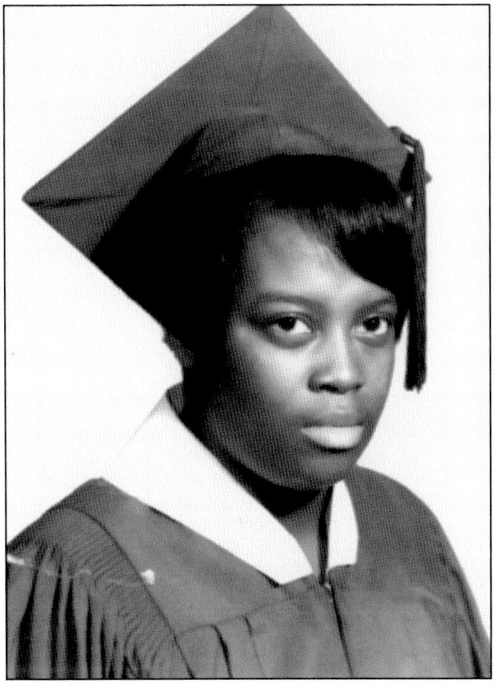

Lauren Frazier graduated from Rogers High School in 1970. (Courtesy of Thelma Garner Myers.)

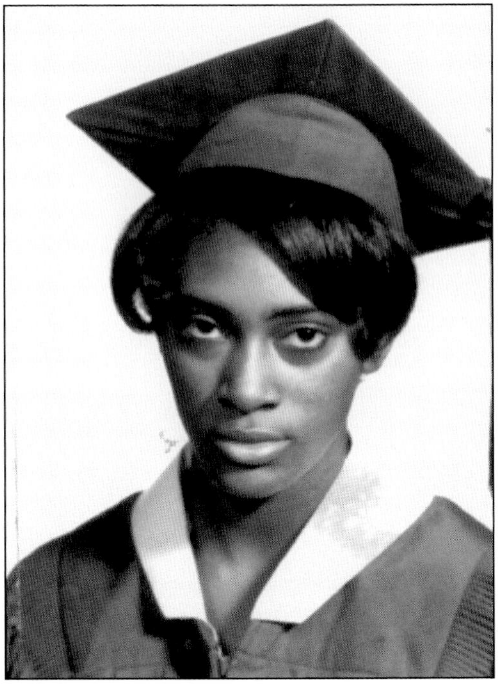

Betty Jean Goldman, class of 1970, is shown in her graduation photo from Rogers High School. (Courtesy of Thelma Garner Myers.)

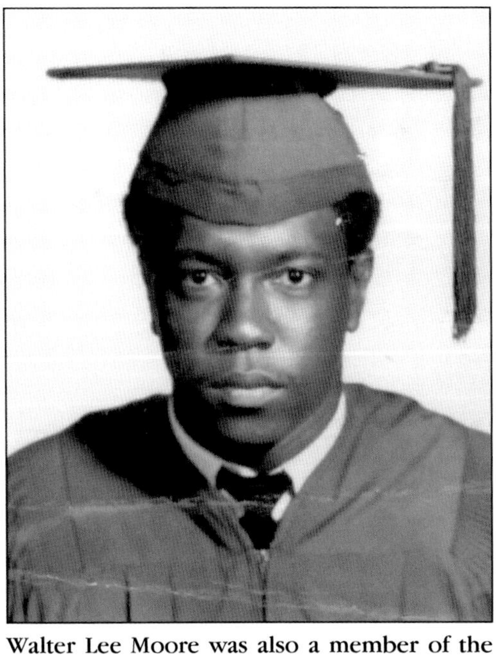

Walter Lee Moore was also a member of the Rogers High School Class of 1970. (Courtesy of Thelma Garner Myers.)

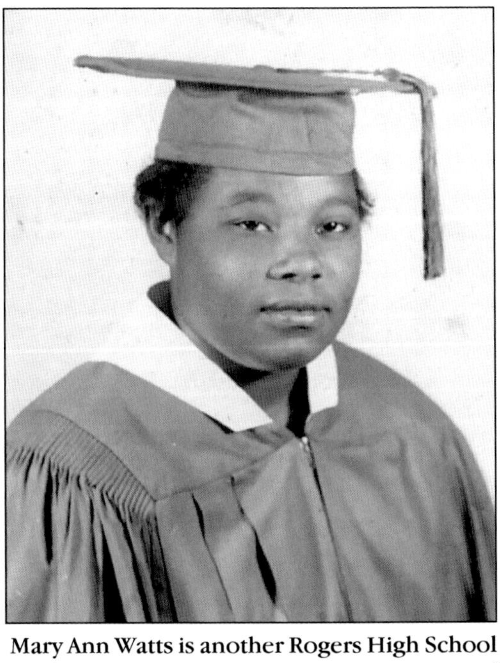

Mary Ann Watts is another Rogers High School graduate in Canton, Mississippi. (Courtesy of James and Francis Sanders.)

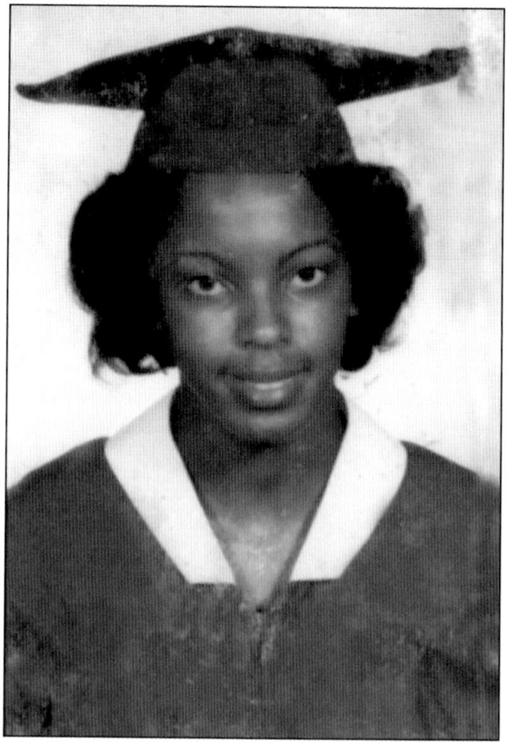

Dianne Ransburg is seen in her graduation photo from Canton High School. She was a member of the Class of 1985. (Courtesy of Stella Berry.)

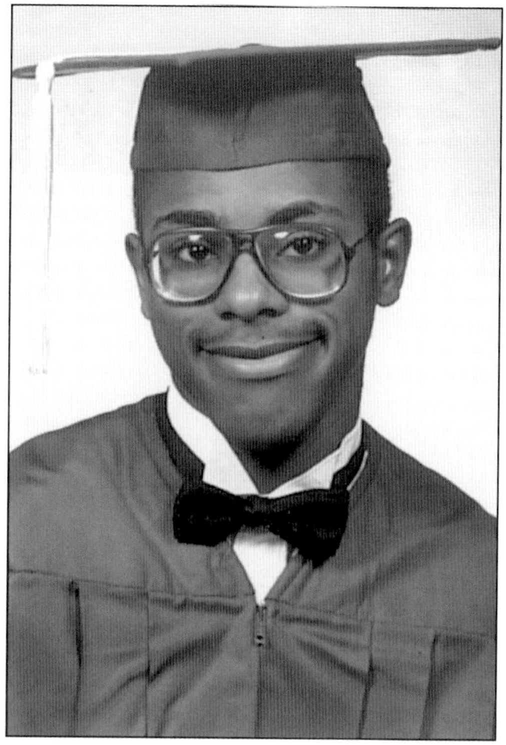

Lawrence Berry's 1988 graduation photo from Madison-Ridgeland High School. (Courtesy of Umble Hawkins.)

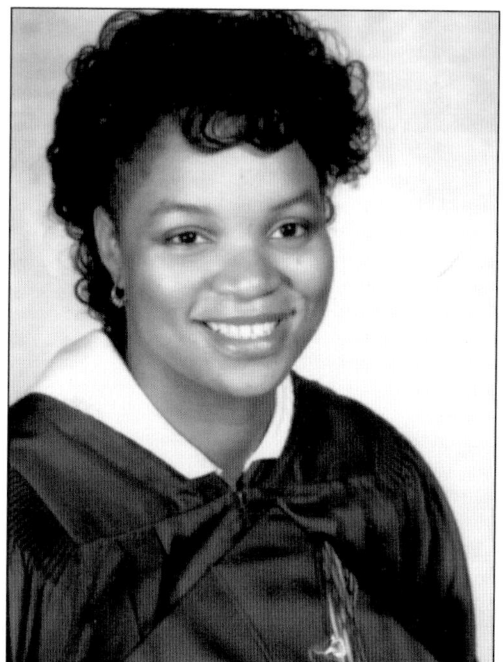

Janet Cheeks is seen in her graduation photo from Canton High School. She was a member of the graduating class of 1988. (Courtesy of Stella Berry.)

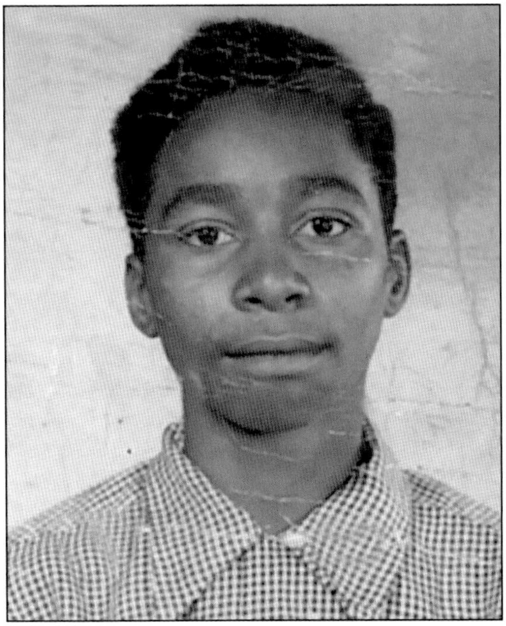

Roosevelt Garner is seen in this 1954 school day picture at the Madison County Training School in rural Madison County. (Courtesy of Tommie Lee Garner.)

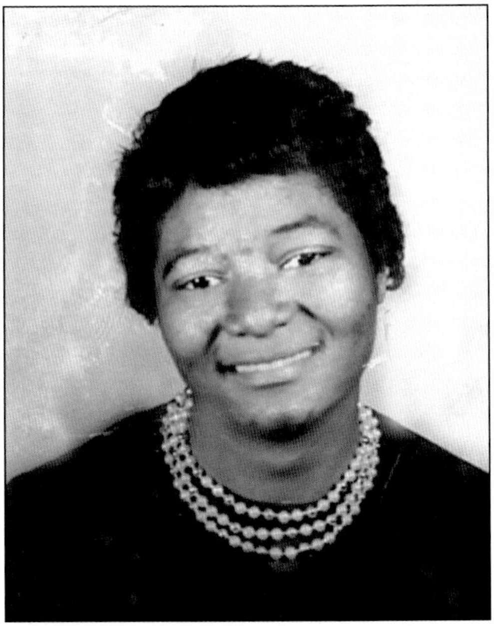

Alice Garner posed for this 1965 school day photo at Rogers High School in Canton. (Courtesy of Tommie Lee Garner.)

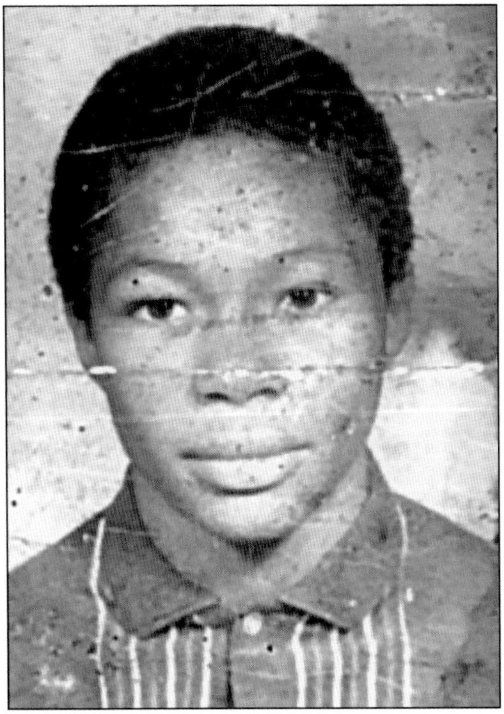

James Garner's school photo was taken in 1952. (Courtesy of Tommie Lee Garner.)

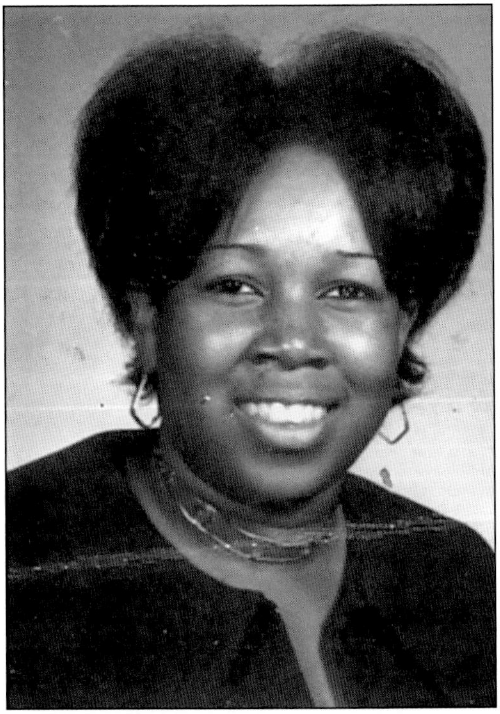

Eliza Ann Miggins is seen in this 1970 school day photo. (Courtesy of Umble Hawkins.)

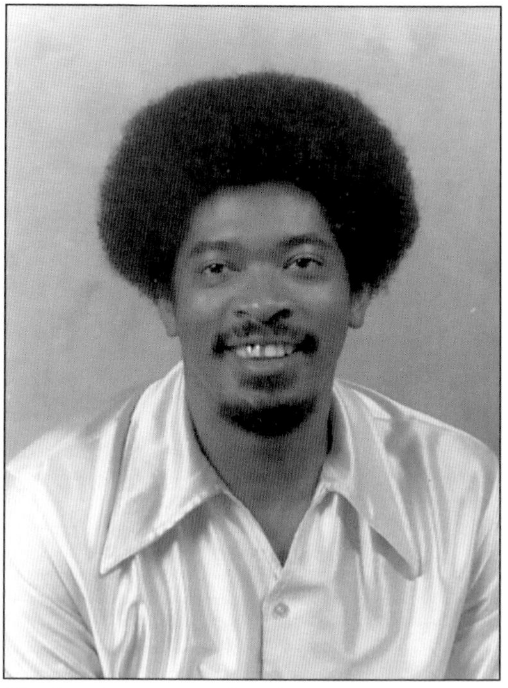

Charles Cain poses for this 1975 school day photo at Canton High School. (Courtesy of Bettie Cain.)

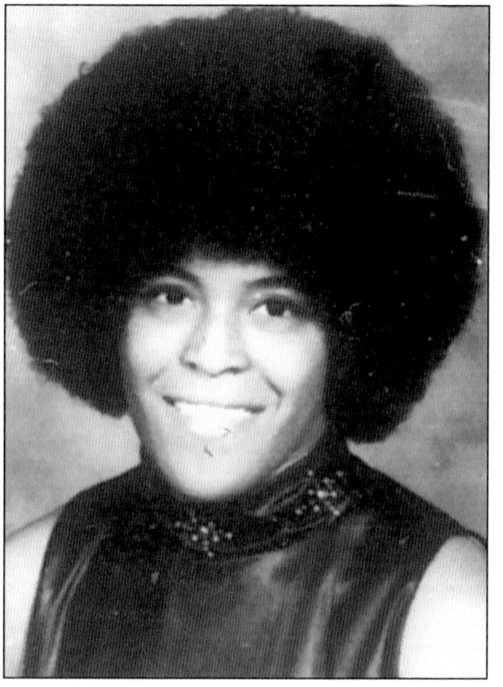

Velma Smith was in the 10th grade at Canton High School when this 1973 photo was taken. (Courtesy of Cora Smith.)

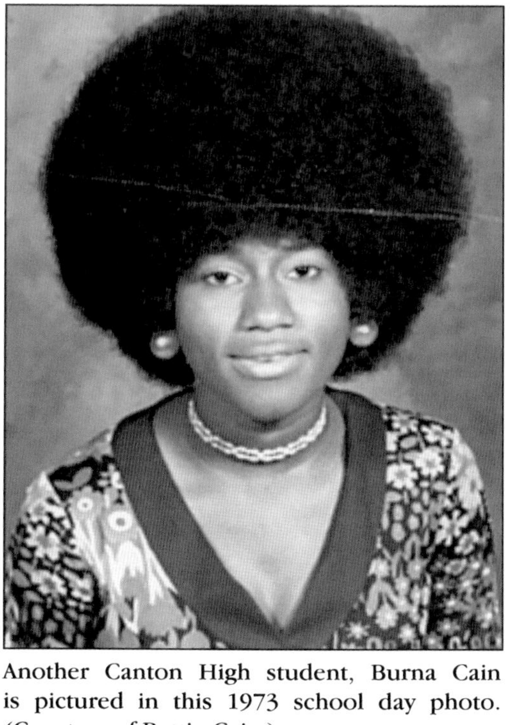

Another Canton High student, Burna Cain is pictured in this 1973 school day photo. (Courtesy of Bettie Cain.)

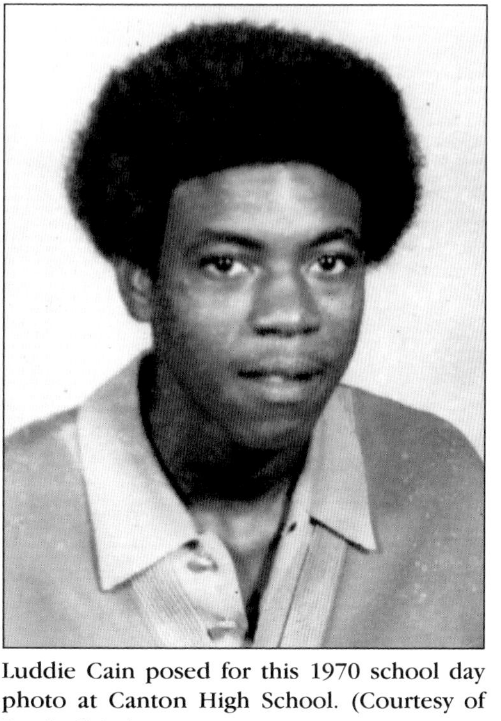

Luddie Cain posed for this 1970 school day photo at Canton High School. (Courtesy of Bettie Cain.)

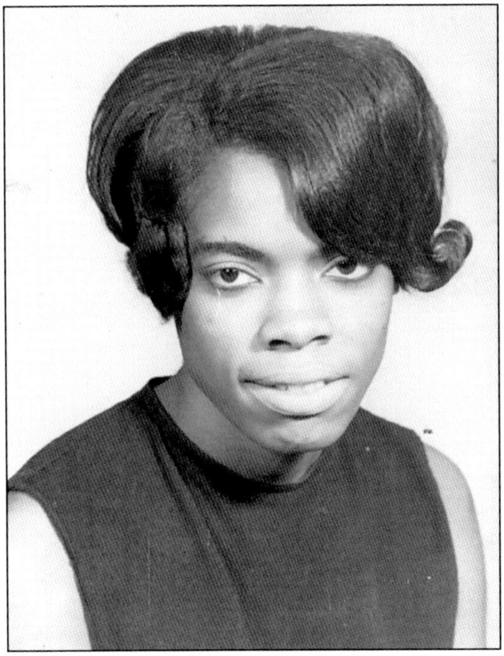

Ora Lee Cain is pictured here in a 1967. She attended Rogers High School. (Courtesy of Betty Cain.)

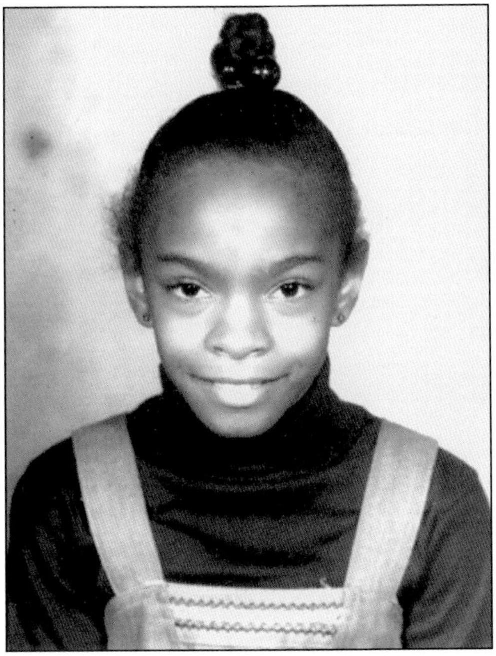

Yolanda Cain is pictured in her 1978 school photo. She attended Canton Public Schools. (Courtesy of Bettie Cain.)

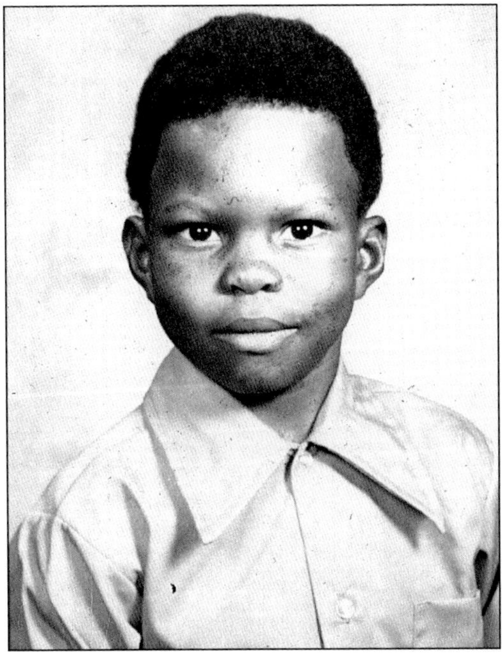

Kelvin Cain attended Holy Child Jesus Catholic School when this photo was taken. (Courtesy of Maggie Cain.)

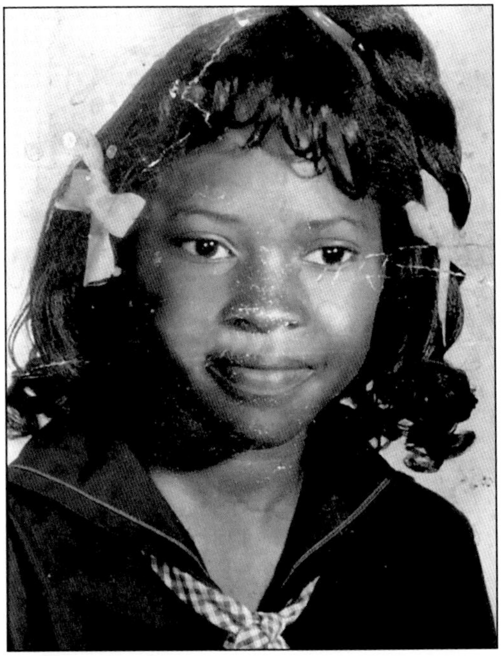

Ethel Cain attended Holy Child Jesus Catholic School when this photo was taken. (Courtesy of Maggie Cain.)

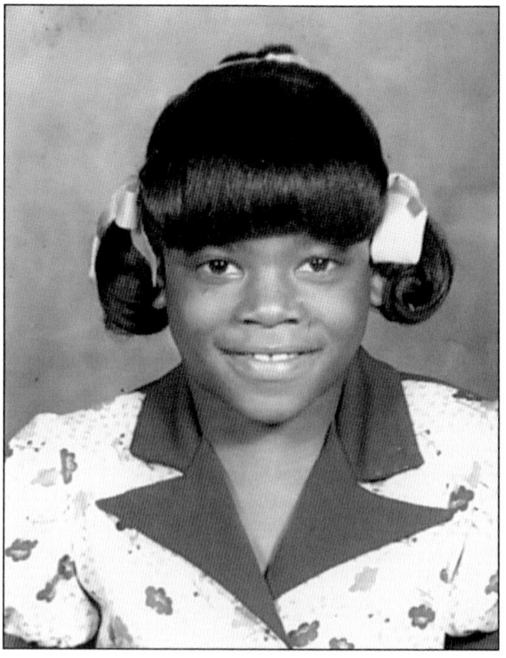

Lisa Tucker posed for a school day photo in 1962. (Courtesy of Umble Hawkins.)

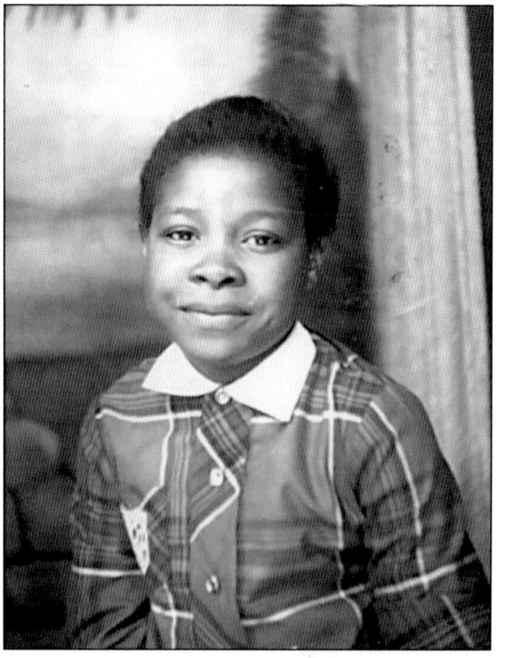

Mary Ann Watts was eight years old when this school photo was taken. (Courtesy of James and Francis Sanders.)

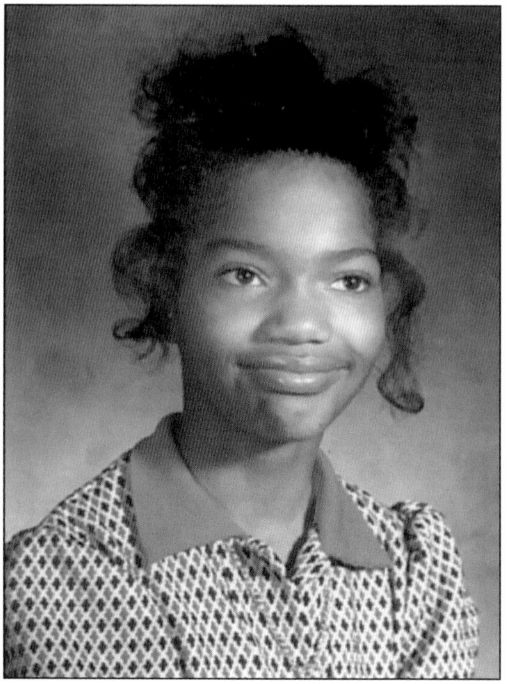

Teresa Garner posed for her school day photo in 1965. She attended Canton Public Schools. (Courtesy of Tommie Lee Garner.)

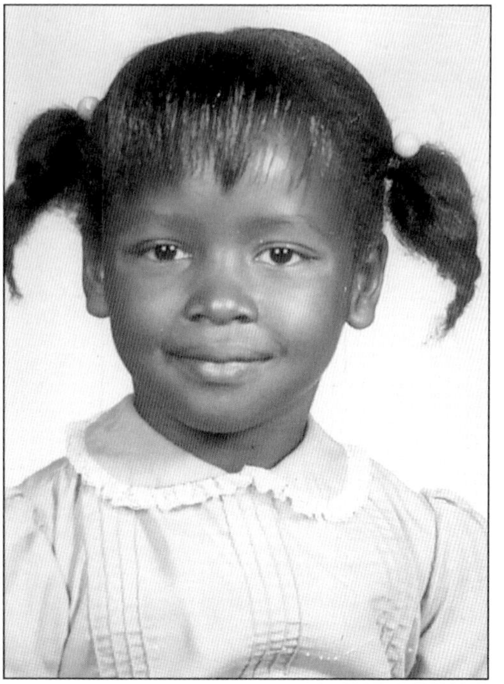

Maxine Sanders was five years old when this school day photograph was taken in 1967. (Courtesy of James and Francis Sanders.)

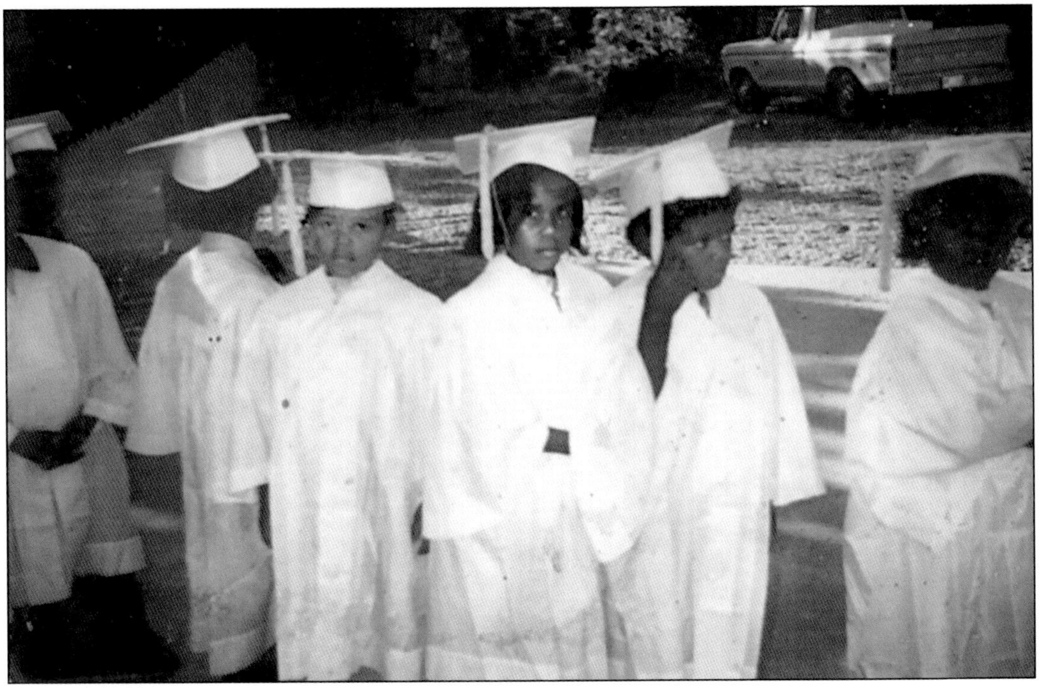

In this 1978 Head Start graduation photo, Clarence Berry is the child pictured to the far left; the other children are unidentified.

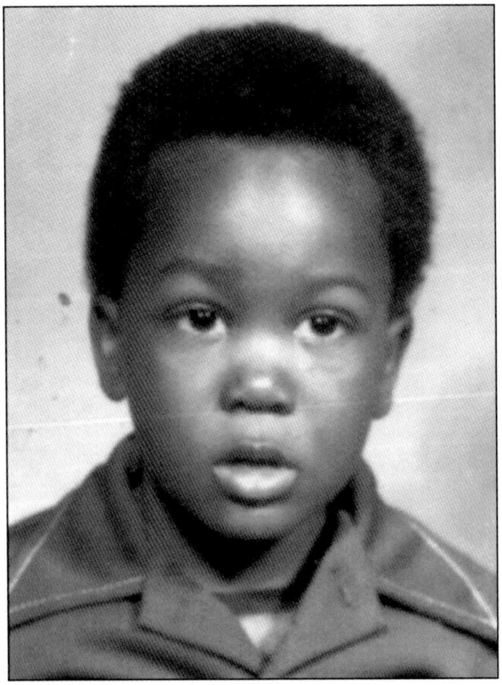

This is Denyatta Garner's 1979 first-grade photo from Canton Elementary School. (Courtesy of Thelma Garner Myers.)

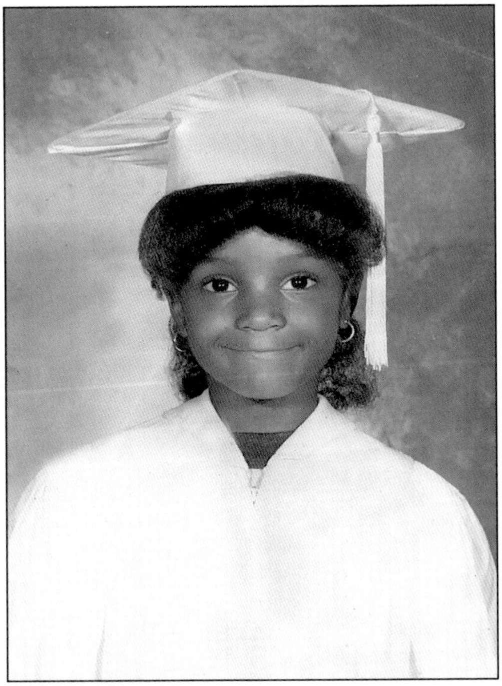

Jennifer Cheeks in seen in this graduation photo from Pleasant Green Headstart in Canton. (Courtesy of Alice Garner Cheeks.)

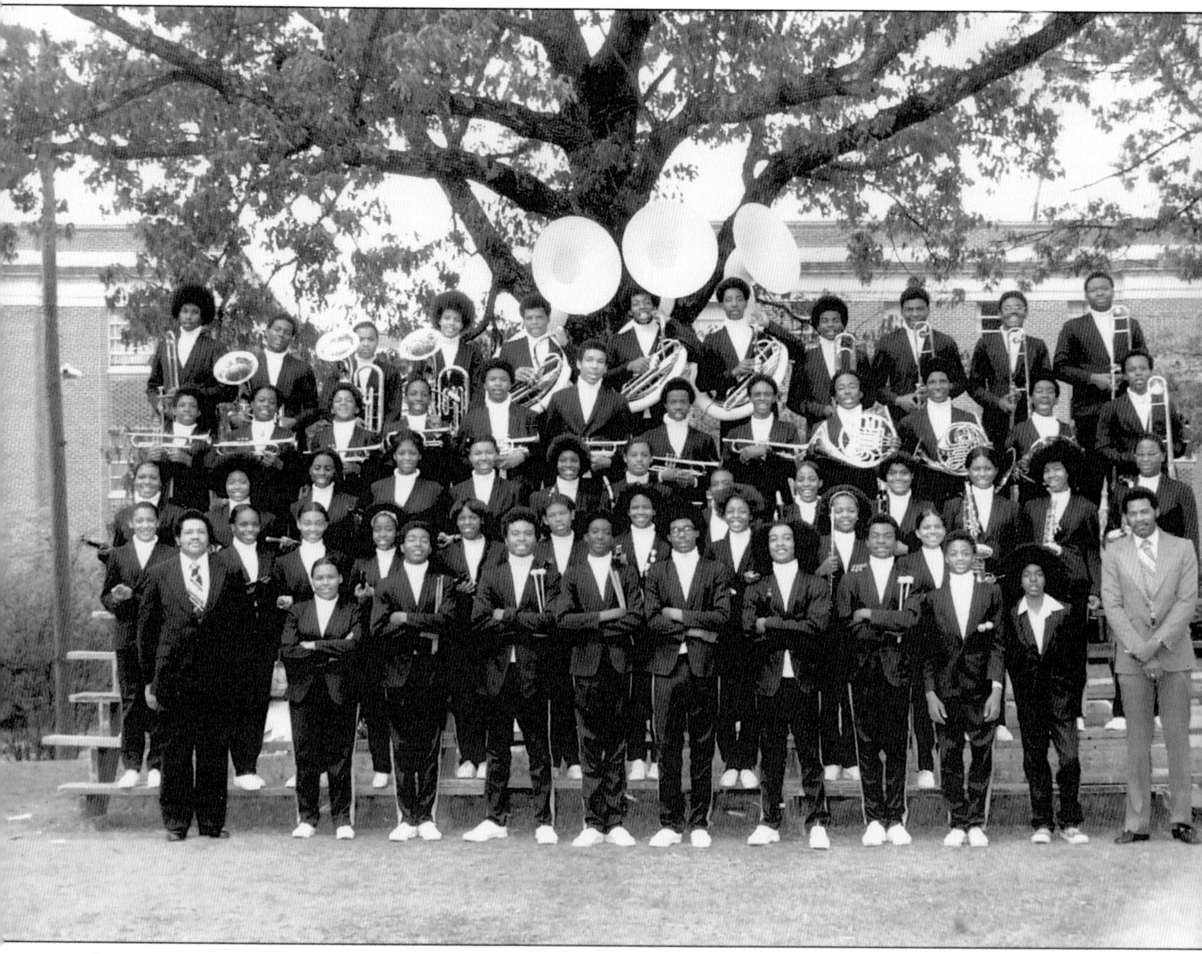

The Canton High School Marching Band is known for its great sound and coordination. The band is also called "The Baby Boom of the South." They acquired their name from their parent band, "The Sonic Boom of the South," which is the Jackson State University Band in Jackson, Mississippi. (Courtesy of James and Francis Sanders.)

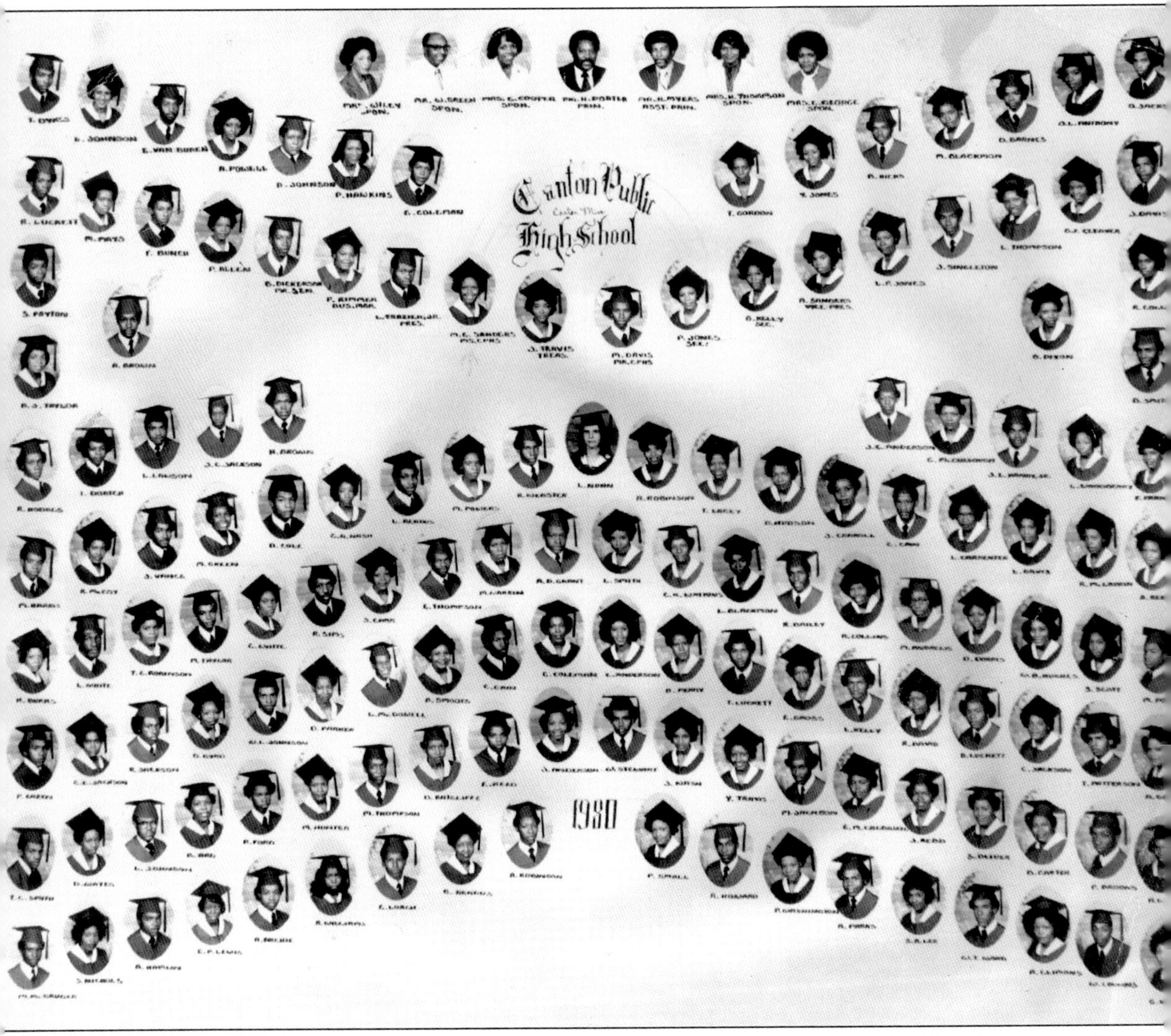

Pictured here are members of the Canton High School Graduating Class of 1980. (Courtesy of James and Francis Sanders.)

Charlie Smith and Thelma Garner pose together for the 1970 Junior and Senior Prom at Canton High School (formerly Rogers High School.). They both dressed in their finest attire for this special occasion. (Courtesy of Thelma Garner Myers.)

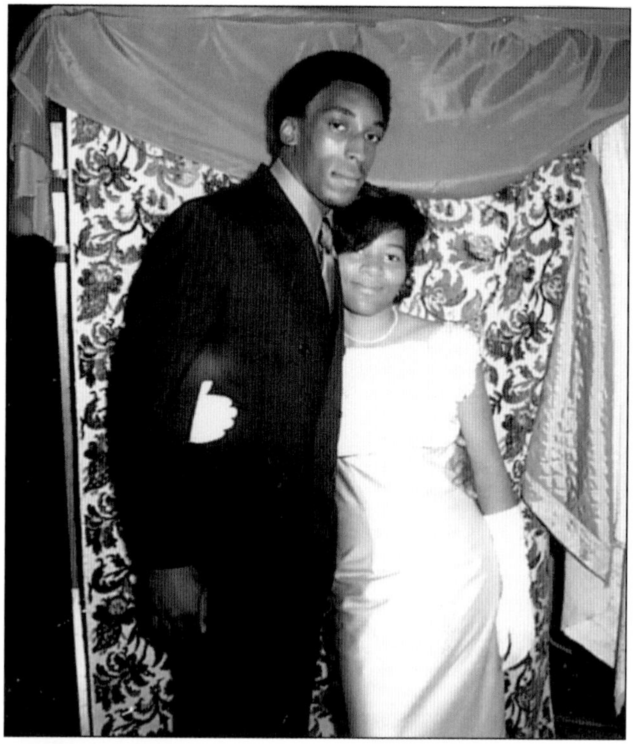

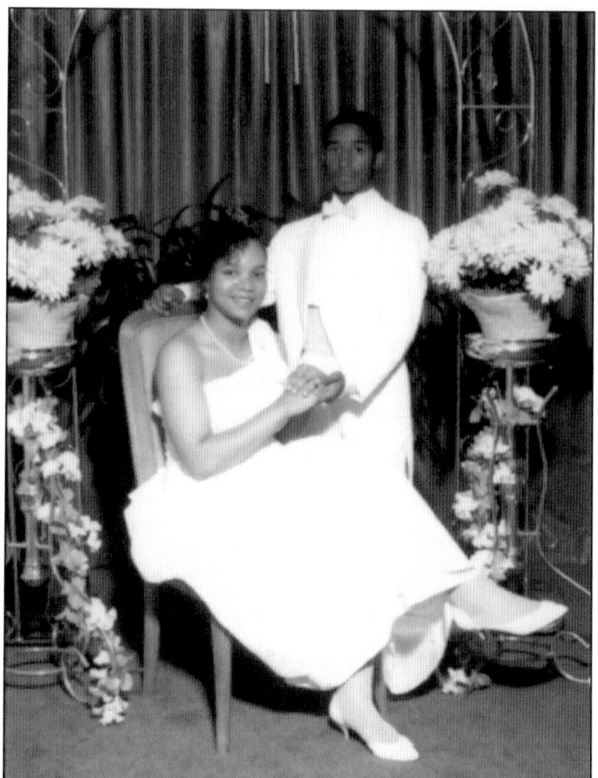

Janet Cheeks and David Berry pose for this Canton High School Junior Senior Prom in 1987. Janet graduated from Canton High School in 1988 and David graduated from Canton High School in 1987. (Courtesy of Stella Berry.)

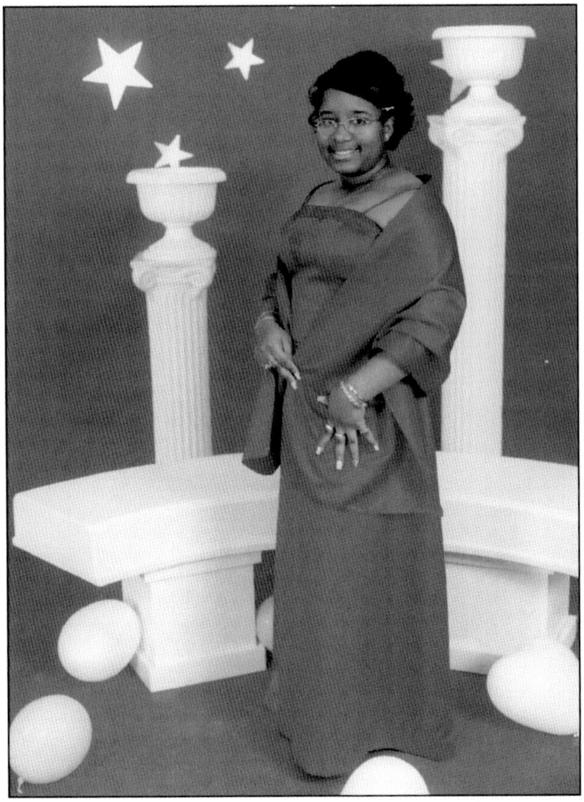

Atanyia L. Cheeks poses gracefully for this photo at the Canton High School Peppermint Ball on February 9, 2002. Atanyia is currently a 10th grader at Canton High School. She is the daughter of Janet Cheeks and David Berry. (Courtesy of Atanyia L. Cheeks.)

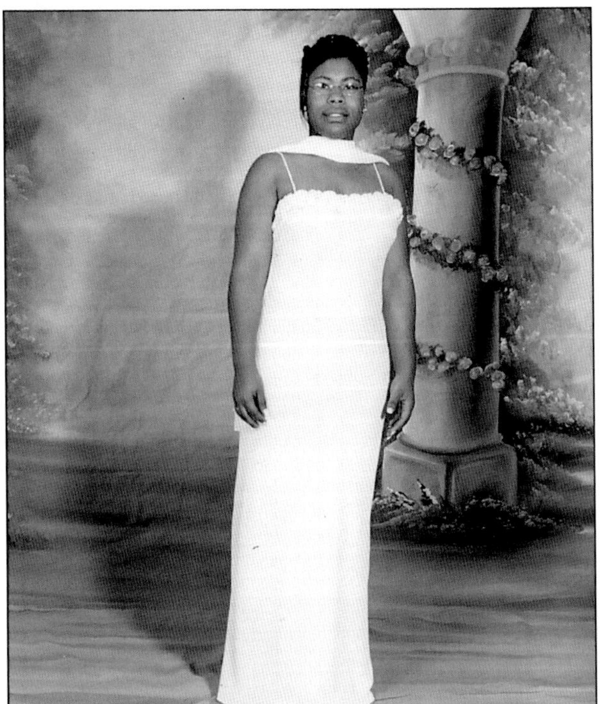

Runsha Sutton poses elegantly for this 2001 photo at Canton High School. She was an honor student and active in JROTC. She is the daughter of proud mother Pamela Sutton. (Runsha was recently a victim of a car accident in Madison County. I wish her Godspeed in her recovery.) (Courtesy of Thelma Cain.)

Four

Civil Rights Era

"The gifts of God should be enjoyed by all citizens in Mississippi. Our only hope is to control the vote."

Medgar Evers, 1963

The Civil Rights movement in Madison County brought droves of people from across the nation to fight for racial equality. The county hosted marches, rallies, and meetings in the 1960s. "Freedom Summer" of 1966 in Canton, Mississippi, was a milestone era. It was the summer that Dr. Martin Luther King Jr. led a march through the county. The most dramatic and horrific scene of the summer occurred when Freedom marchers tried to pitch a tent to lodge women and children on the grounds of McNeal Elementary School. When the tent was hoisted, National Guard soldiers fired tear gas from the roof of the school into the crowd; many were injured by the tear gas cannons. Churches were also targets of bombings and threats. This chapter honors a small portion of the great number of heroes—men and women who stood in the face of such horrific events—to fight for Civil Rights in Madison County and the entire country.

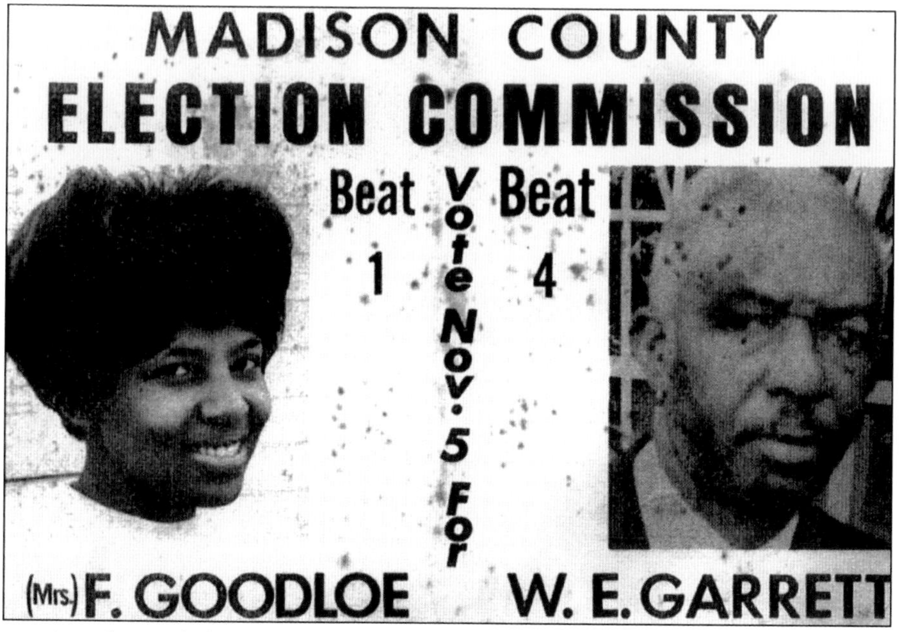

This campaign photo of Flonzie Goodloe of Beat 1 and W.E. Garrett of Beat 4 was used to try and get more African Americans to the polls to vote on election day. (Courtesy of Flonzie Brown.)

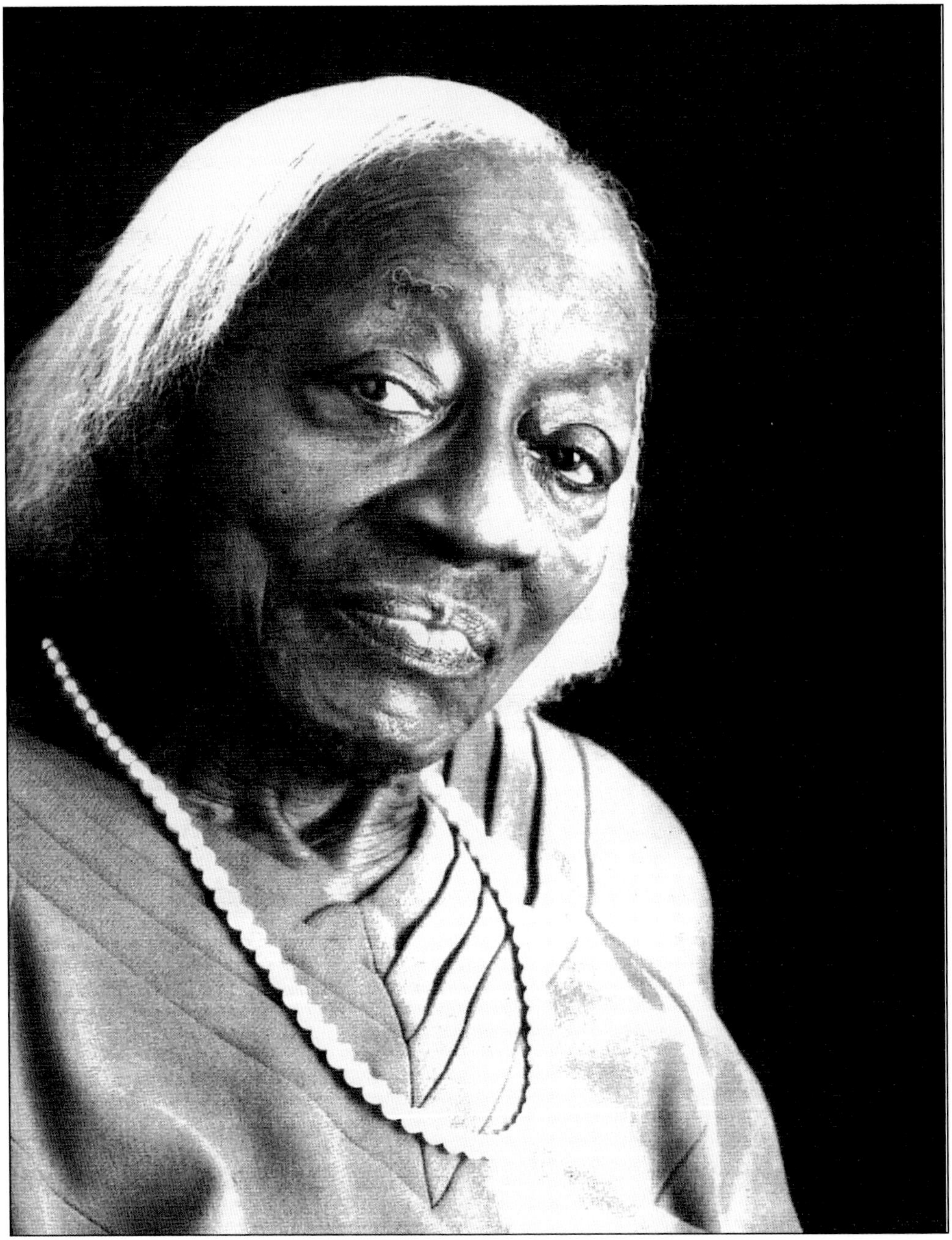

Annie Devine was one of Madison County's leading women in Civil Rights. She was a trailblazer for justice and equality for African Americans in Madison County. She and other Civil Rights leaders organized the Canton office for Congress Of Racial Equality (CORE) in 1963. In 1964, Devine and other Civil Rights workers organized Canton's first Freedom Day on February 28. More than 350 African-American residents arrived at the Madison County Courthouse demanding their voting rights. Through arrests, fire hoses, attack dogs, and tear gas, Devine and the movement prevailed. Madison County is a better place for African Americans because of the efforts of Devine and others like her. (Courtesy of Carrie Smoot.)

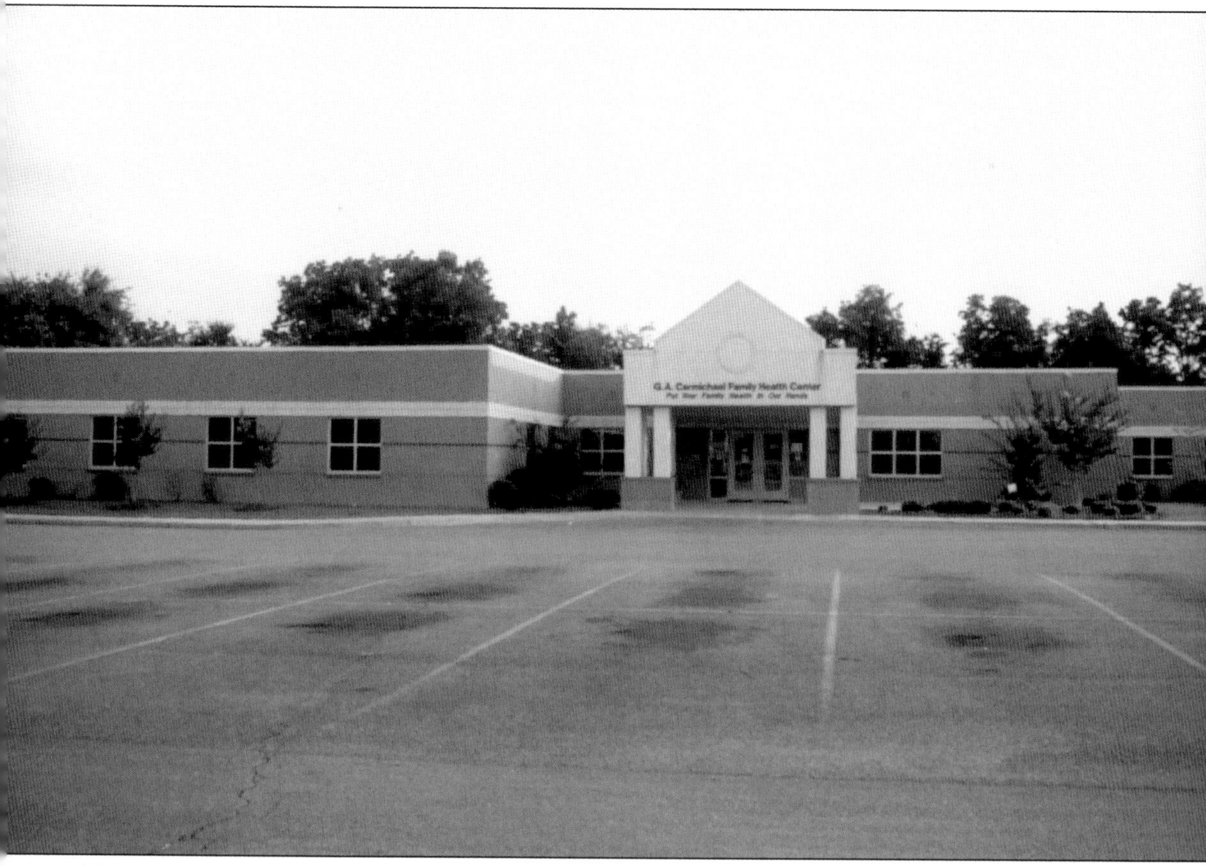

The G.A. Carmichael Family Health Center is named after one of Canton's great doctors. Dr. George Carmichael was a native of Canton, Mississippi. He was a graduate from Meharry Medical College in Nashville, Tennessee. Upon graduating from Meharry, Dr. G.A. Carmichael came back to Canton to practice medicine. He began his practice in 1934 on Hickory Street. If he needed to hospitalize his patients, he had to send them to Yazoo City to a black hospital. Dr. Carmichael continuously applied to the board of directors to be on staff at the Kings Daughters Hospital in Canton, but was repeatedly turned down. The last time he applied, he was accepted but with one stipulation: he could enter through the front door but his patients had to enter through the rear doors. Dr. Carmichael thanked the hospital board of directors for accepting him on their staff, but he declined their offer because his patients could not enter through the front door of the hospital. Dr. Carmichael continued to send his patients 30 miles to Yazoo City's Afro Hospital. He practiced medicine in Canton for 50 years. (Courtesy of the Author.)

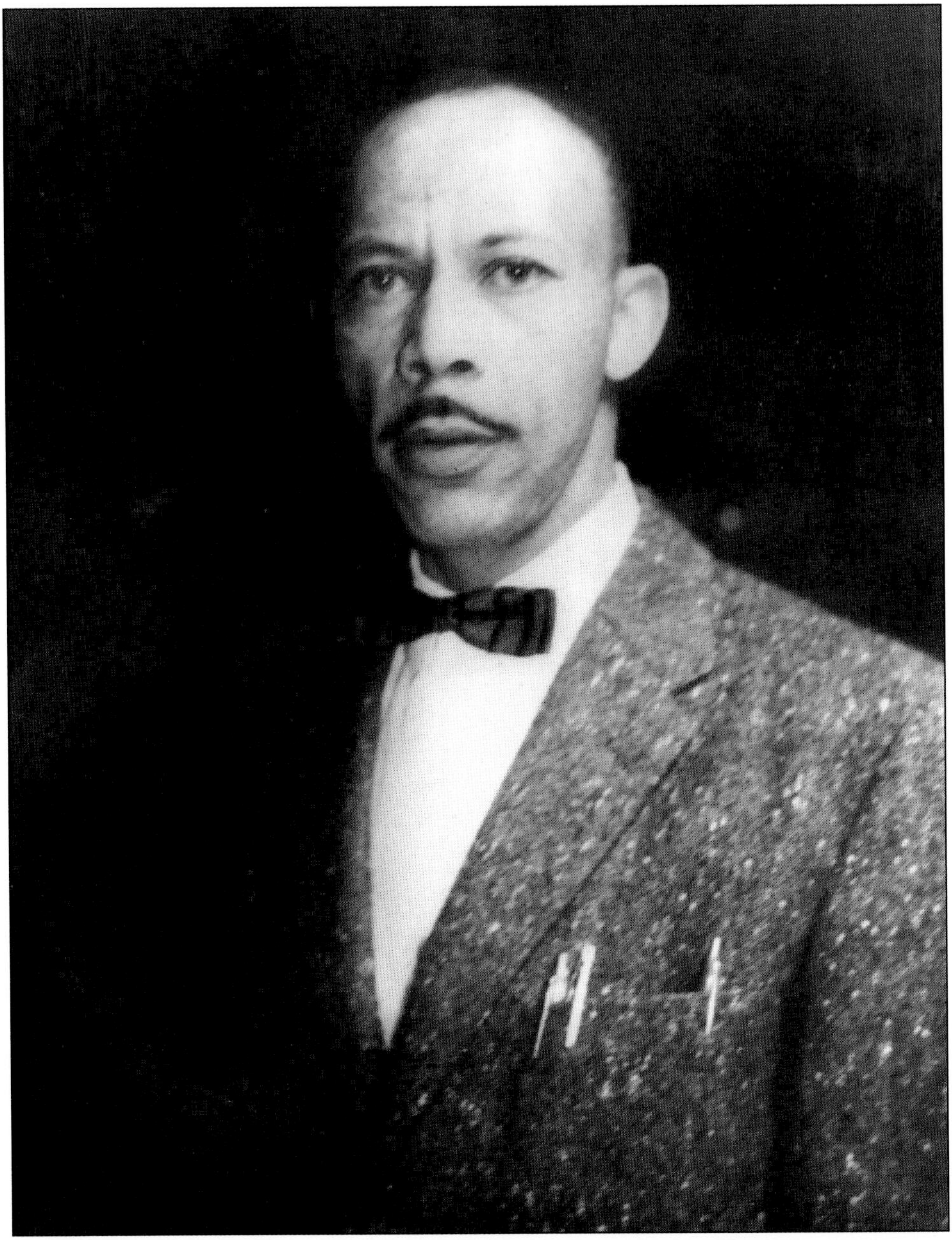

Eddie E. Coney, born January 8, 1923 in Madison County, was married to Clarice Dillon. Coney was a Civil and Human Rights Activist and served as manager of the Flora Parrish State 4-H Club Camp from 1952 to 1965. Coney was dedicated to protecting his family. During the 1966 Freedom Summer tear gas incident by the National Guard at McNeal Elementary School, Eddie Coney stood boldly on his front porch with rifle in hand, ready to protect his family and his dwelling. Marchers running to the Coney home for shelter literally picked him up and brought him into his house away from the gas. He would go to almost any extreme to protect his family. During that same event, Coney housed and fed 127 Civil Rights marchers during the summer of 1966. His wife, Clarice, is pictured on page 71. (Courtesy of Clarice Coney.)

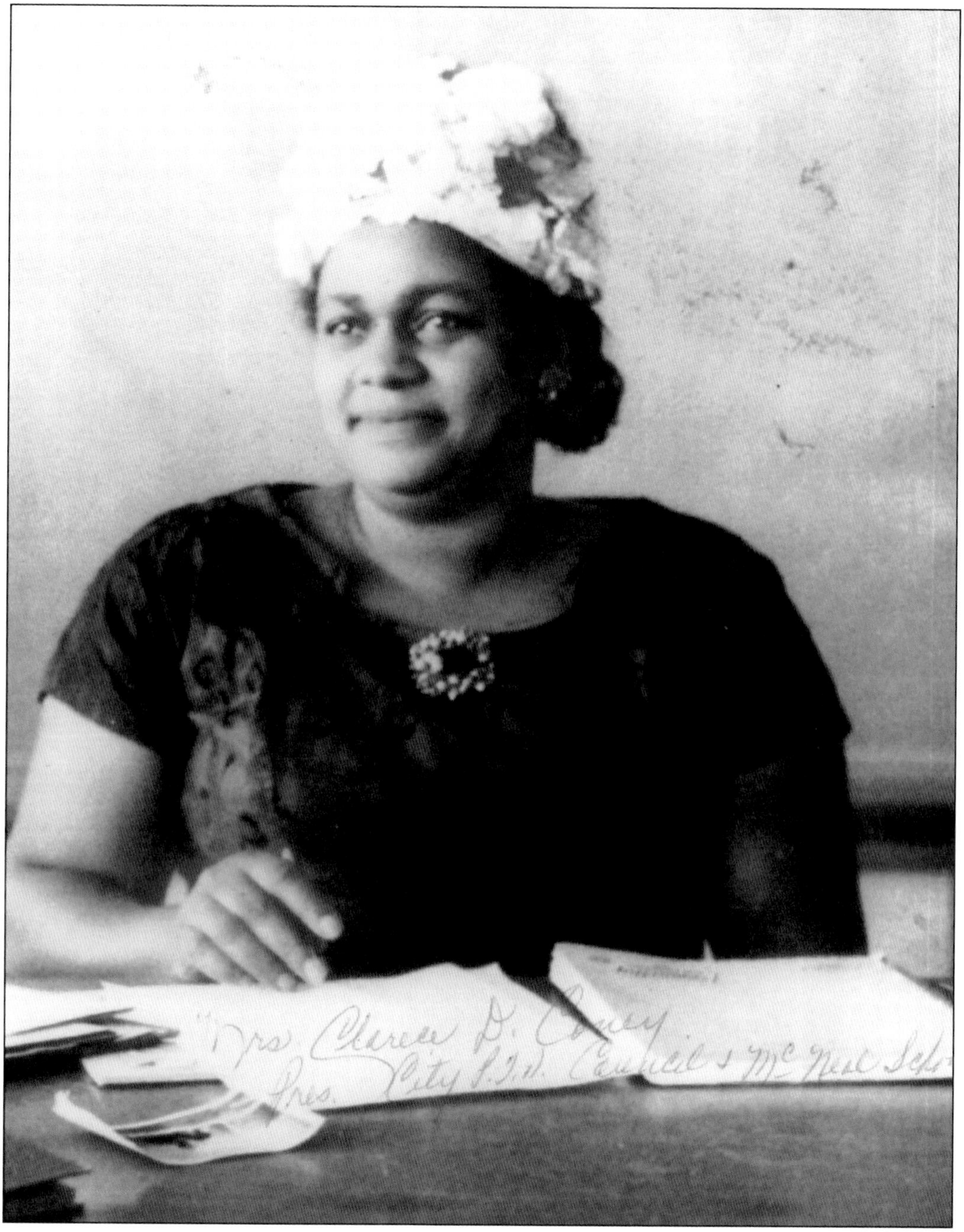

Mrs. Clarice Dillon Coney is a retired educator. She served in the education field for over 33 years and she continues to educate youth in Madison County. Mrs. Coney was a Civil Rights Activist in Madison County where she assisted in voter education and registration. She is a member of CORE, COFO, and the NAACP. She presently serves as manager for elections in District 4 Precinct 5, and is actively affiliated with various clubs and organizations on state and local levels. She is also a practicing psychometrist in the State of Mississippi. Her late husband, Eddie, is pictured on page 70. (Courtesy of Clarice Coney.)

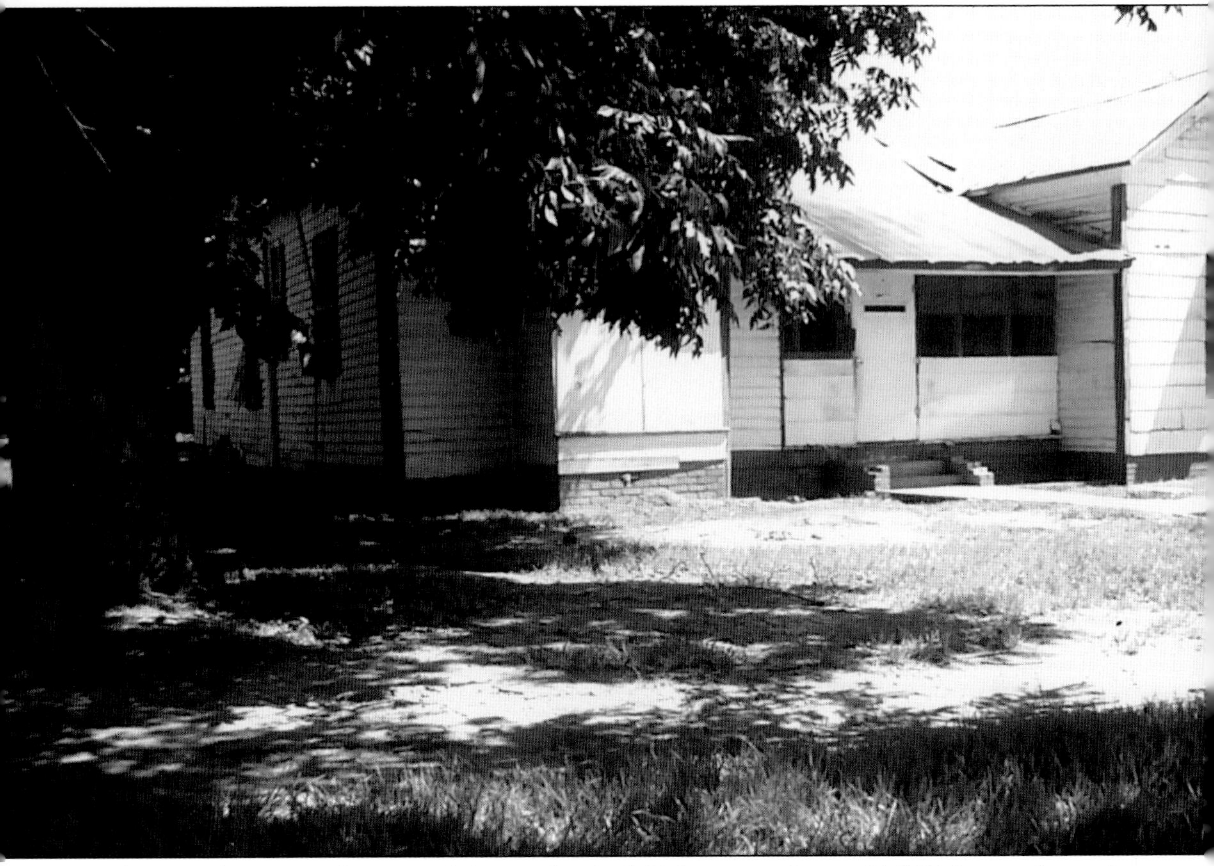

The "Freedom House" was used during the Civil Rights era to house Civil Rights workers who came to Madison County. Located on Lutz Street (now George Washington Drive) in Canton, the house was donated to the "freedom riders" and other Civil Rights organizations by Mr. George Washington. The Freedom House was the target of bombings, vandalism, and threats during the Civil Rights Movement. (Courtesy of the Author.)

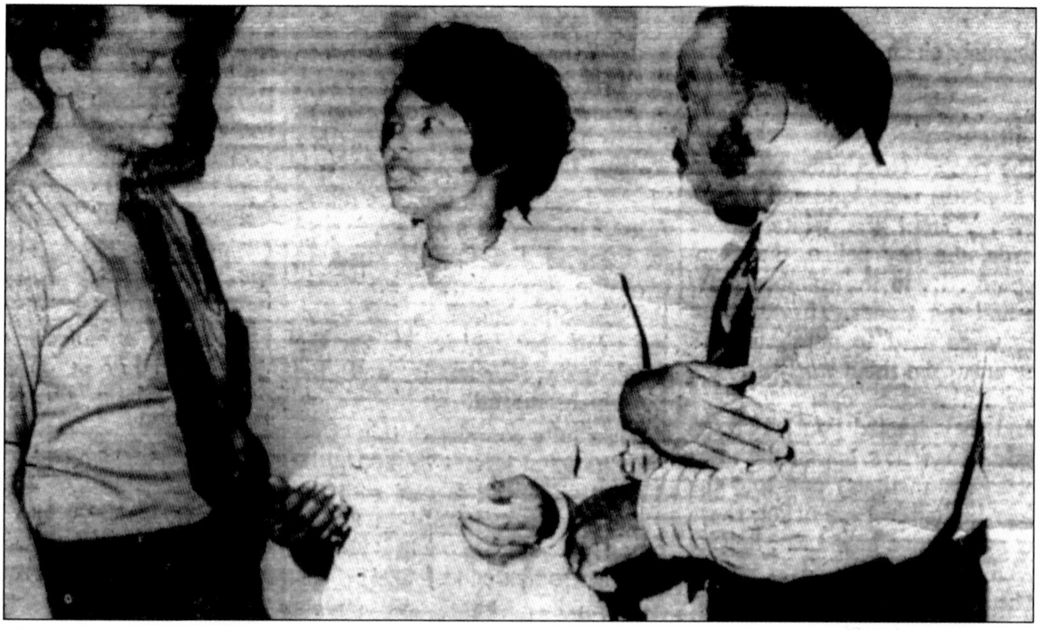

This 1971 photo shows, from left to right, Julian Bonds (state of Georgia legislator), Flonzie Goodloe (Madison County elections commissioner), and John Lewis (executive director of the Voter Education Project). Julian Bonds spoke at the Madison County Courthouse to a crowd of more than 1,000 people, even though local papers reported only 250 people attended. He spoke on the importance of voting rights and voter education in the African-American community.

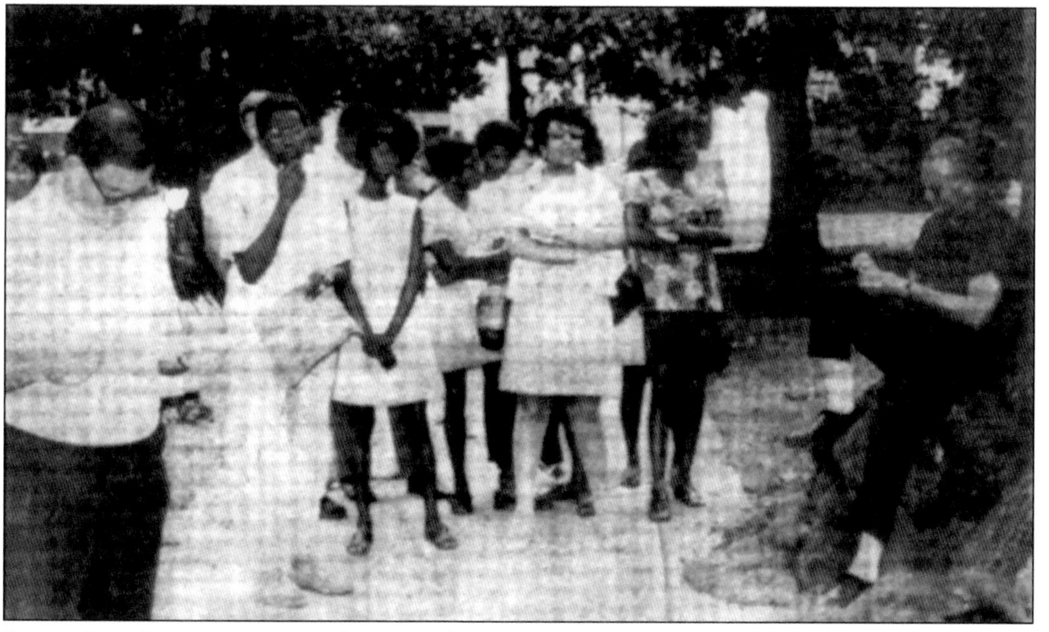

Jimmy Swan's campaign speech is heard by a few local blacks who gathered at the Madison County Courthouse on June 27, 1971. He was a Democrat running against a very powerful Republican. Swan wanted the vote of local blacks to ensure a win in the election. (Courtesy of Flonzie Goodloe Brown.)

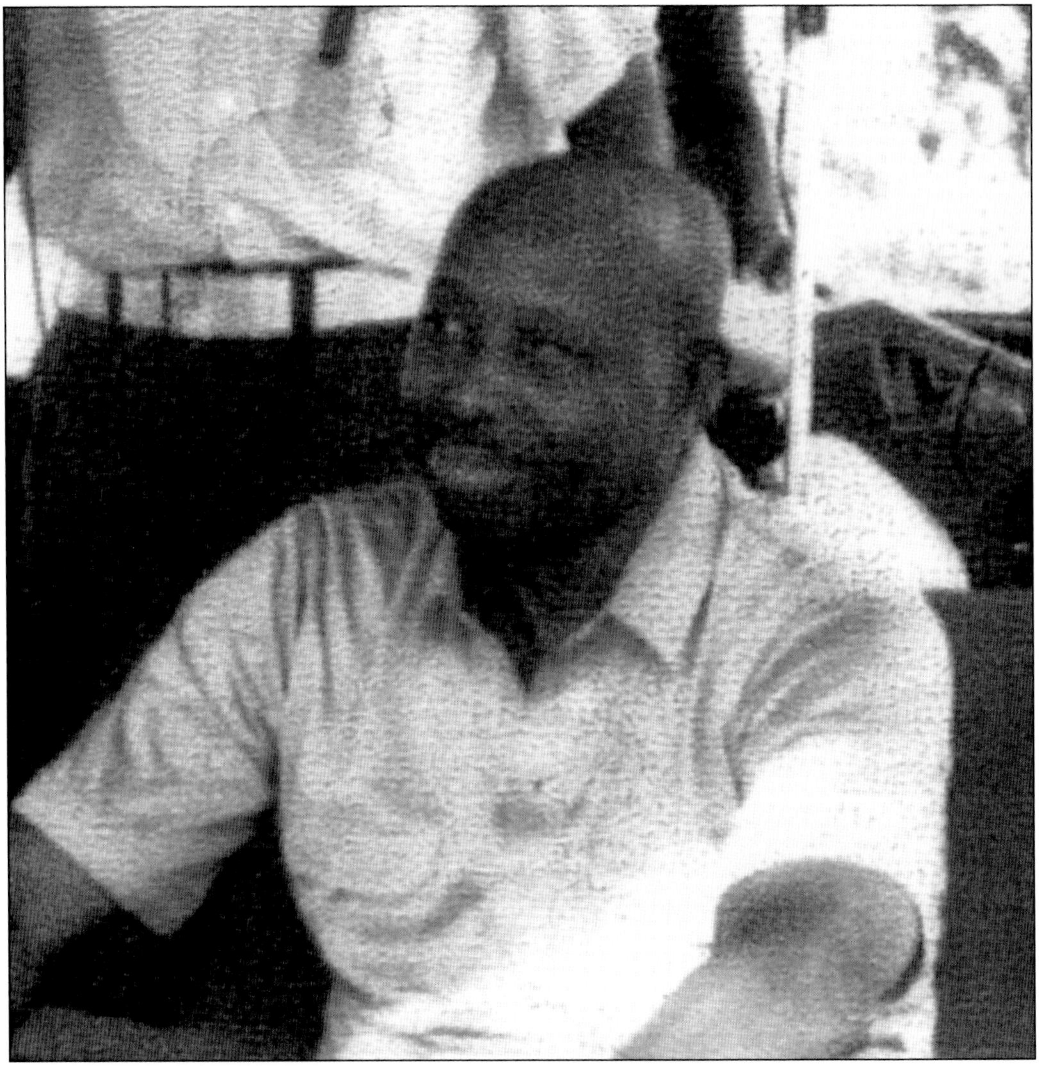

C.O. Chinn was born on September 18, 1919 in the Sharon Community of Madison County. He married Minnie Lou Dearon and they bore four children. Chinn is said to be "the last of the great frontiersmen" for his work and dedication to Civil Rights. Chinn is thought of as the "father" of Civil Rights in Madison County. He was one of the organizers of the Madison County CORE chapter, and headed many Civil Rights marches, rallies, and meetings in the county. Chinn was responsible for helping public places in Madison County become desegregated and for making racial equality mandatory in all facets across the county. During his lifetime, he was recognized for his work with Head Start, PTA, community service, and Civil Rights. In recognition for his contributions, the city of Canton declared May 2, 1999 as C.O. Chinn Day. (Courtesy of James Cheeks.)

Five

SOCIAL GATHERINGS

"I have a great belief in the future of my people and my country."

Marian Anderson, 1960

African Americans in Madison County often enjoyed "get togethers." Social gatherings were normal forms of entertainment. People often gathered after church, on Friday nights at local nightclubs, and at the homes of families and friends. Social gatherings provided a time for bonding outside of work. The people seen in this chapter are captured enjoying the nightclubs, homes, and family functions of their choosing. It was a refreshing event to get dressed up and enjoy the simple things in life. From church functions to weddings to everyday family gatherings, Madison County's black community found ways to gather and celebrate .

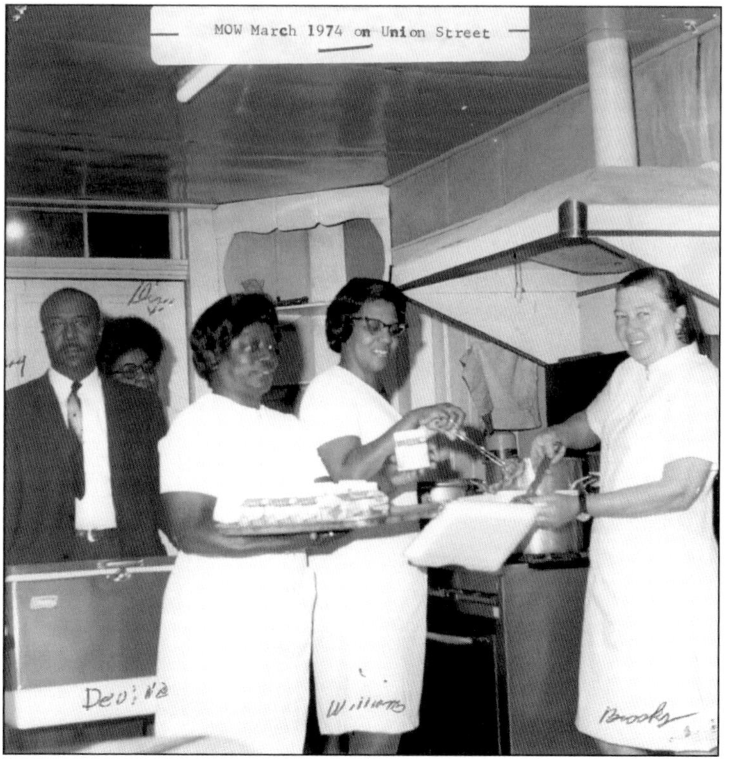

Meals-On-Wheels workers pictured from left to right in 1974 are Thomas Perry, Ruth Luckett, Annie Devine, Leslie Williams, and Melba Brooks. Canton citizen Ruth Luckett started this program in Madison County in 1972. The program serves meals to elderly residents in Canton, Flora, Madison, and Ridgeland. (Courtesy of Ruth Luckett.)

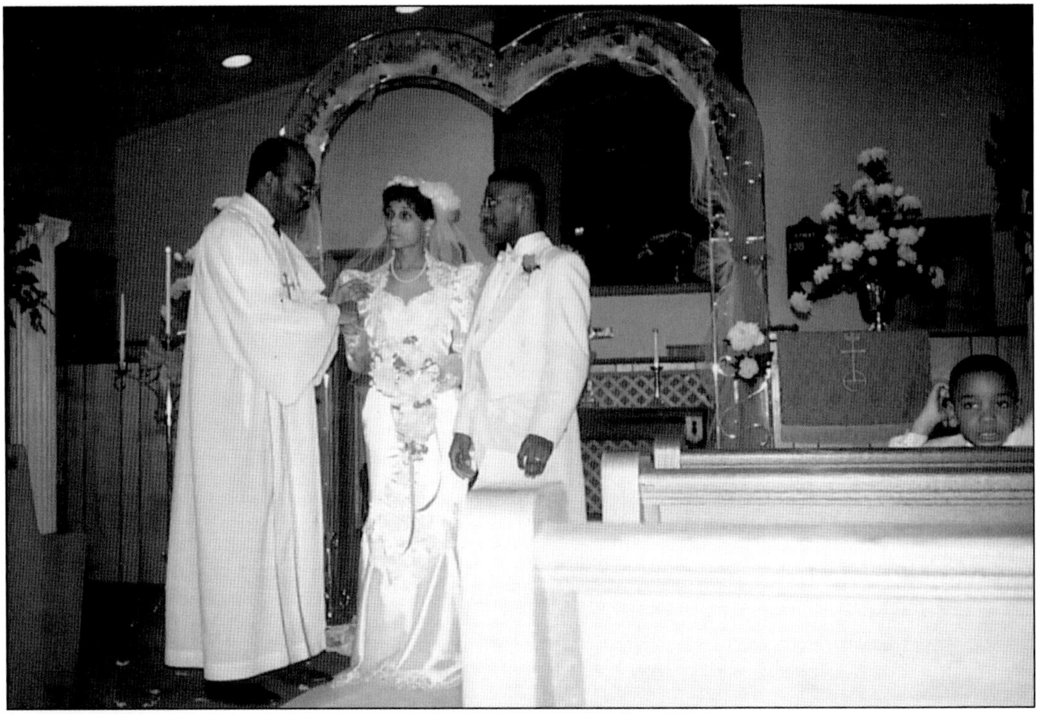

Alexis and Lawrence Berry's 1992 wedding is shown here. Lawrence is a native of Madison County. He grew up attending the Harvey Chapel Missionary Baptist Church and was educated in the Madison County Public Schools. (Courtesy of Annie B. Berry.)

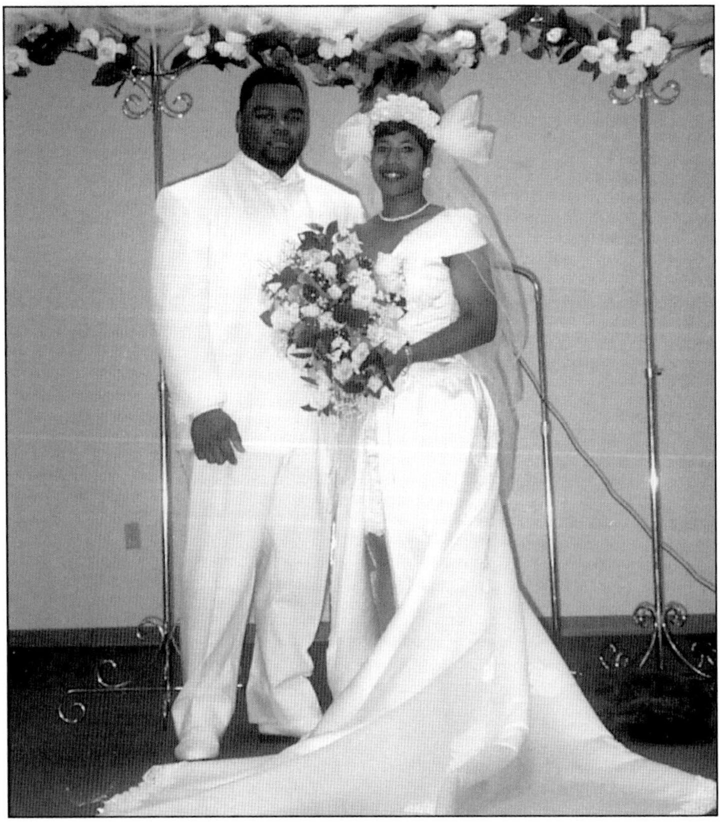

Pamela Sutton and Fredrick Rush married in May of 1997. (Courtesy of Thelma Cain.)

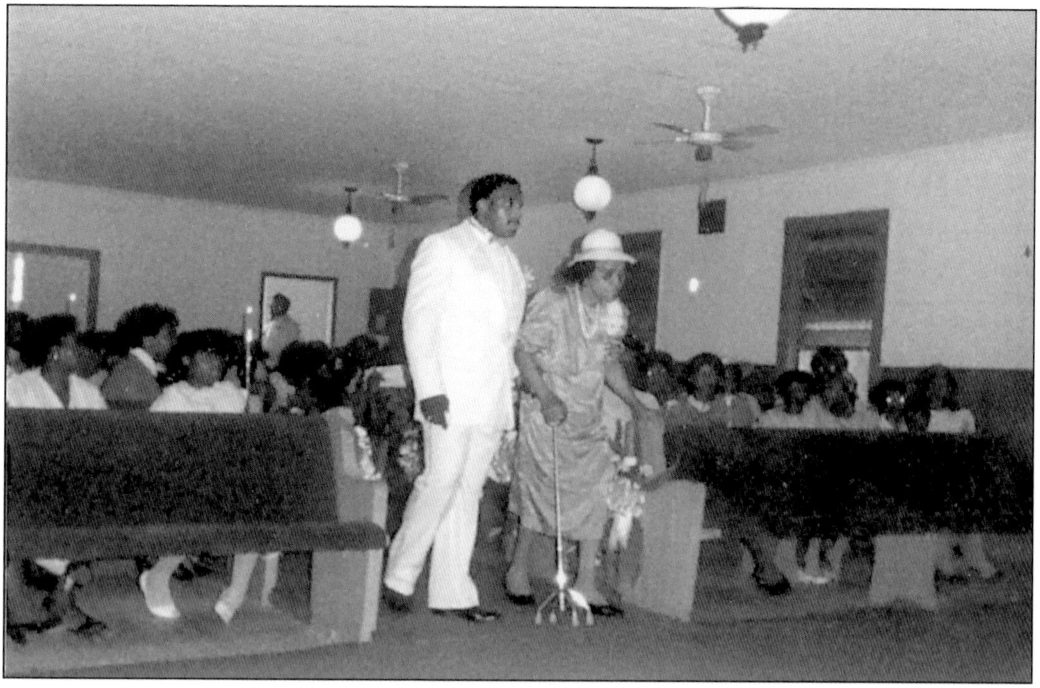

Charlie Smith is seen escorting his mother, Ernestine "Teen" Smith, to her seat at the wedding ceremony of his sister and her daughter, Velma Smith. The Smith family is native to Madison County and lived southwest of Canton for many years. L.C. Smith farmed, owned, and operated a neighborhood convenient store in his later years.

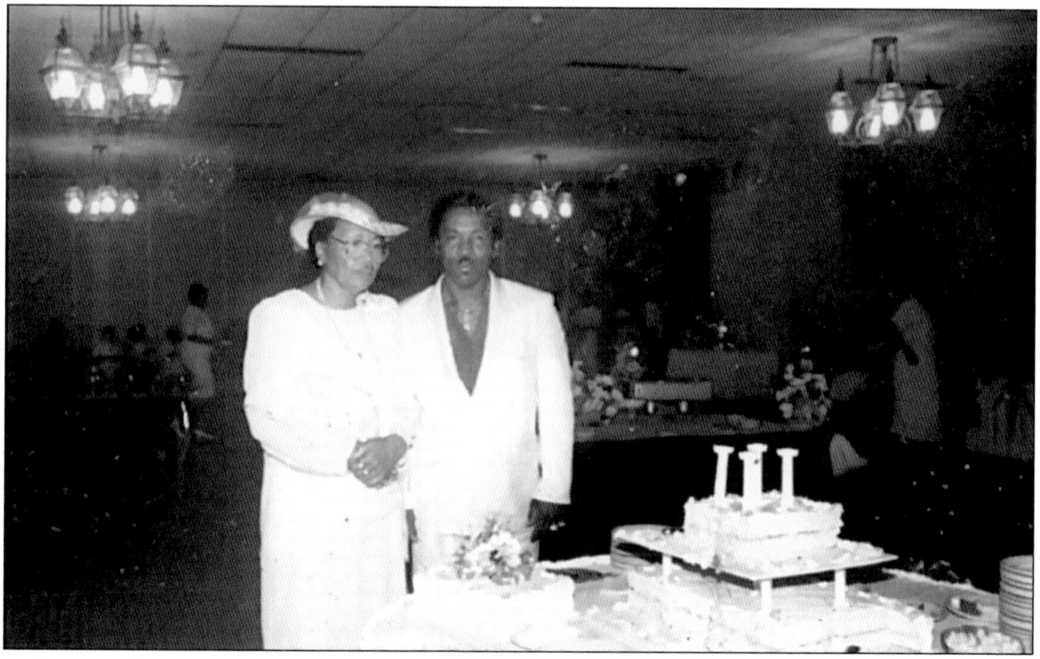

Callie Bouldin and her son Ben Bouldin are seen at Richey Bouldin's wedding. (Courtesy of Callie Bouldin.)

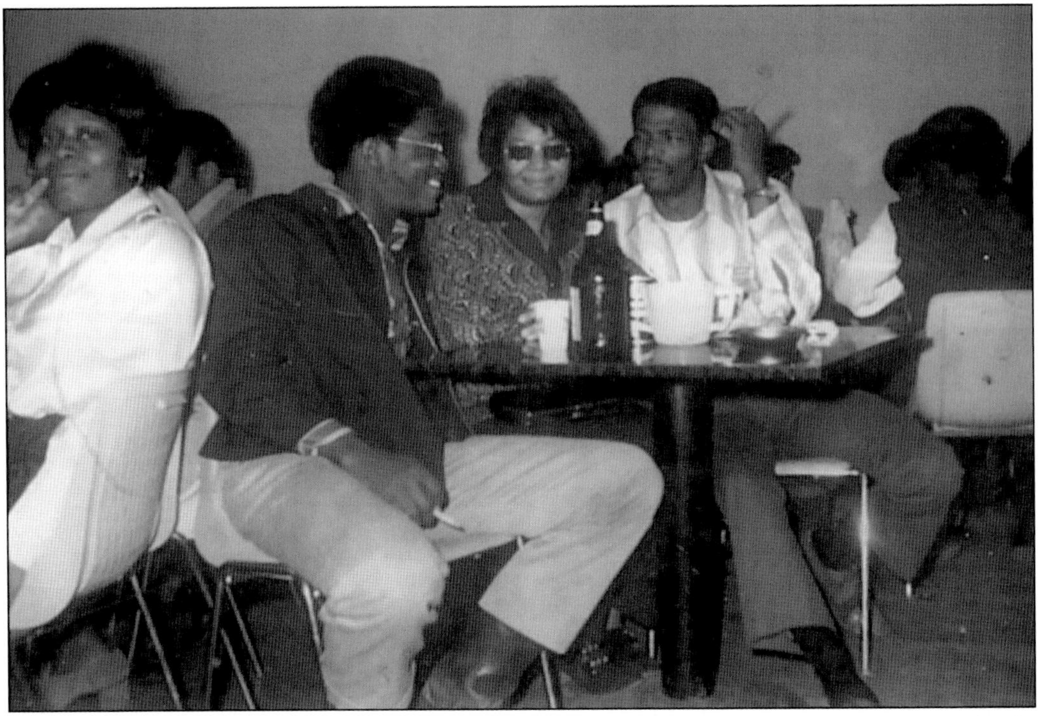

Pictured from left to right are unidentified, L.C. Cheeks, Alice Garner Cheeks, and James Cheeks at Johnnie Sims nightclub in Canton. This photo was taken in the 1970s. (Courtesy of Thelma Garner Myers.)

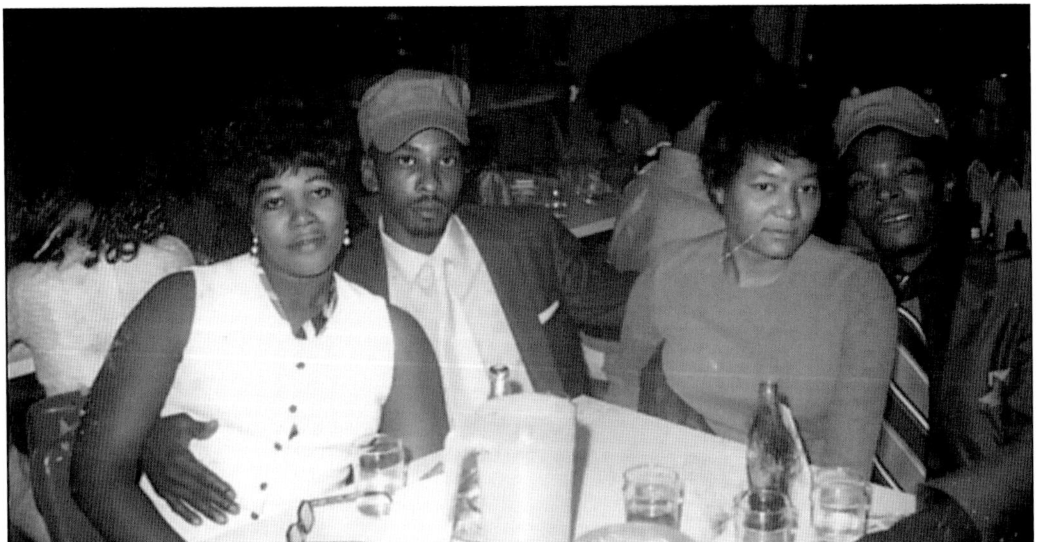

Pictured from left to right are Mrs. and Mr. Luckett and Alice and James Cheeks. The couples enjoy a night out on the town at Johnnie Sims, one of Canton's most popular nightclubs in the 1970s. Johnnie Sims was known for its music and food. On any given night, crowds of people would be in the small club enjoying the night. The club was torn down in the mid-1990s. (Courtesy of Thelma Garner Myers.)

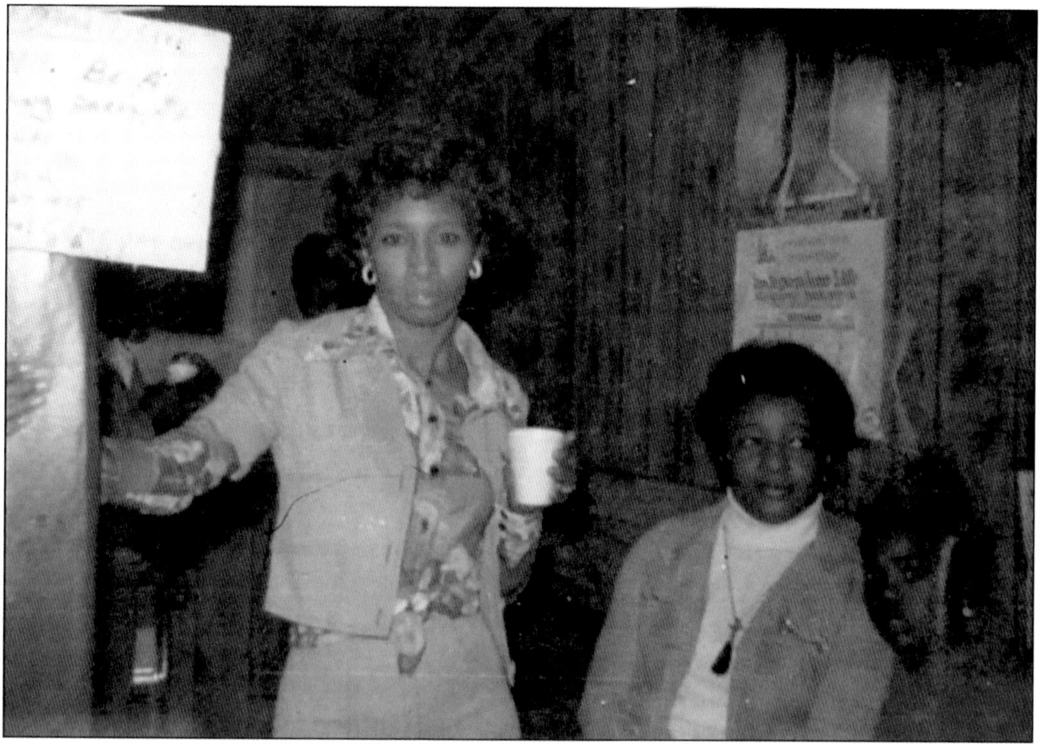

Rosie Bell Lipsey enjoys a night out at the Cain's Cafe. This was a popular nightclub that African Americans in the community often frequented. (Courtesy of Umble Hawkins.)

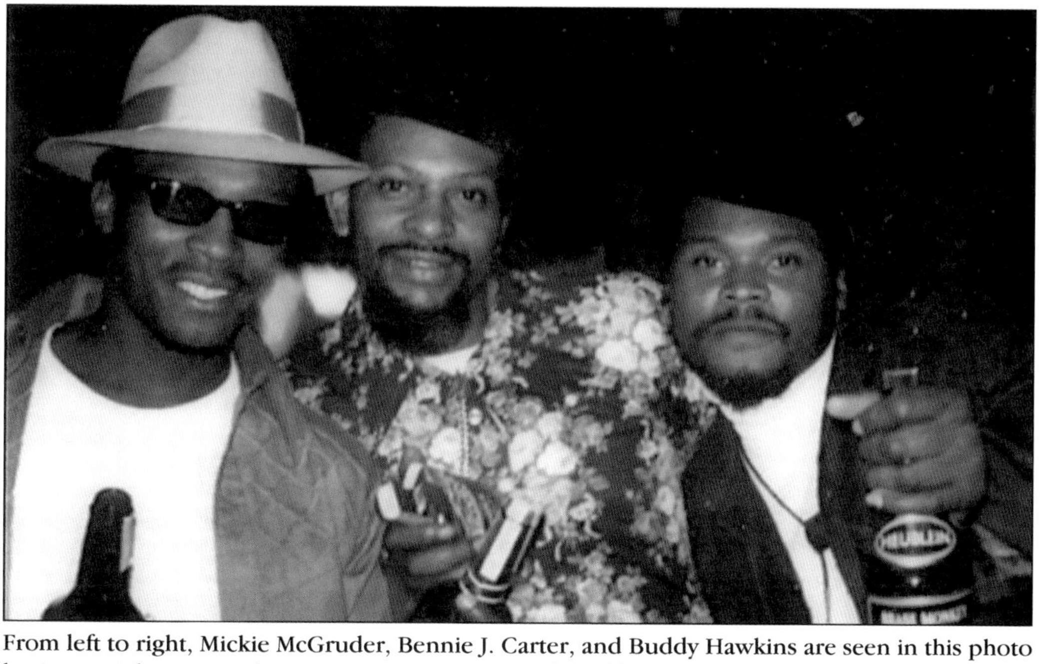

From left to right, Mickie McGruder, Bennie J. Carter, and Buddy Hawkins are seen in this photo having a night out on the town. Bennie Carter and Buddy Hawkins are deceased. (Courtesy of Umble Hawkins.)

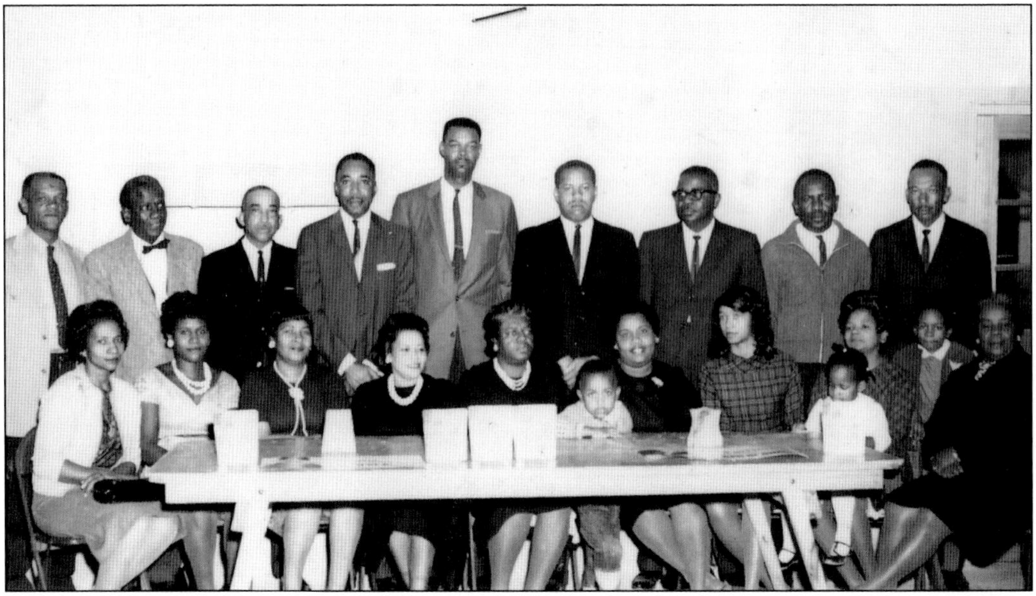

This is a 1957 March of Dimes meeting. From left to right are (front row) Mr. Ellis, Thomas Jordan, R.M. Mackey, Edward Jackson, Mr. Parker, Dr. Summers, James Thomason, and James Goodloe; (second row) Wealther Cox, Fred Luckett Jr, Ruth Luckett, Mrs. T.L. Jordan, and Louise Wales. (Courtesy of Ruth Luckett.)

The top of the picture (not seen) reads "Meals on Wheels Promotes Togetherness." Pictured in this photo are Ruth Luckett (top), Aridell Jones (right), and Arthur Tate (left). This photo was taken in 1974. (Courtesy of Ruth Luckett.)

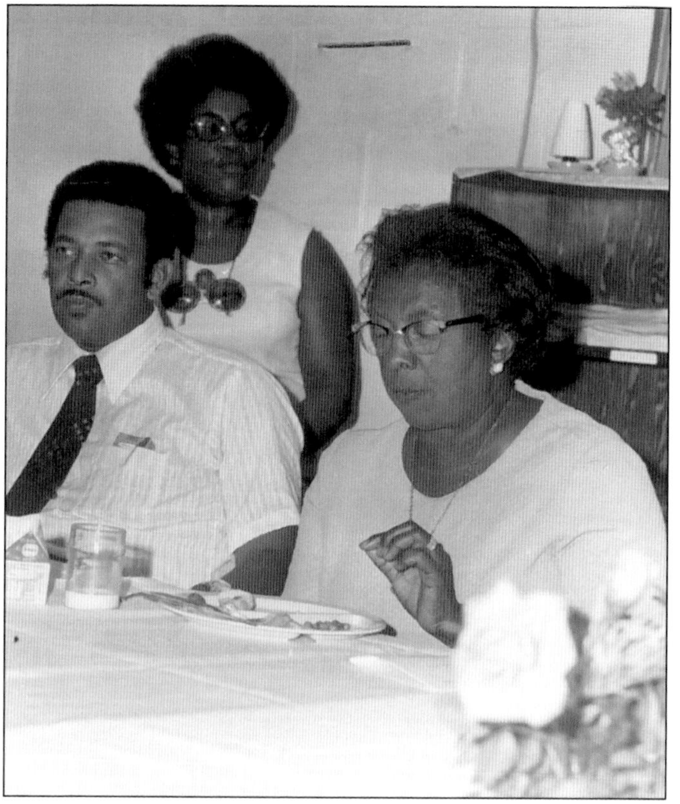

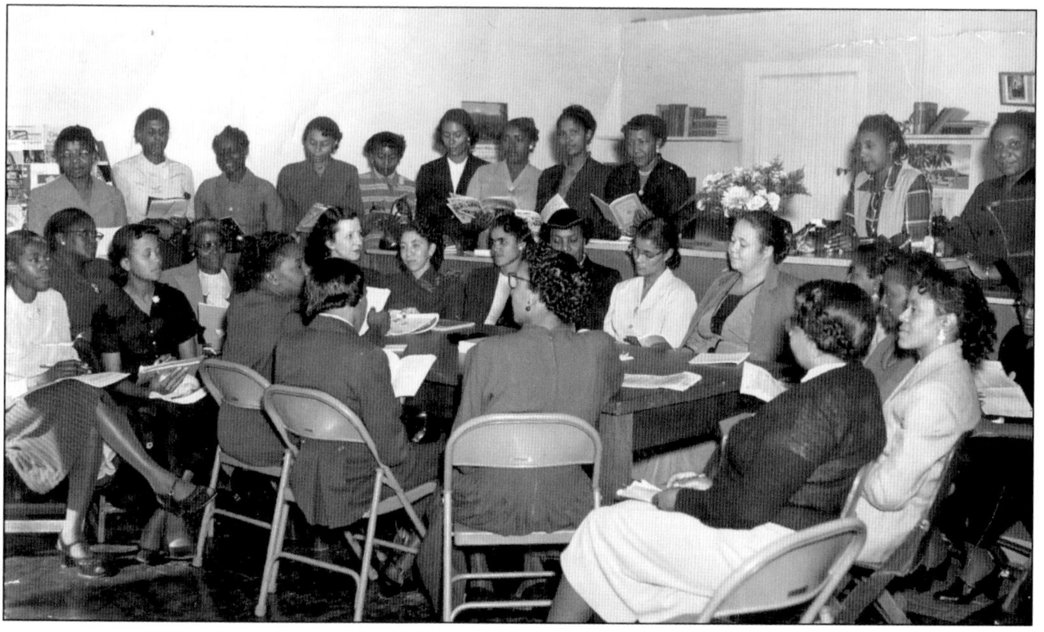

This photo was taken at a teachers' workshop in Madison County. Many well-known educators would participate in enrichment workshops throughout the school year. (Courtesy of Ruth Luckett.)

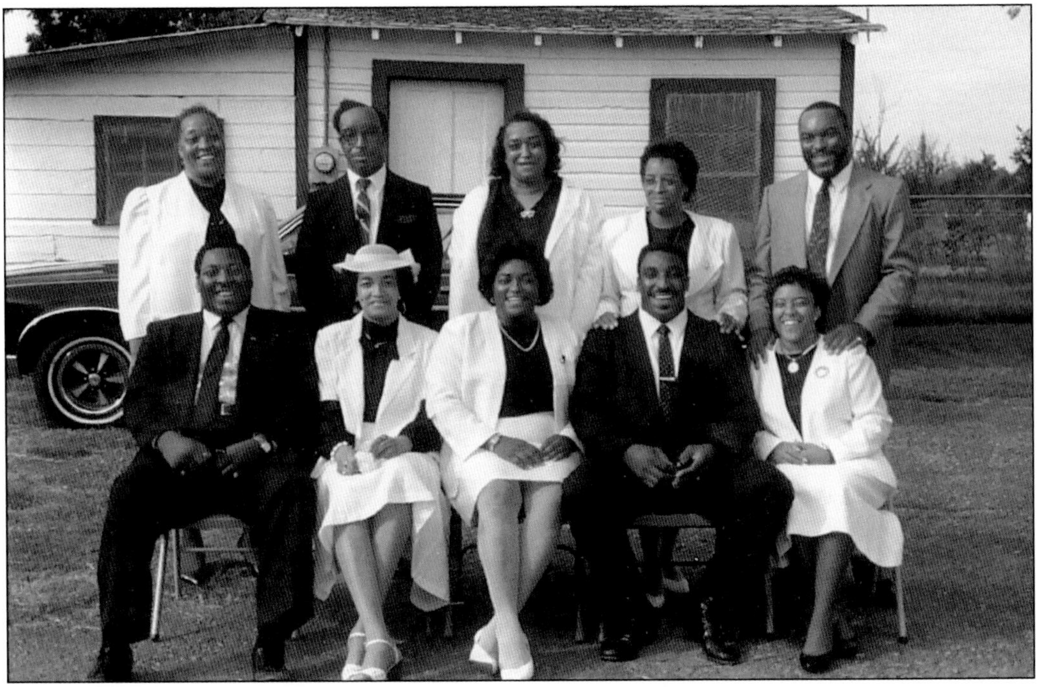

The children of L.C. Smith Sr. and Earnestine Smith gather at the family home on Old Jackson Road for this family photograph. Seen from left to right are (front row) Melvin, Bernice, Gloria Steen, Charlie, and Velma; (back row) Everlene, L.C., Angie Bell, Ruby, and Willie. (Courtesy of Tommie Garner.)

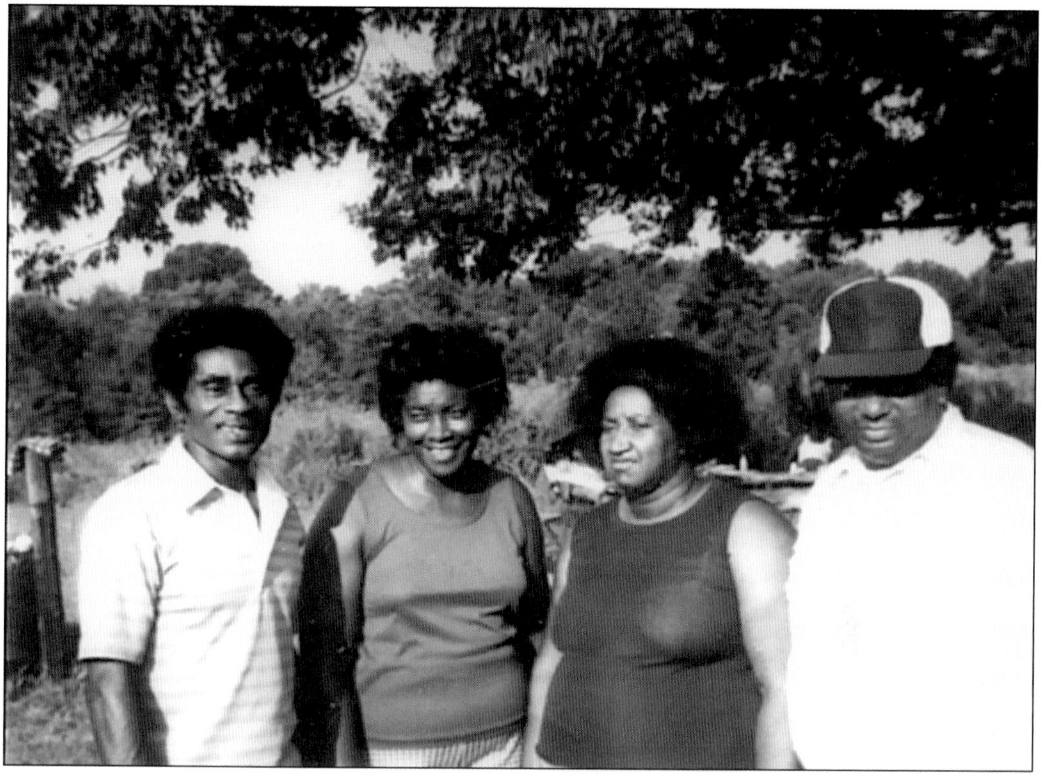

From left to right are William Cain, Bettie Cain, Delois Holmes, and Freddie Holmes. The two couples posed for this photo at the Cains' home. Delois and Bettie were sisters; Bettie is the only person in this photo still living. She continues to reside in Madison County. (Courtesy of Bettie Cain.)

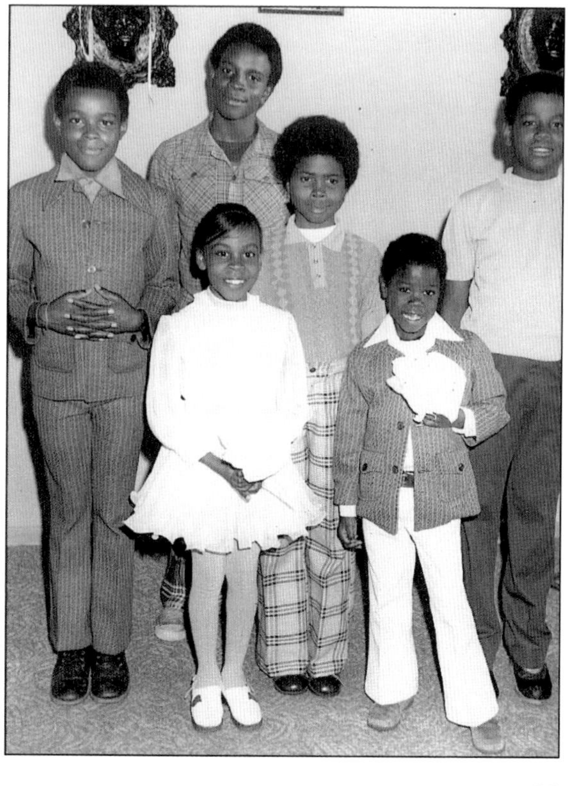

Pictured here are the grandchildren of William and Bettie Cain. From left to right are Claire Cain, Willie Earl Cain, Michael Cain, James Cain, Fay Cain, and Claudy Cain. (Courtesy of Bettie Cain.)

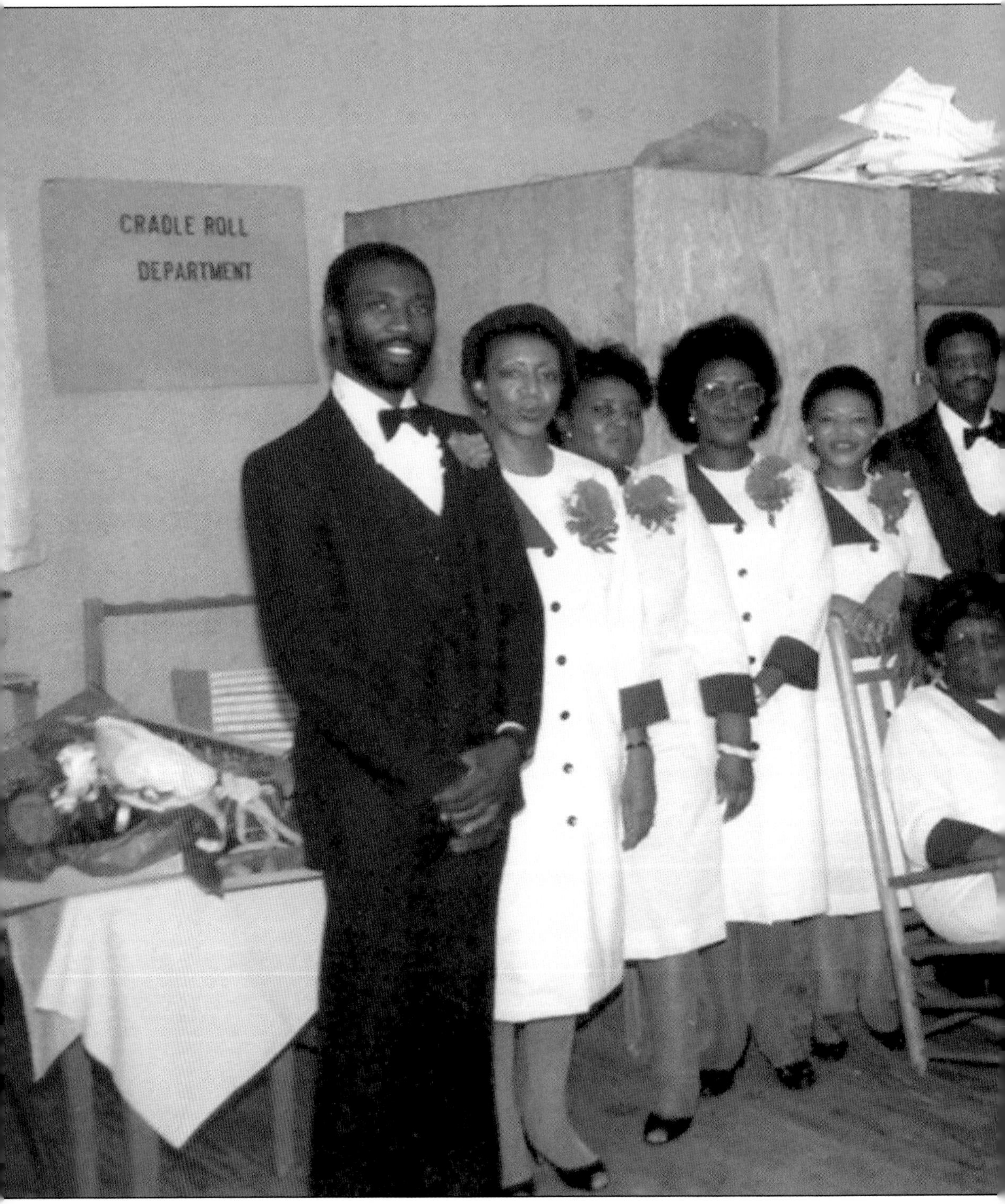

The Sims family of Madison County is seen posing for this family photo. J.B. and Juanita Sims are the parents of 13 children, 12 of which are pictured here. From left to right are James Sims, Georgia, Airedell, Mildred, Casaundra, Oscar, Theresa, Juanita, J.B. Jr., Weedell, Lessie, and

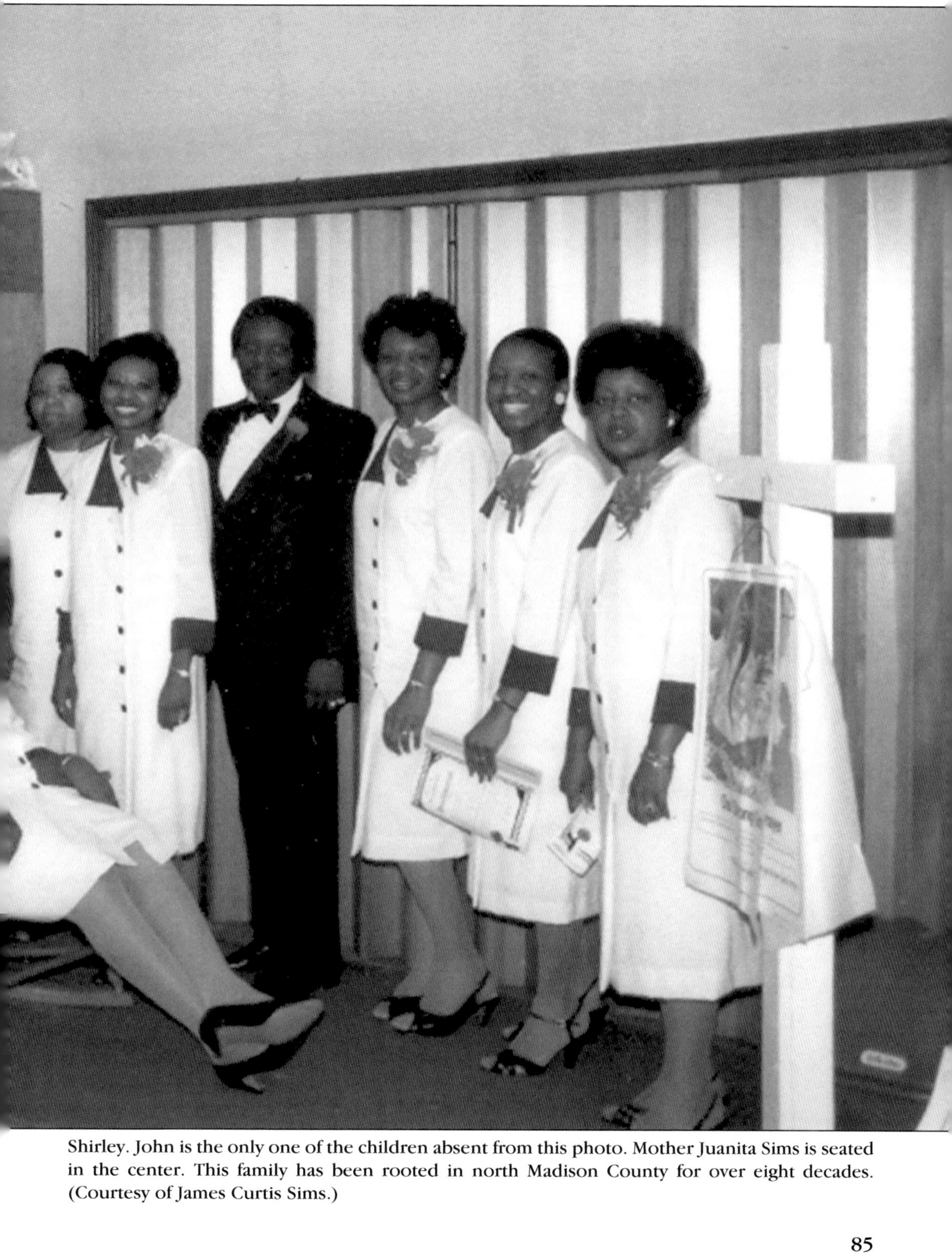

Shirley. John is the only one of the children absent from this photo. Mother Juanita Sims is seated in the center. This family has been rooted in north Madison County for over eight decades. (Courtesy of James Curtis Sims.)

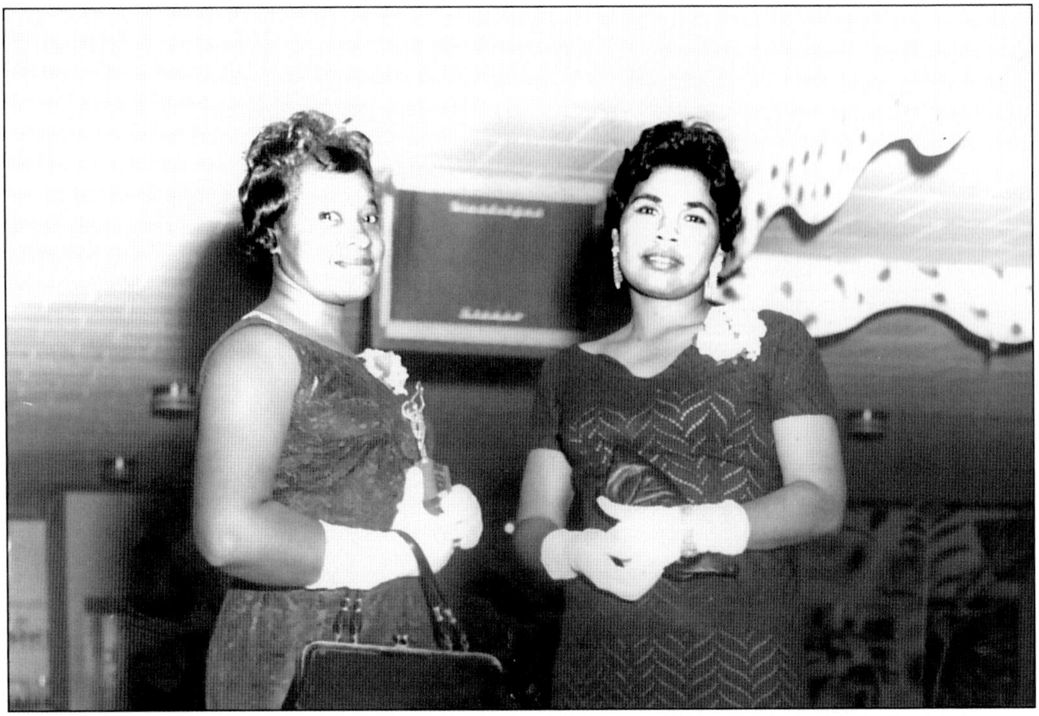

Cora Smith and Bettie Robinson are pictured in 1962. (Courtesy of Cora Smith.)

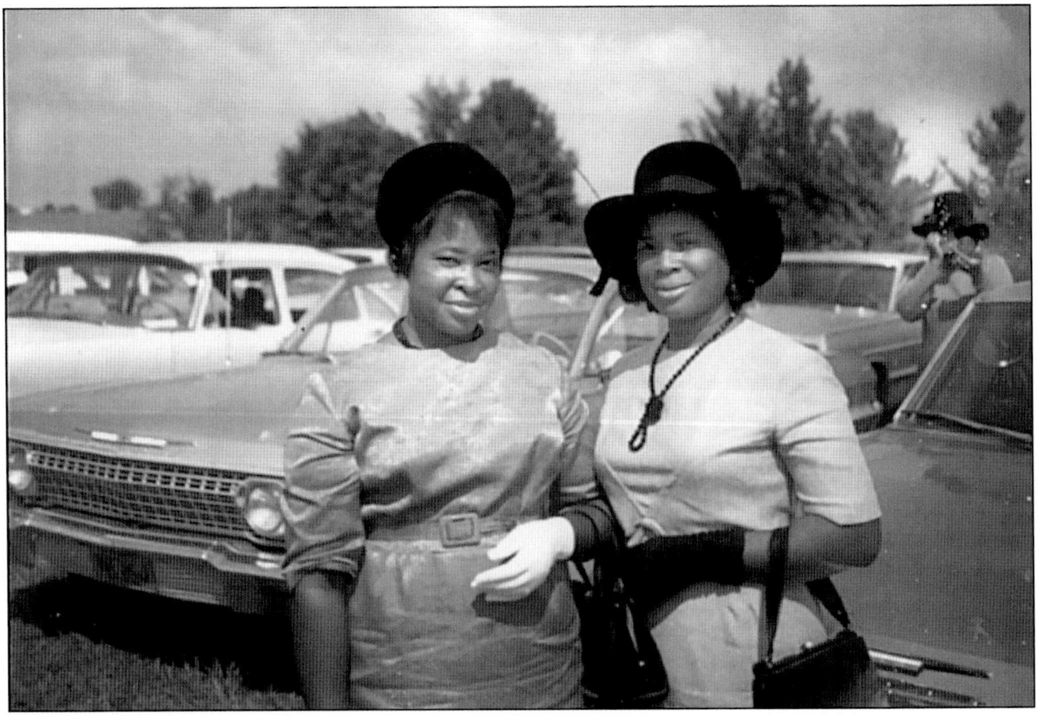

Cora Smith and Doris Bouldin are seen in the 1960s at the Harvey Chapel Missionary Baptist Church. (Courtesy of Cora Smith.)

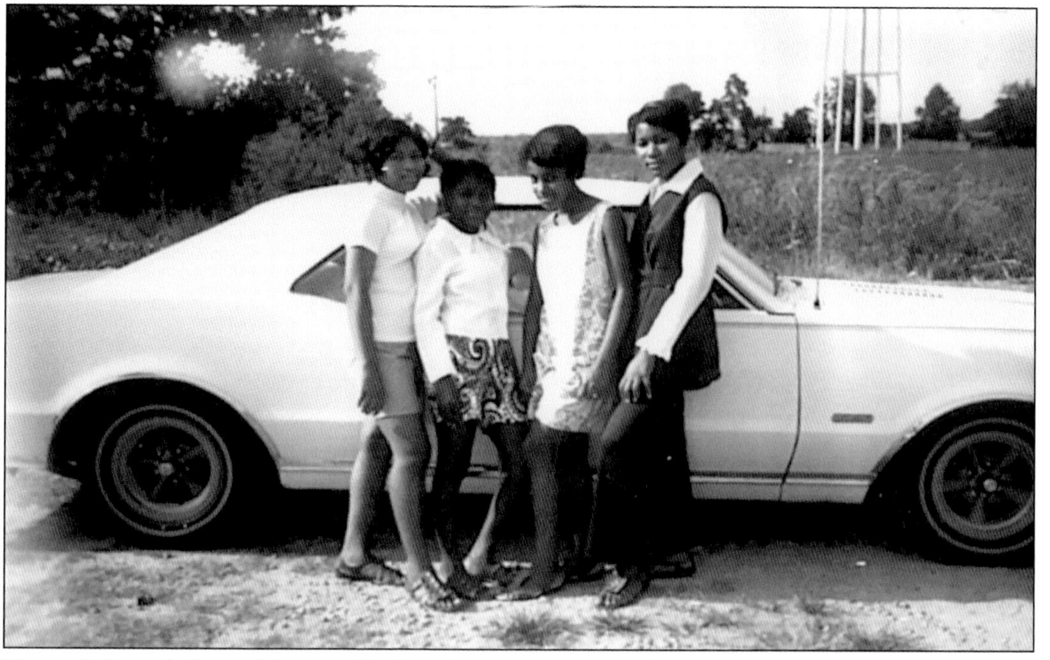

Pictured from left to right are Thelma Garner, Doris Beale, Ernestine McLaurin, and Velma Garner. This photo was taken in the summer of 1969 in the Garner family's yard. (Courtesy of Thelma Garner Myers.).

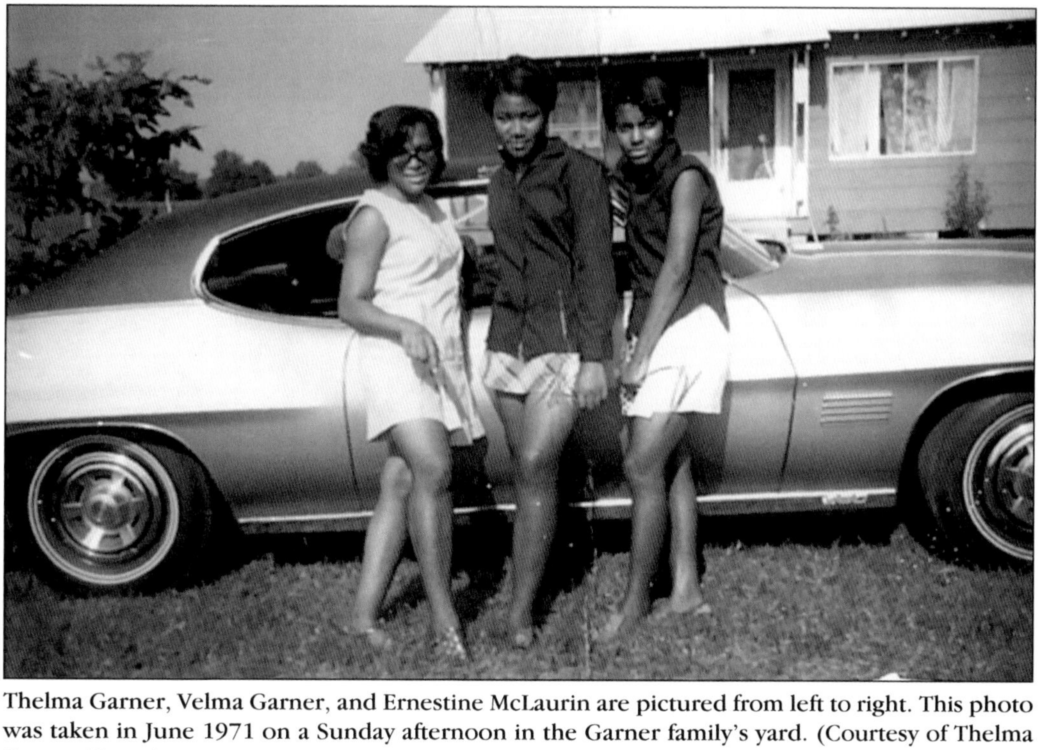

Thelma Garner, Velma Garner, and Ernestine McLaurin are pictured from left to right. This photo was taken in June 1971 on a Sunday afternoon in the Garner family's yard. (Courtesy of Thelma Garner Myers.)

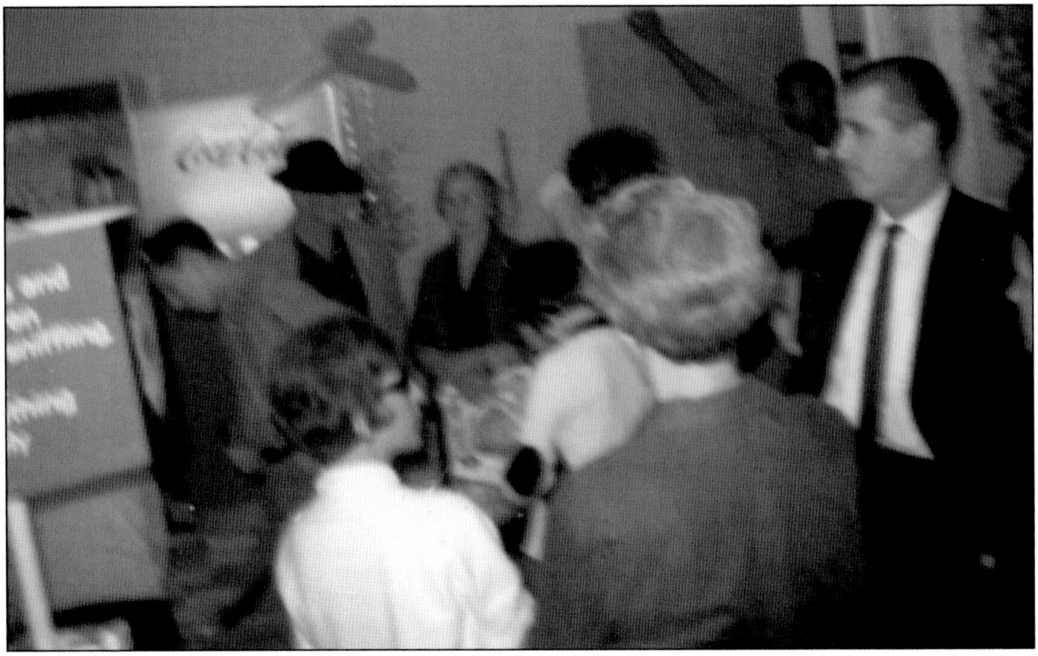

This photo was taken on October 1, 1961 at the grand opening of Jacobs Drug Store on Main Street in the city of Madison. Seen standing in the doorway is teenager Billy Gilbert. He was a helper in the store for several years. Gilbert has since enjoyed success as a pastor, barbershop owner, and electronic equipment repair shop owner. Also pictured in this photo are, from left to right, (background) Billy Bennet, Stuart Hoy, and Mrs. E.D. Cox; (foreground) Virginia Brockmann, Modena Cain (back to camera), and Walter Burns Sr. The opening of this store was such a spectacular affair because there were few stores between Canton and Jackson and this made shopping more convenient for people in the Madison area. (Courtesy of Polly S. Jacobs.)

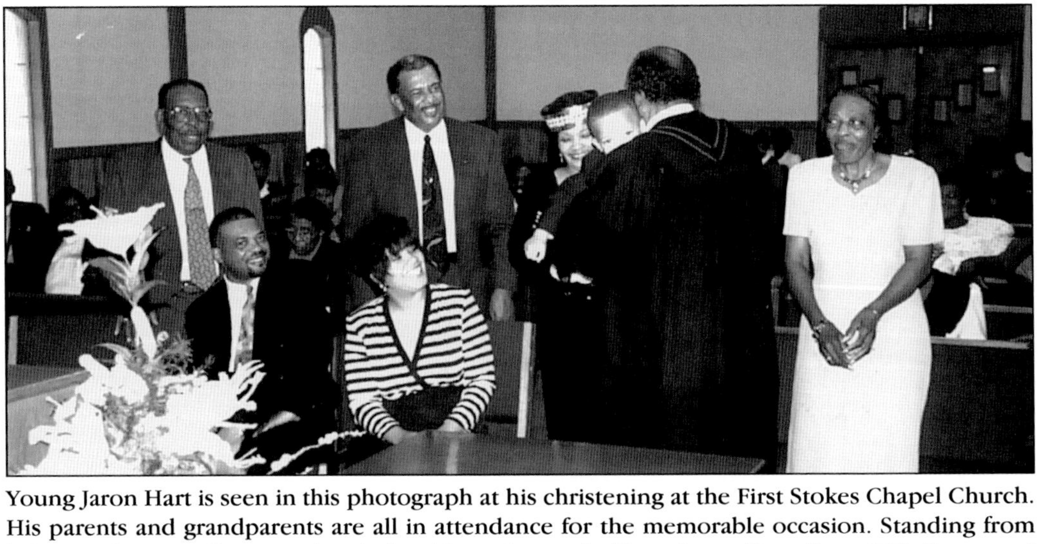

Young Jaron Hart is seen in this photograph at his christening at the First Stokes Chapel Church. His parents and grandparents are all in attendance for the memorable occasion. Standing from left to right are Bilbo Hart Sr., Arthur Tate, Conswela Tate, Jaron Hart, Rev. C.H. Pope, and Dessiree Hart. Sitting from left to right are Jaron's parents, Bilbo Hart Jr. and Rita Hart. (Courtesy of Mary L. Hart.)

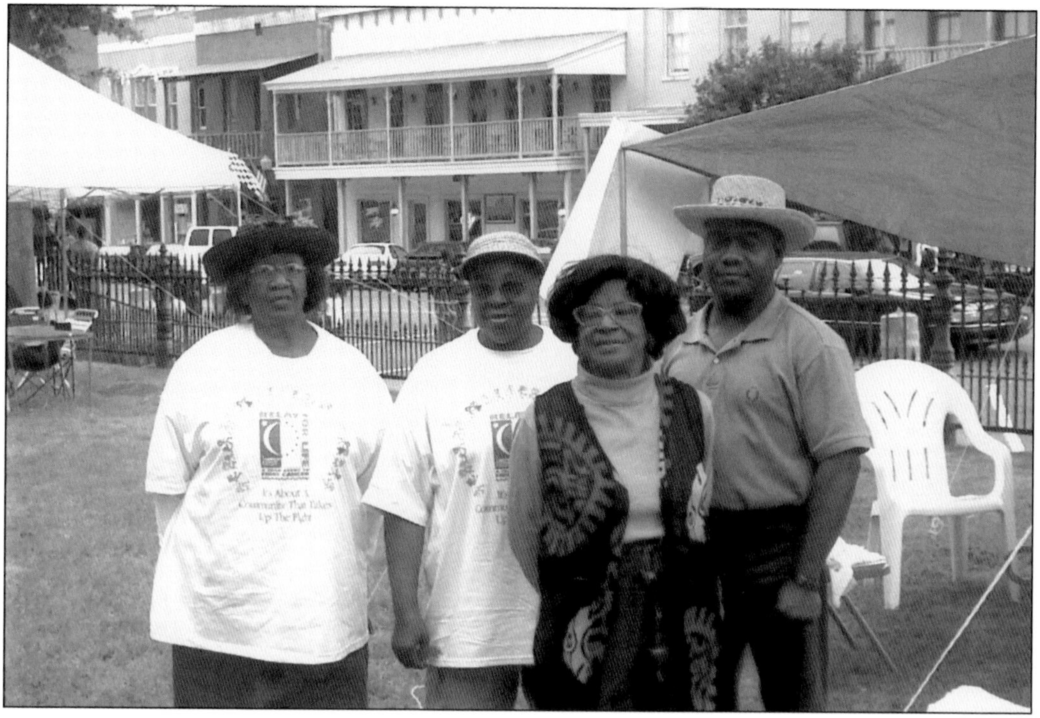

Pictured from left to right are Bessie Alexander, Cora Smith, Virginia Hell, and Earl Hell. The group gathered on the courthouse lawn in Canton to participate in a "Walk for Cancer" event. (Courtesy of Cora Smith.)

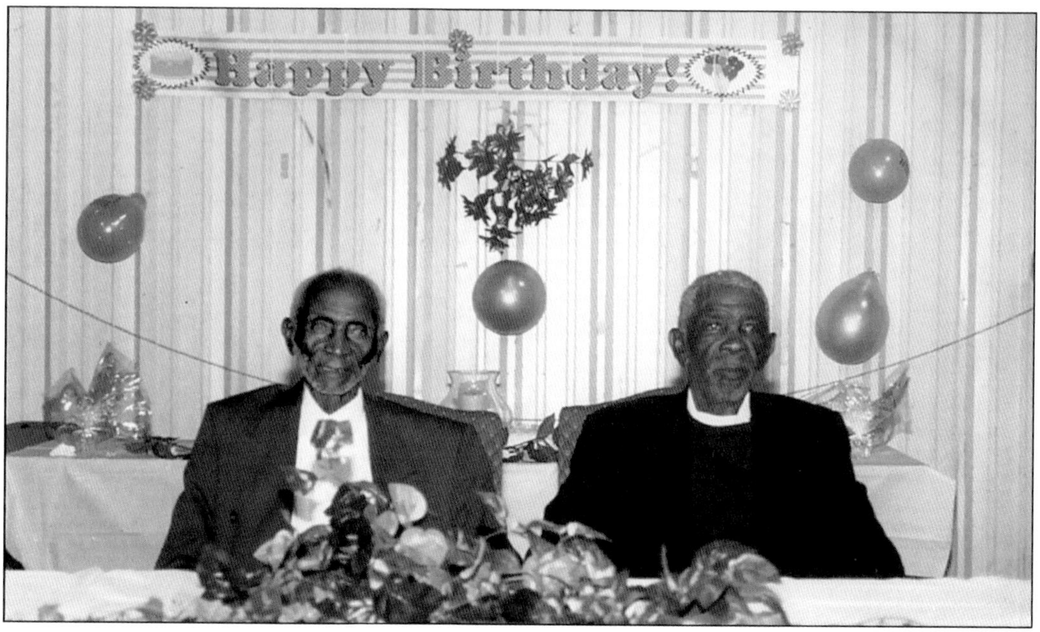

Larkin Woodruff, age 100, and Clarence Woodruff, age 88, posed for this photograph in 2001 as they celebrated their birthdays. Clarence is now deceased and Larkin continues to reside in Canton. (Courtesy of Bennie Smith.)

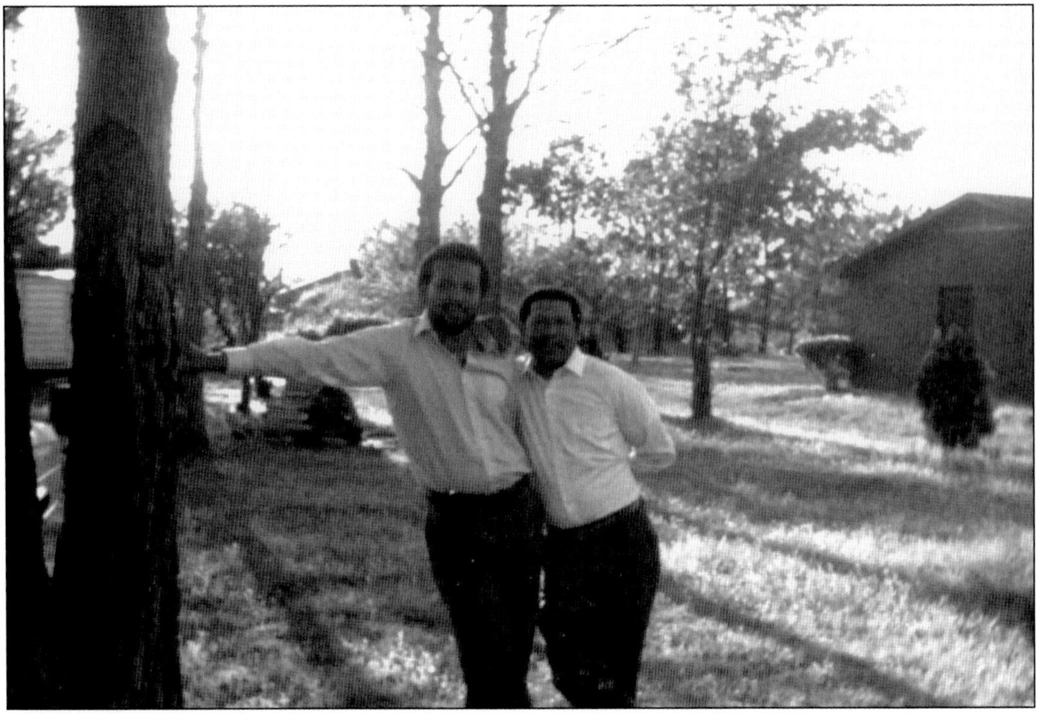

Bilbo Hart Jr. and his uncle Comador Hart pose for a photo at Bilbo's home. (Courtesy of Mary L. Hart.)

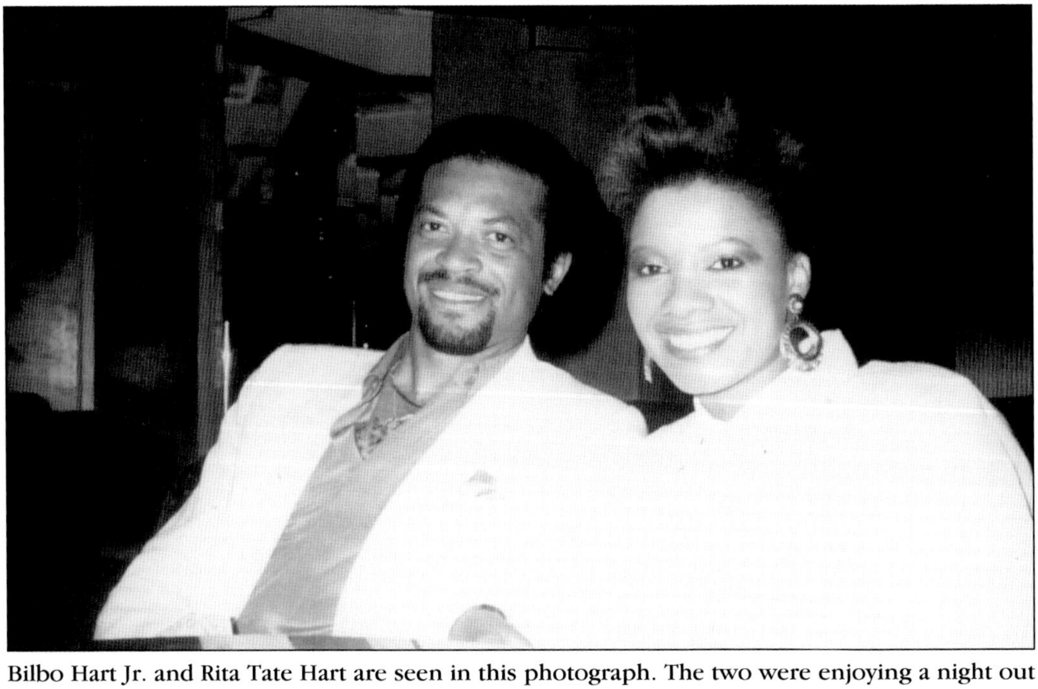

Bilbo Hart Jr. and Rita Tate Hart are seen in this photograph. The two were enjoying a night out on the town. They are the proud parents of two children, Jaron and Jill Hart. (Courtesy of Mary L. Hart.)

Six

FACES OF MADISON COUNTY

"America is woven of many strands. I would recognize them and let it so remain. Our fate is to become one and yet many. This is not prophecy, but description."

Ralph Ellison, 1952

The faces seen in this chapter are those of ordinary people who have lived in Madison County, the men and women who make the county what it is today. They have worked in the fields and plants of the county. They shop in the local grocery stores and attend the churches. They are not famous, but they all give Madison its distinct character. I would like to pay great respect to the everyday people of Madison County.

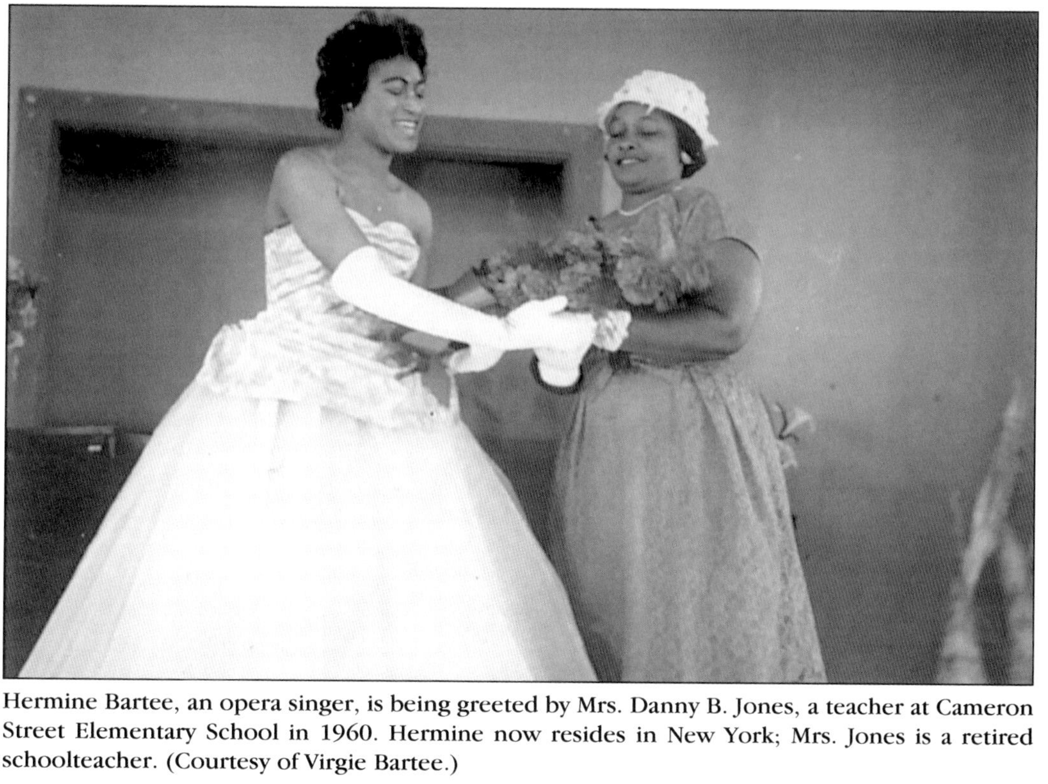

Hermine Bartee, an opera singer, is being greeted by Mrs. Danny B. Jones, a teacher at Cameron Street Elementary School in 1960. Hermine now resides in New York; Mrs. Jones is a retired schoolteacher. (Courtesy of Virgie Bartee.)

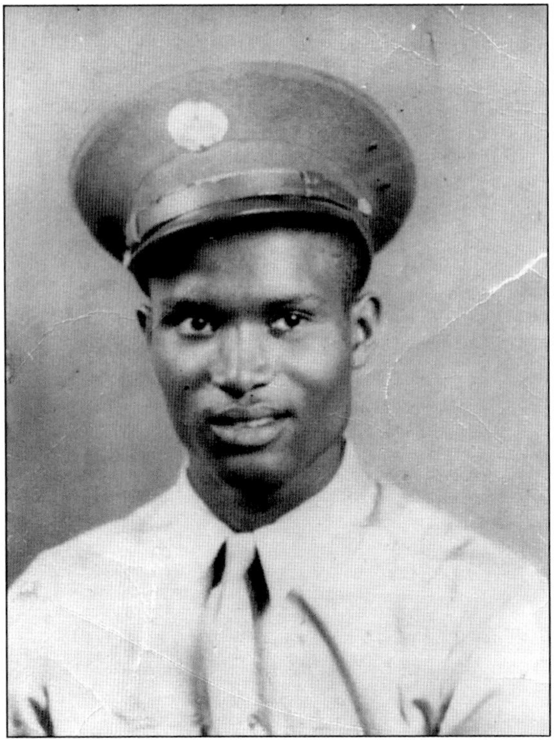

Landres Cheeks is seen in 1944. He was 21 years old when this photo was taken at Camp Shelby in Hattiesburg, Mississippi. (Courtesy of Landres Cheeks.)

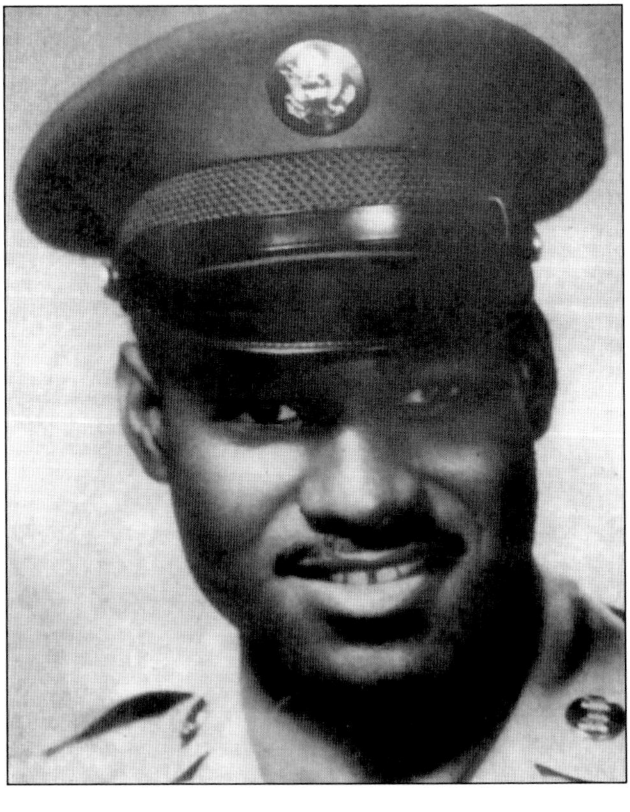

Arthur Garner served in the United States Army for less than a year. Due to illness, he was medically discharged. (Courtesy of Thelma Garner Myers.)

Robert Thompson was a member of the United States Army and he served proudly in World War I. He was 32 years old when this photo was taken. (Courtesy of Alice Reed.)

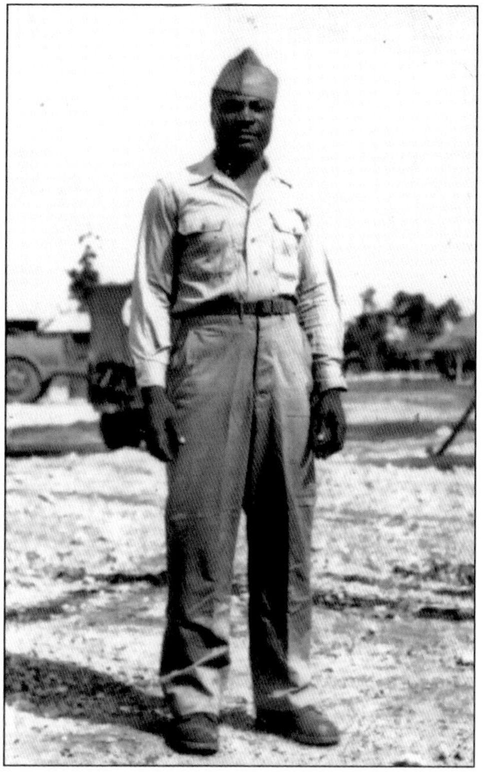

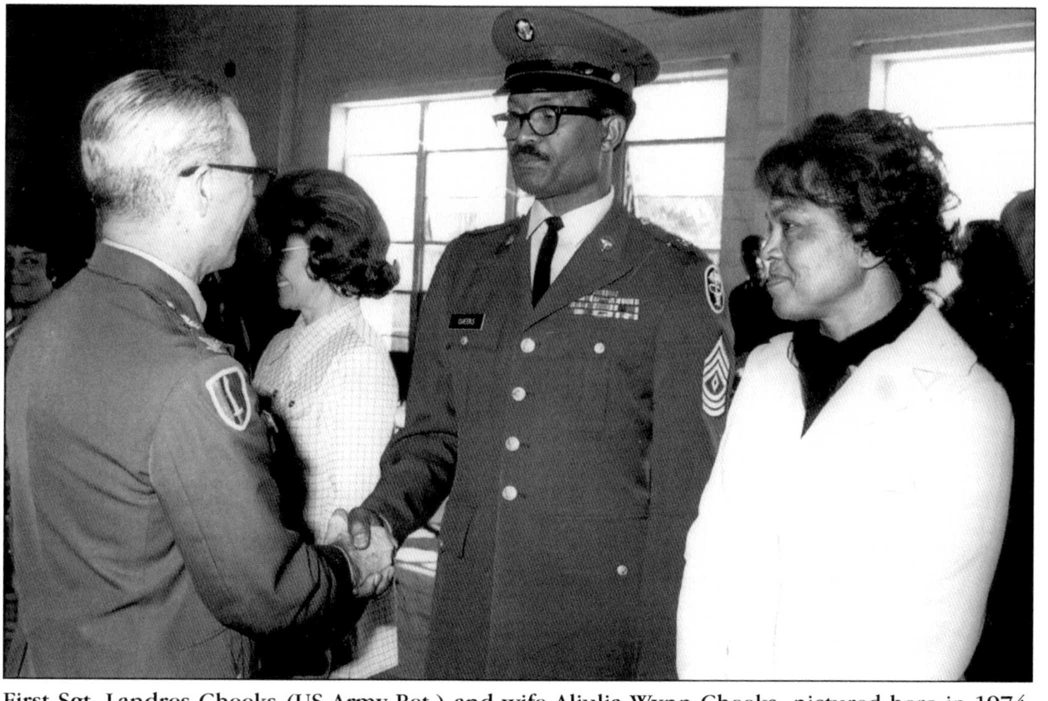

First Sgt. Landres Cheeks (US Army Ret.) and wife Aljulia Wynn Cheeks, pictured here in 1974, currently serve as community volunteers in Canton, Mississippi. (Courtesy of Landres Cheeks.)

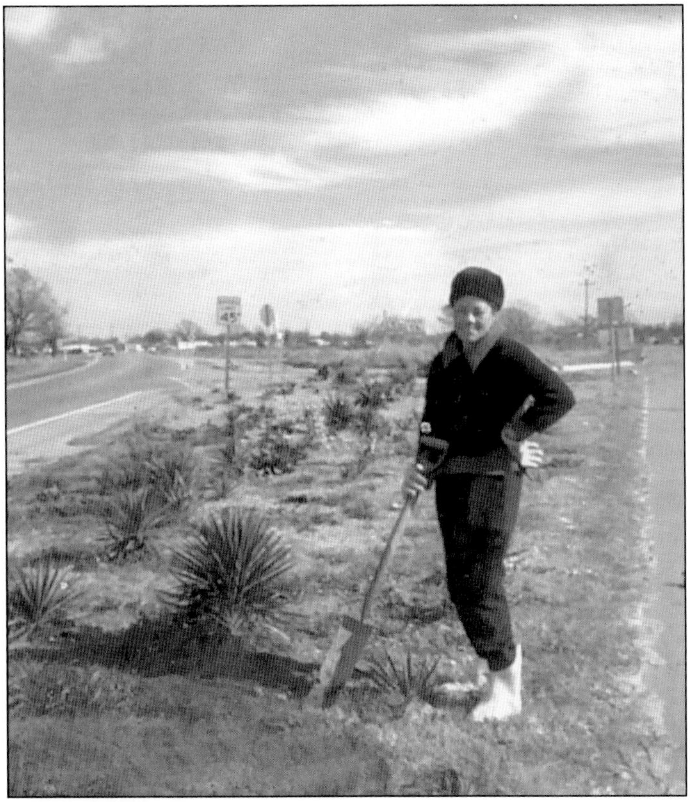

Zettie Bouldin is seen in this photograph taken in January of 1975. "Aunt Zet," as she was called, was fond of children, the church, and the community. She was in church every Sunday morning, shouting for joy and praising God. (Courtesy of Tommie Garner.)

Mr. and Mrs. John Garner are pictured in 1980. The couple took this photograph in front of their family home on Ragsdale Road in Madison County. (Courtesy of Tommie Garner.)

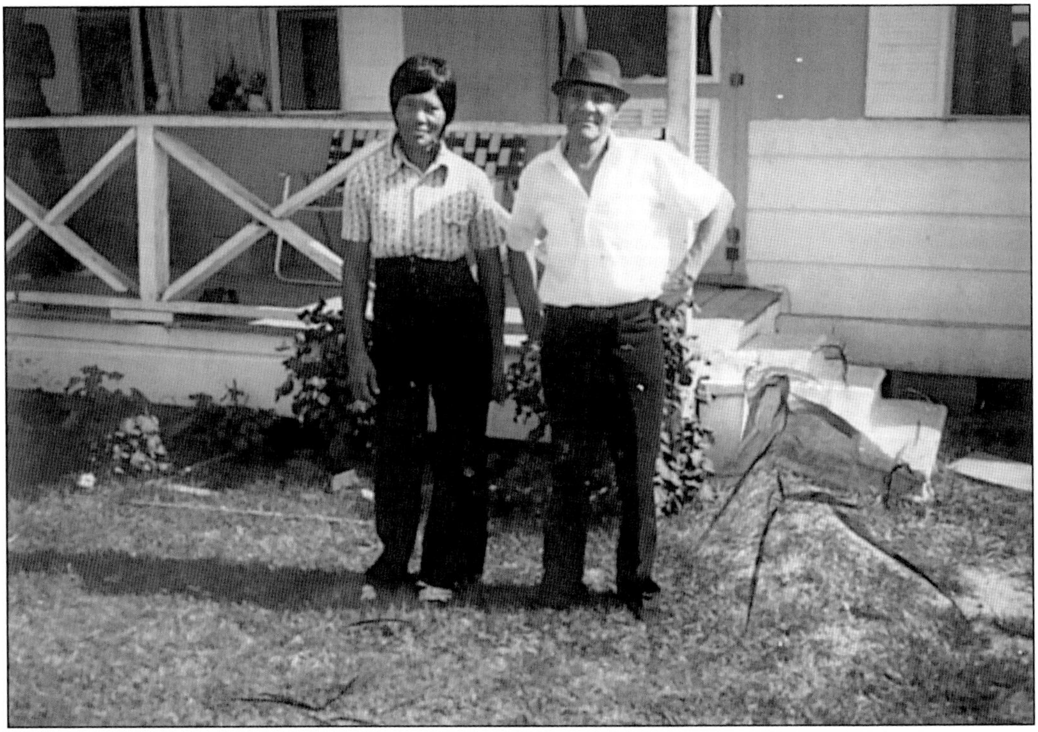

Mandy Carson Payton posed for this 1960 photograph. She was a native of Madison County, where she married and became a housewife and mother. (Courtesy of Tommie Garner.)

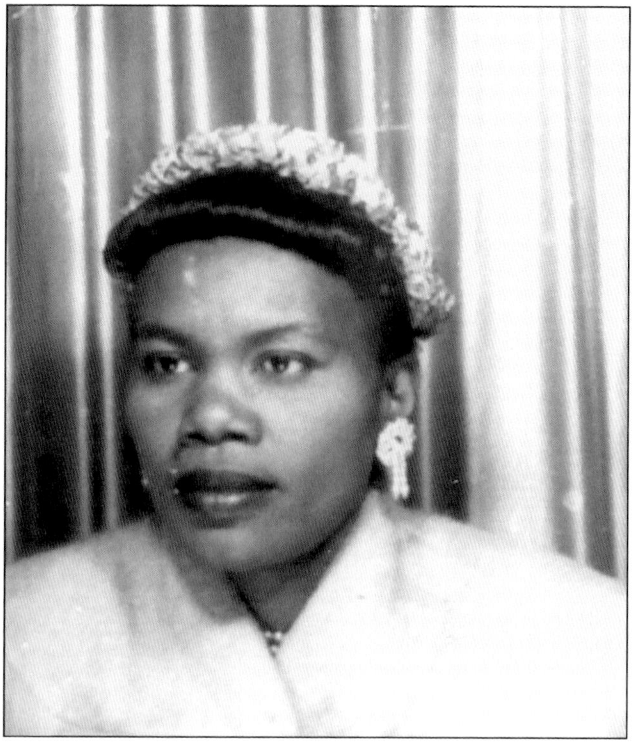

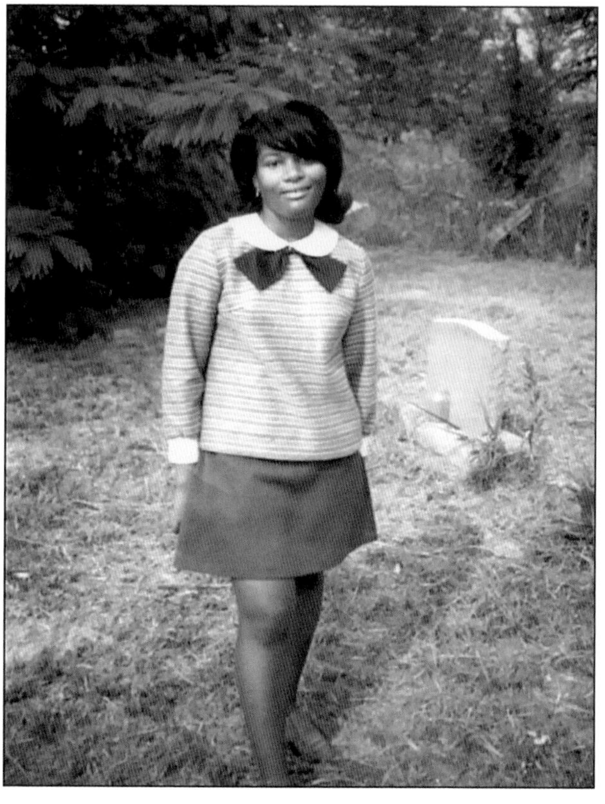

Thelma Garner poses for this Sunday afternoon photo in 1969. Like many people, Thelma would have camera in hand to take pictures of friends and family after church services. She and her family attend Harvey Chapel Missionary Baptist Church south of Canton. (Courtesy of Thelma Garner Myers.)

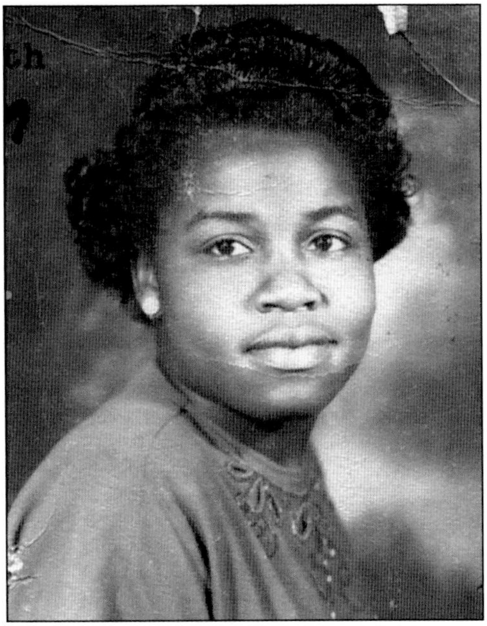

Ruth Luckett graduated from Cameron Street High School in 1949. (Courtesy of Ruth Luckett.)

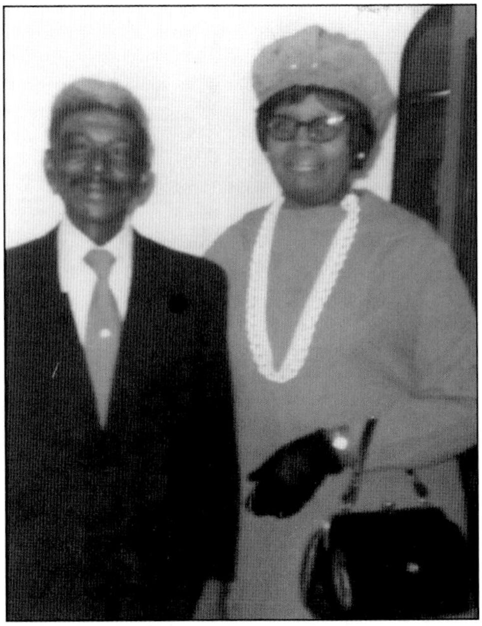

J.B. (born 1904) and Juanita (born 1914) Sims married in 1930. They were the parents of 13 children. He worked as a farmer and she as a housewife and mother. They attended Mount Zion Cobbsville Church. (Courtesy of James Curtis Sims.)

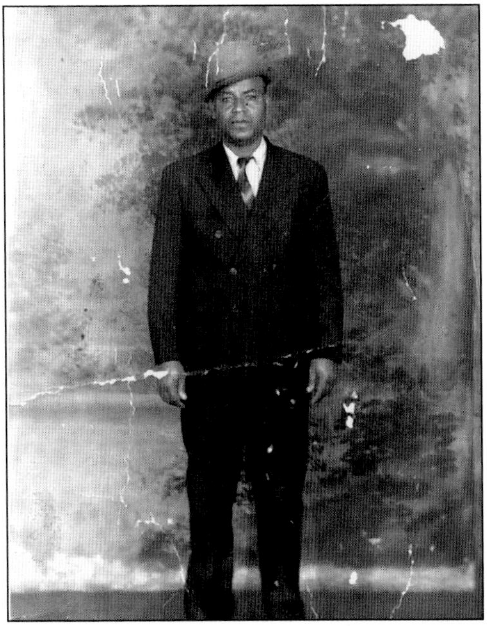

Jimmy Cheeks stands for this 1940s photo. His wife Amelia is seen to the right. (Courtesy of Landres Cheeks.)

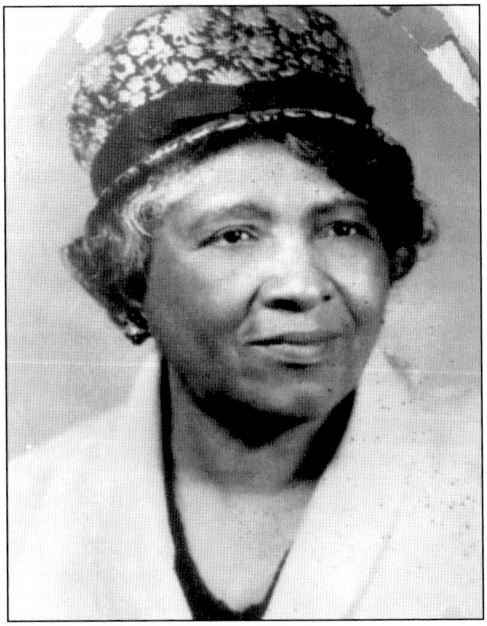

Amelia Jackson Cheeks, born in 1902, is pictured in 1964. She passed away in 1990. (Courtesy of Landres Cheeks.)

L.C. Smith stands proudly beside his first truck. L.C. was and still is an active farmer in Madison County, and he comes from a large family of sisters and brothers. A deacon at the Harvey Chapel Missionary Baptist Church, L.C. and his wife of many years continue to reside in Madison County. (Courtesy of Cora Smith.)

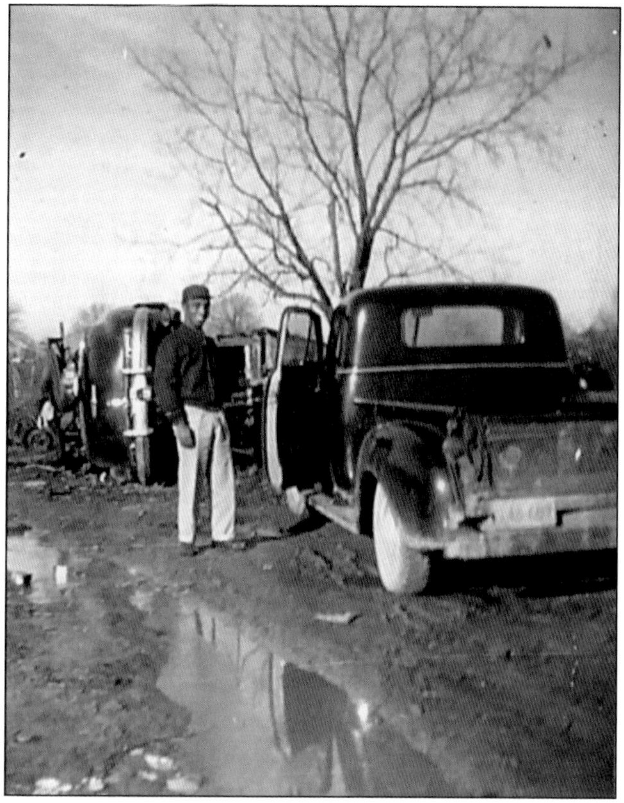

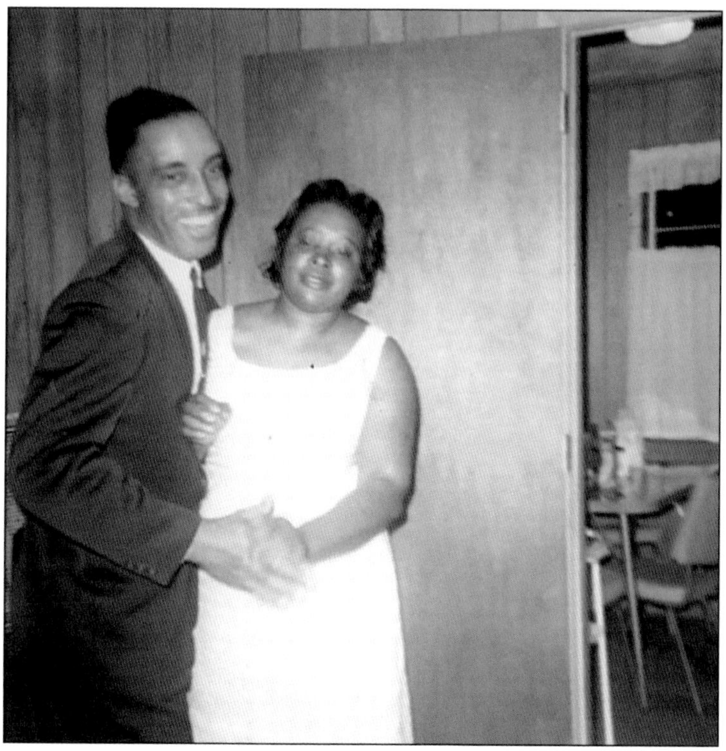

L.C. and Cora Lee Smith are pictured at home in 1960. Both active in the church, L.C. and Cora have now been married 44 years. (Courtesy of Cora Smith.)

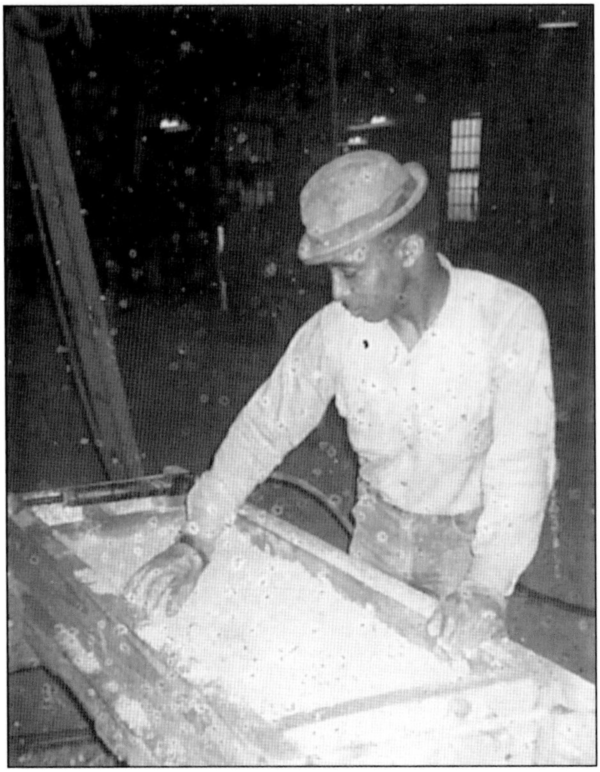

L.C. Smith is seen at his first job at the Jackson Stone Co. in Jackson, Mississippi in 1965. Many Madison County residents sought employment in neighboring Hinds County. (Courtesy of Cora Smith.)

This photo was taken of L.C. Smith on his farm in Madison County in 1981; his grandson sits on top of the horse. (Courtesy of Cora Smith.)

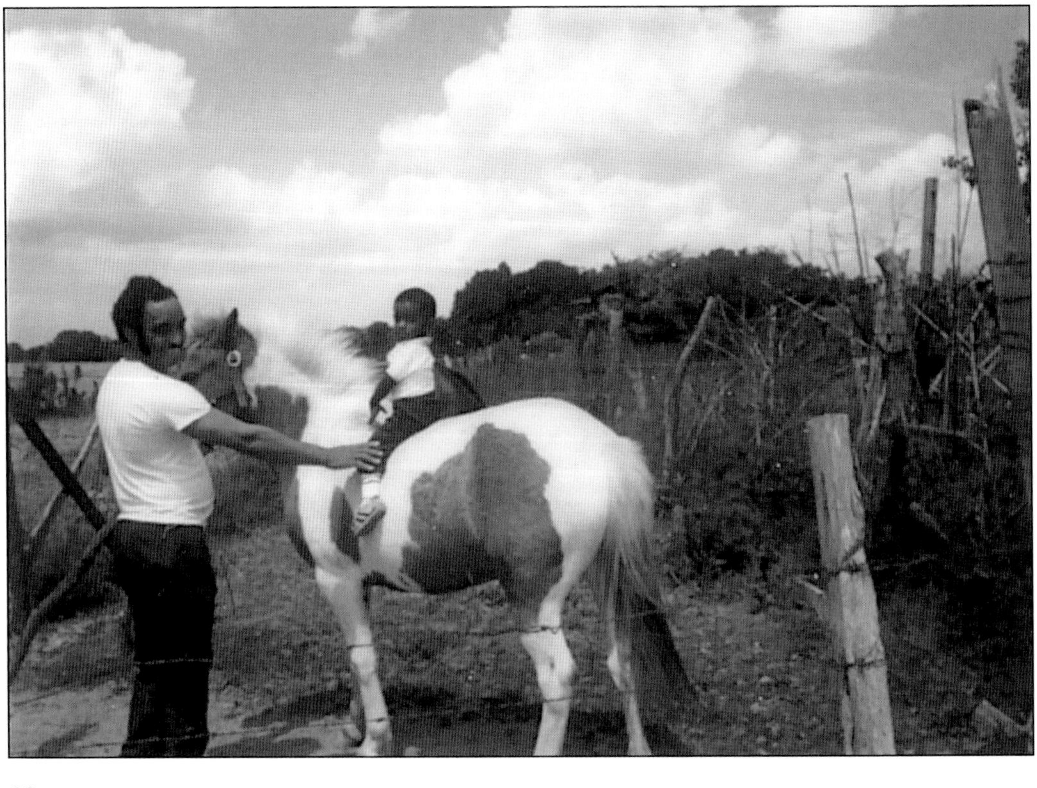

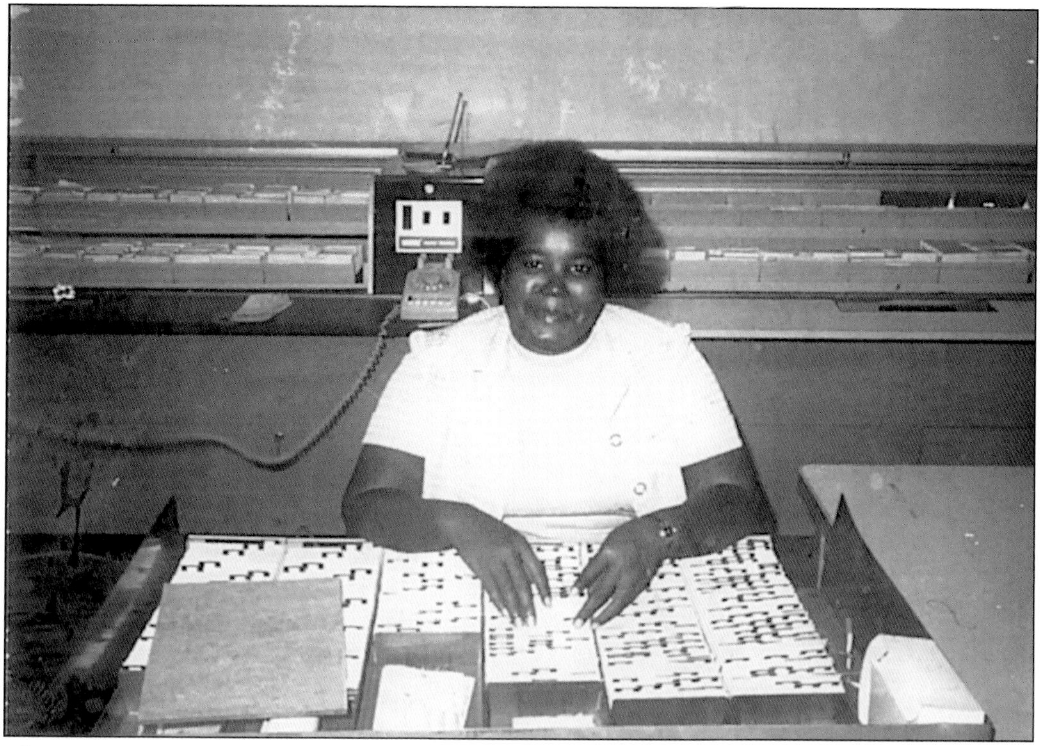

Gloria Smith, daughter of L.C. and Cora Smith, is seen is this photograph. She was a graduate of Canton High School. (Courtesy of Cora Smith.)

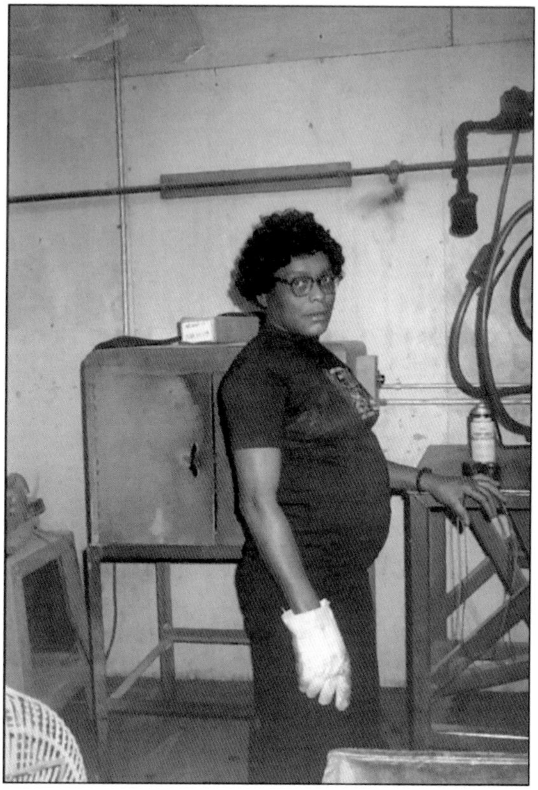

Annie Bell Berry is seen in this photograph working at Jack Evans factory making coils and cut-off valves. She remains employed there to this day, after 28 years of service. (Courtesy of Annie B. Berry.)

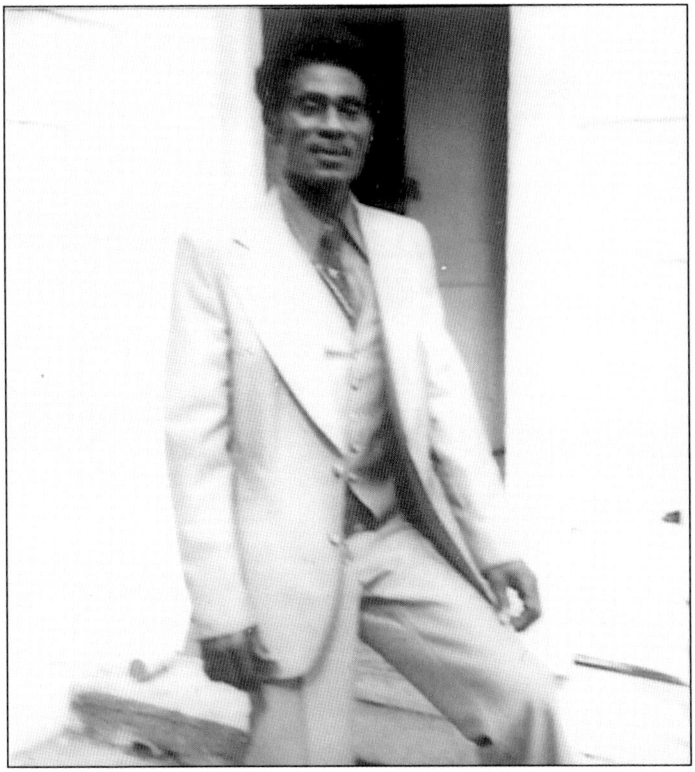

William Cain took time out for this photo at the Harvey Chapel Missionary Baptist Church in 1980. He was a deacon and Sunday school superintendent at this church until his death. (Courtesy of Bettie Cain.)

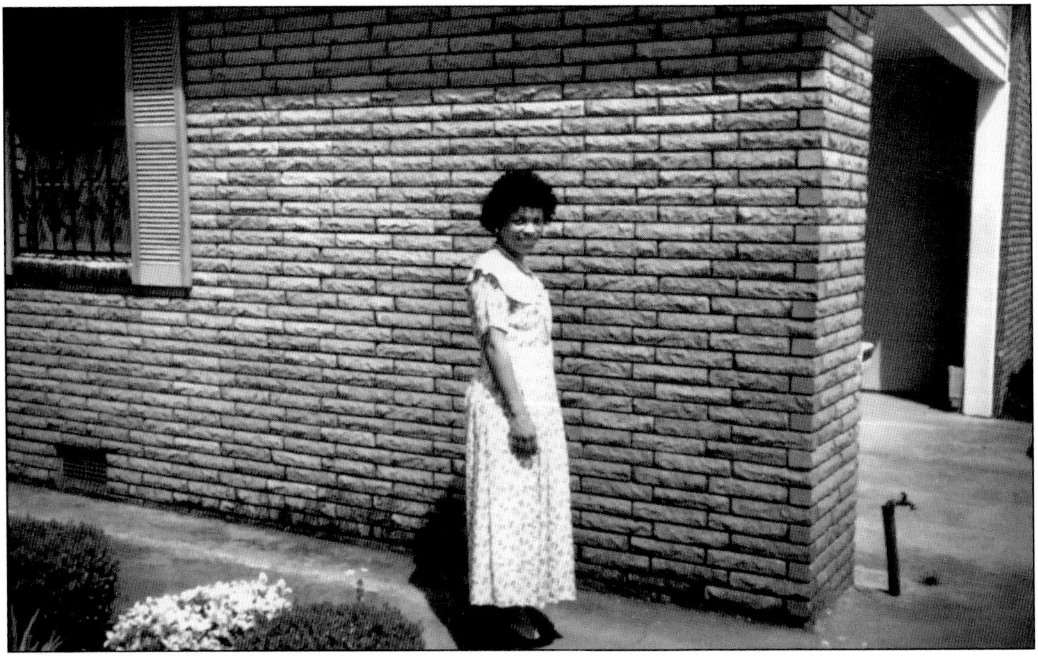

Mary L. Hart poses in front of the family home for this photograph. Mary was a 1978 graduate from Canton High School. She currently resides in Canton. She is the mother of one son, Frederick Hart. (Courtesy of Mary L. Hart.)

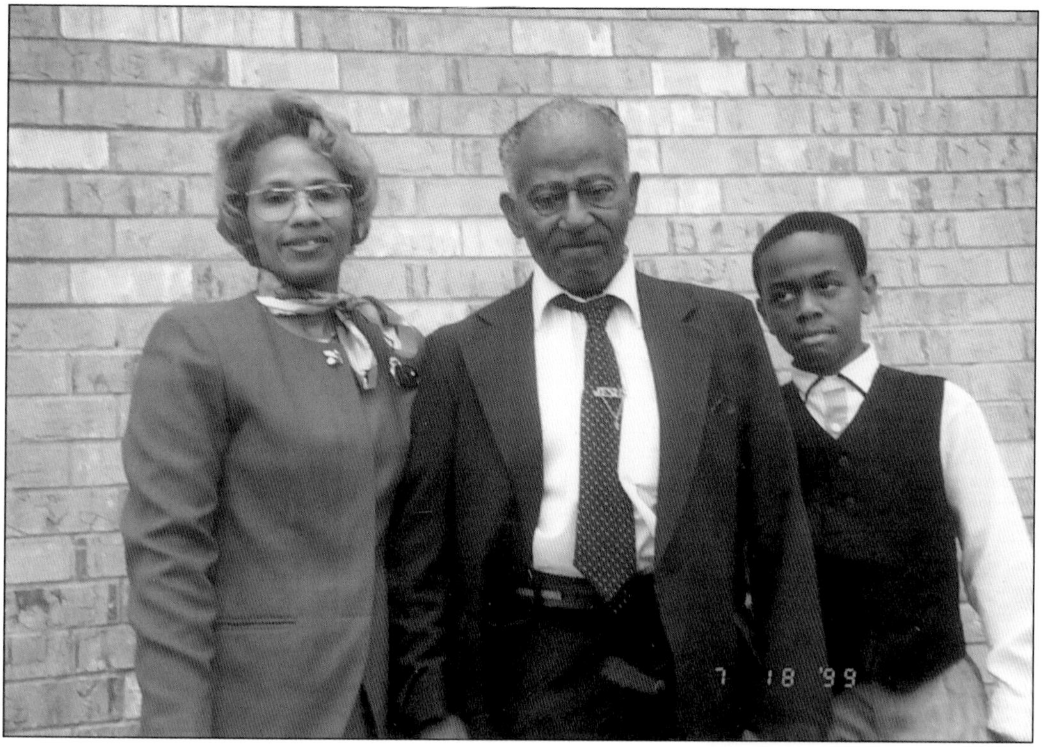

LeAndrew Cain, daughter Burna Cain Bess, and grandson Derrick Bess are shown at the Harvey Chapel Missionary Baptist Church. (Courtesy of Thelma Cain.)

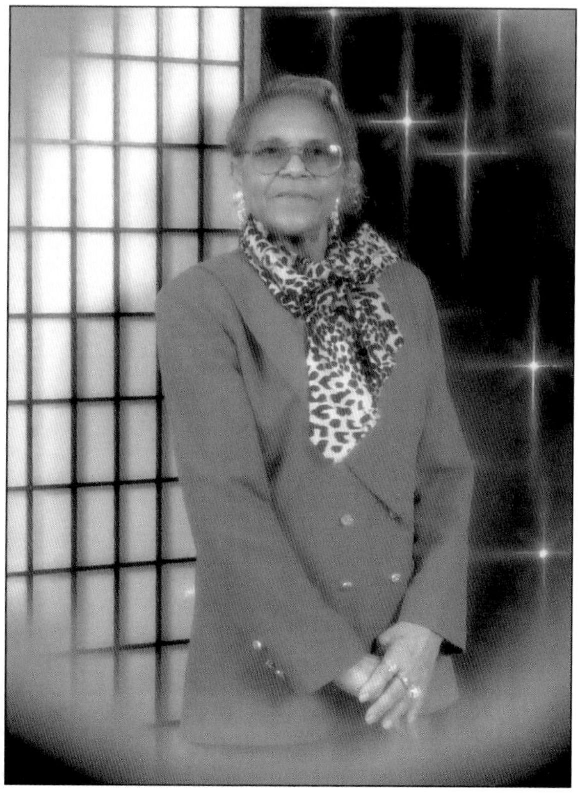

Thelma Cain is the daughter of Tempia and Dave Winfield. An active member of the Harvey Chapel Missionary Baptist Church, she is a part of several auxiliaries within the church. She is the mother of eight children. Mrs. Cain currently resides in Canton, Mississippi. (Courtesy of Thelma Cain.)

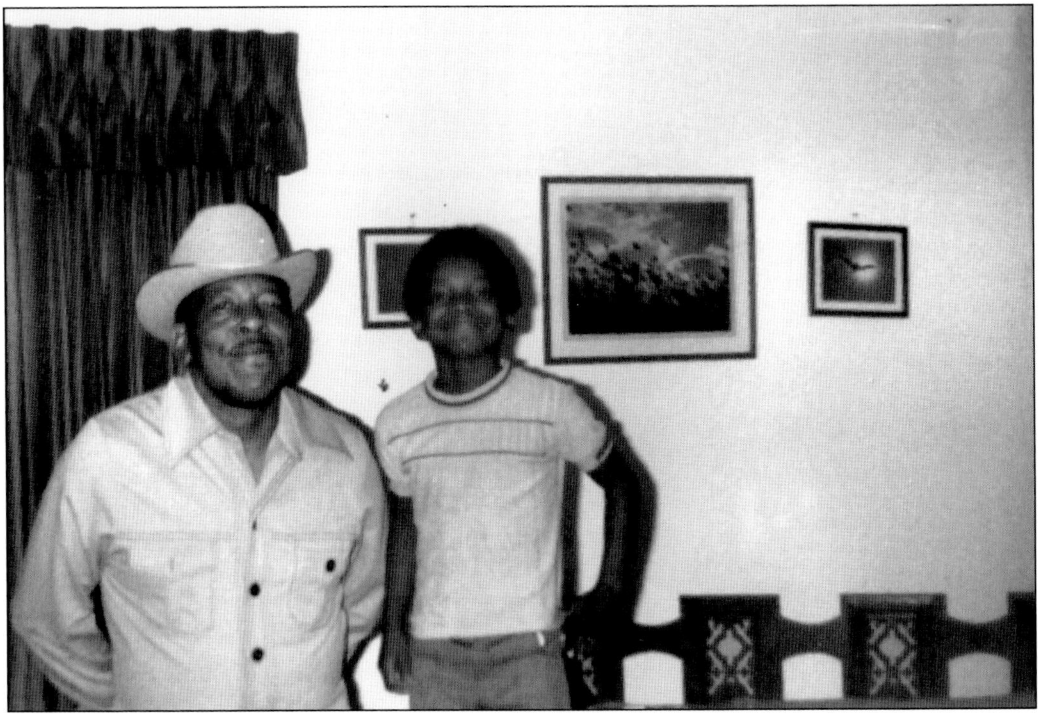

Bilbo Hart and his grandson Frederick Hart are seen in this 1982 photo. Both are natives of Madison County, where they continue to reside. (Courtesy of Mary L. Hart.)

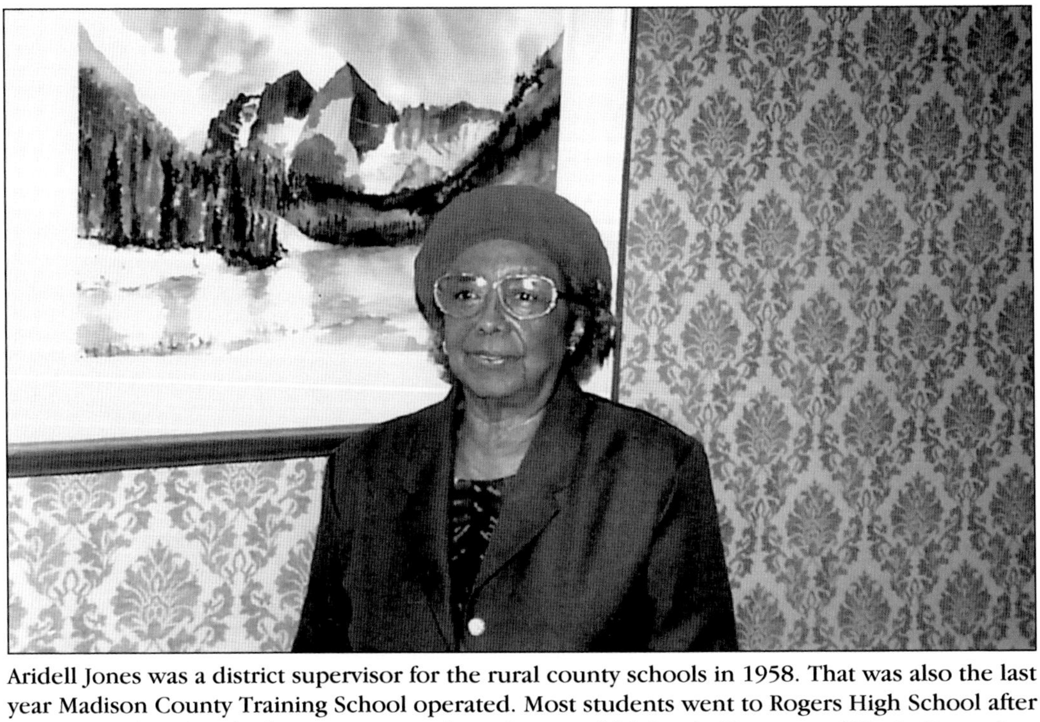

Aridell Jones was a district supervisor for the rural county schools in 1958. That was also the last year Madison County Training School operated. Most students went to Rogers High School after the school closed and others went to Madison Rosenwald School. (Courtesy of Virgie Bartee.)

Odell Cain, daughter of William and Bettie Cain, posed for this 1980 photograph. She is currently residing in Chicago, Illinois. (Courtesy of Bettie Cain.)

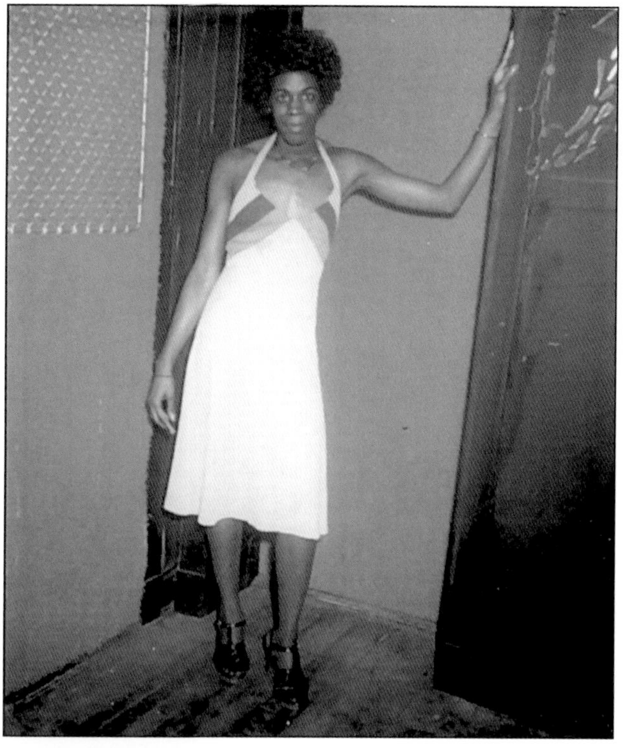

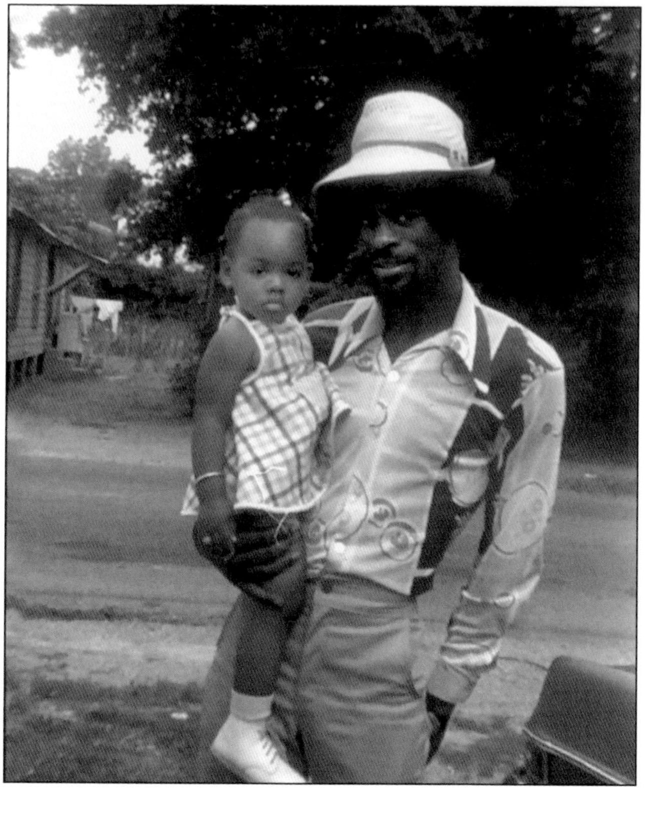

Joseph Cain proudly holds his baby daughter Kim for this 1977 photograph. (Courtesy of Bettie Cain.)

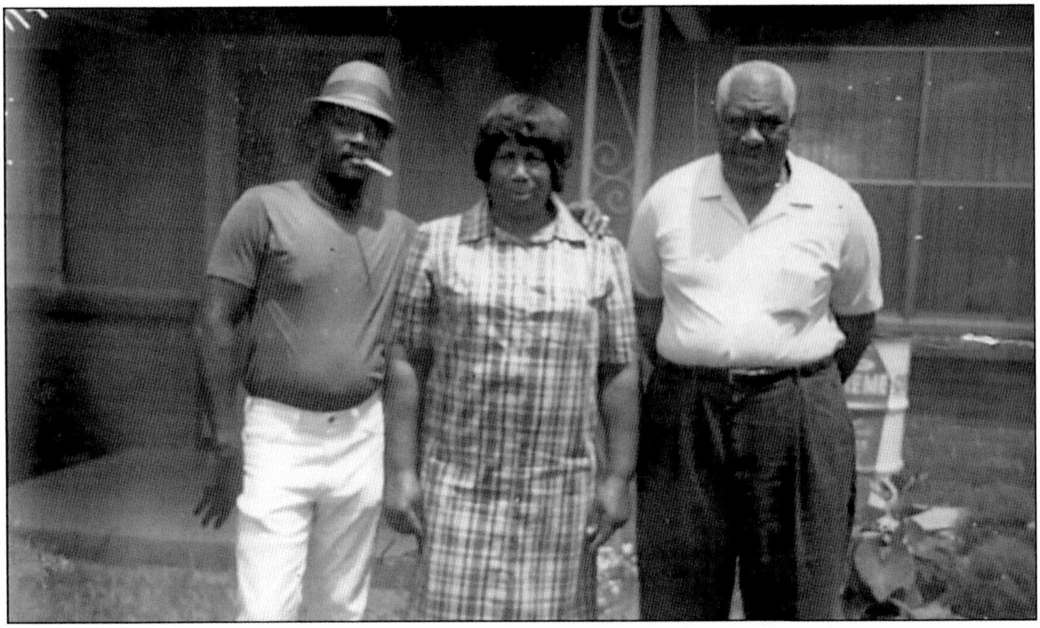

From left to right, Willie Davis, his mother Varie Robinson, and her husband Willie Robinson are pictured in front of the Robinsons' home. (Courtesy of Umble Hawkins.)

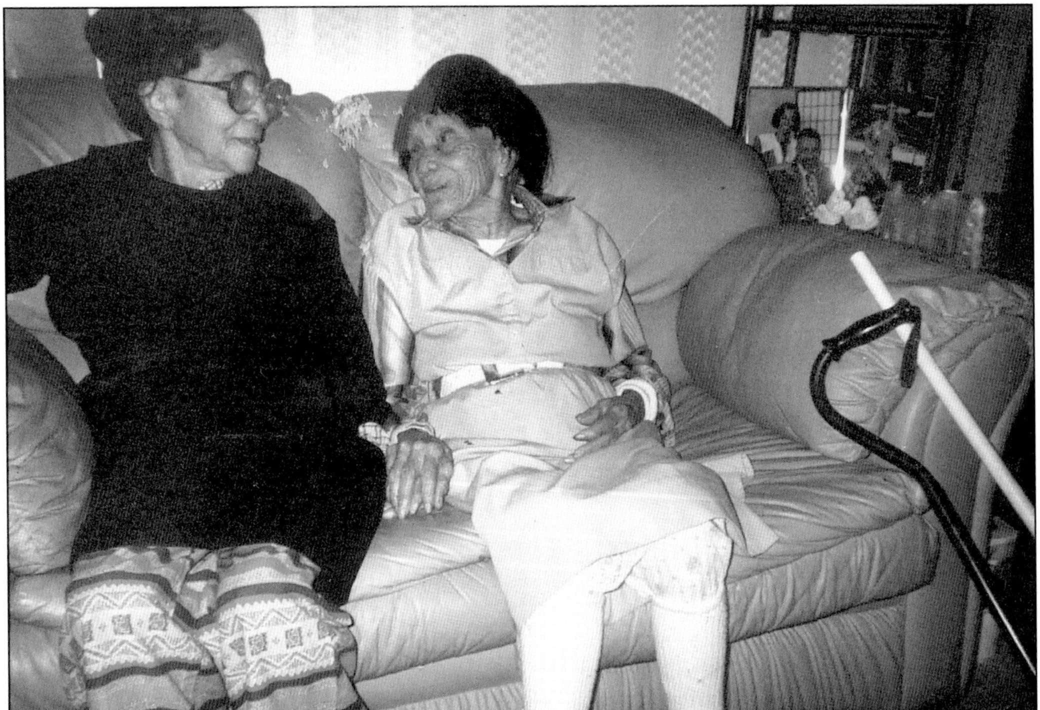

Winnie Day and Hattie Cauthern are pictured in 1997. Winnie Day lives in Evansville, Indiana. Hattie Cauthern, who is 108 years old, lives in Gluckstadt. Ms. Hattie is one of the oldest African Americans living in Madison County. (Courtesy of Callie Bouldin.)

Eva Archie poses for this photograph with her daughter, Grace Archie Bouldin. Eva was an active member of the Harvey Chapel Missionary Baptist Church. She was affiliated with several auxiliaries in the church until her death. Grace continues to reside in Madison County and she is also an active member of the Harvey Chapel Missionary Baptist Church. (Courtesy of Callie Bouldin.)

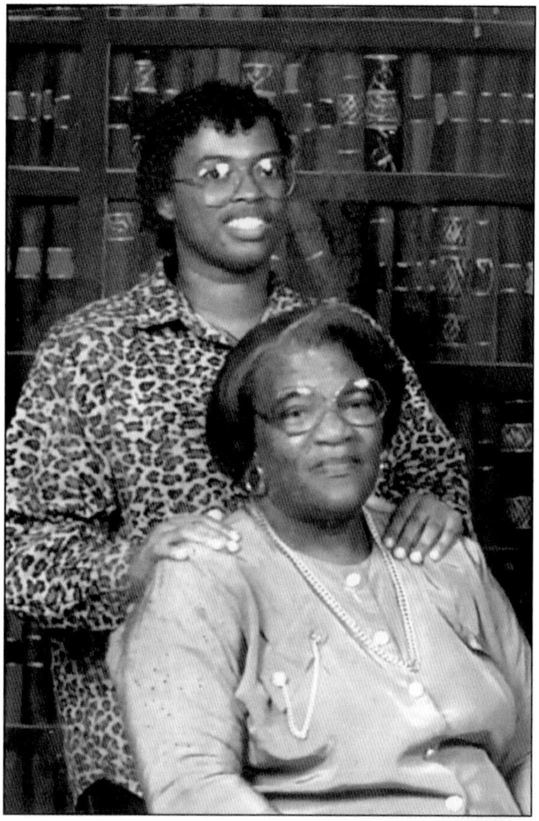

The grandchildren of Alice Teen Berry gather at her home for this photograph. This house was 125 years old, but it was torn down in 2002 to make way for road expansion. (Courtesy of Annie B. Berry.)

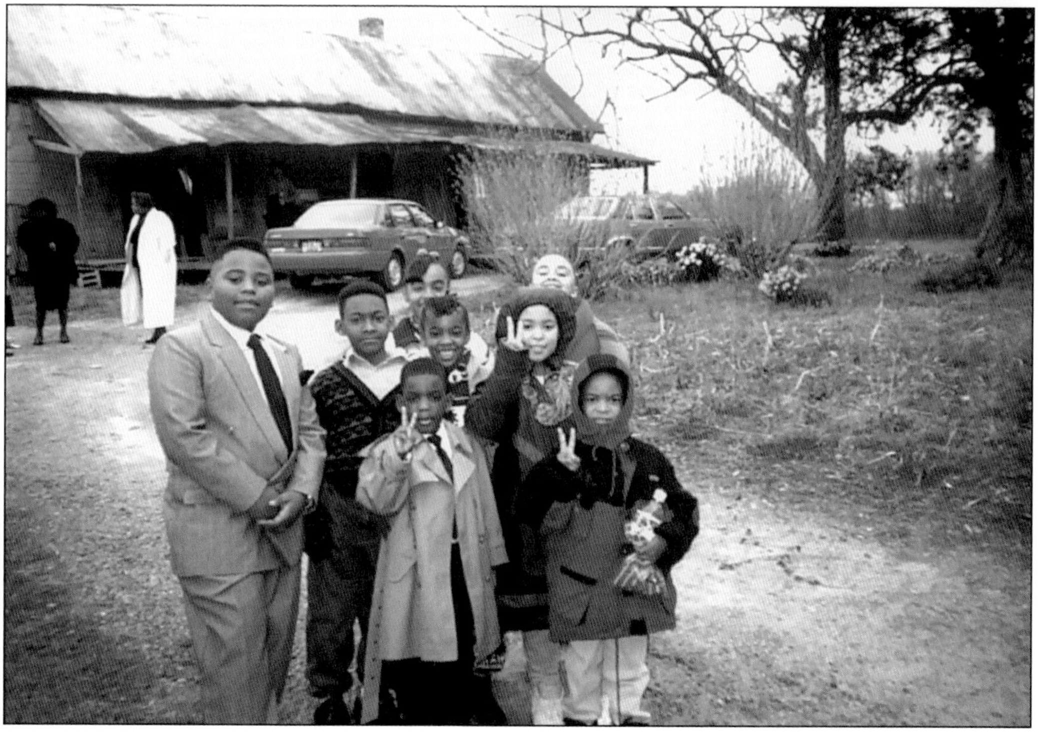

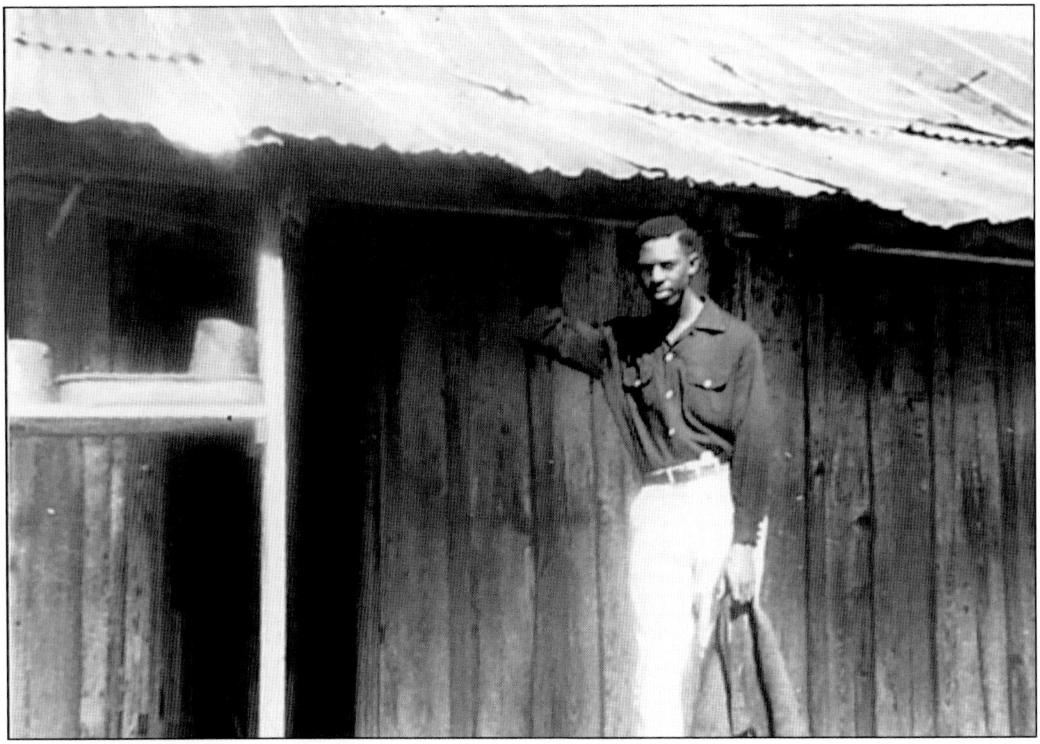

L.V. Lipsey is seen in this 1957 photograph at 20 years old. Notice the old wood house with the tin roof. (Courtesy of L.V. Lipsey.)

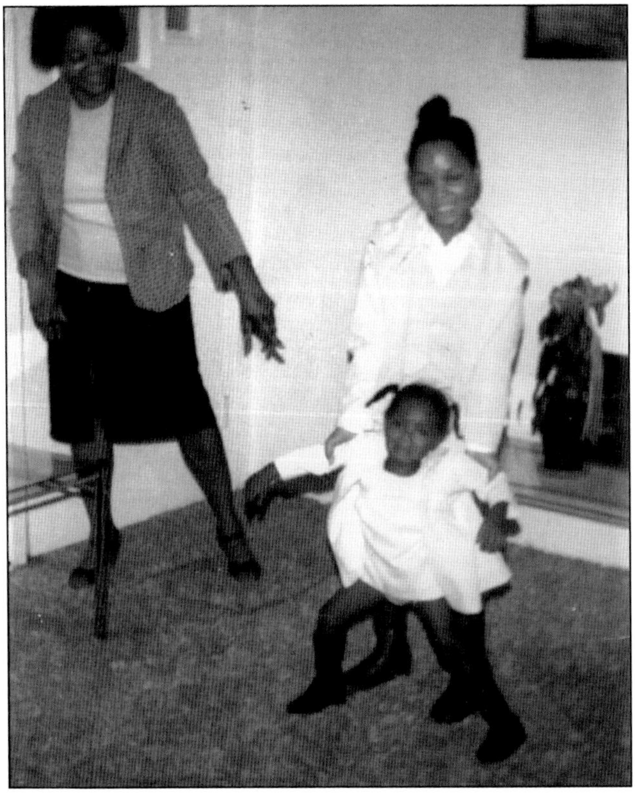

Alice Cheeks is seen in this photograph with her two daughters, Janet and Jennifer Cheeks. Janet is the child smiling and Jennifer is the child frowning. (Courtesy of Alice Cheeks.)

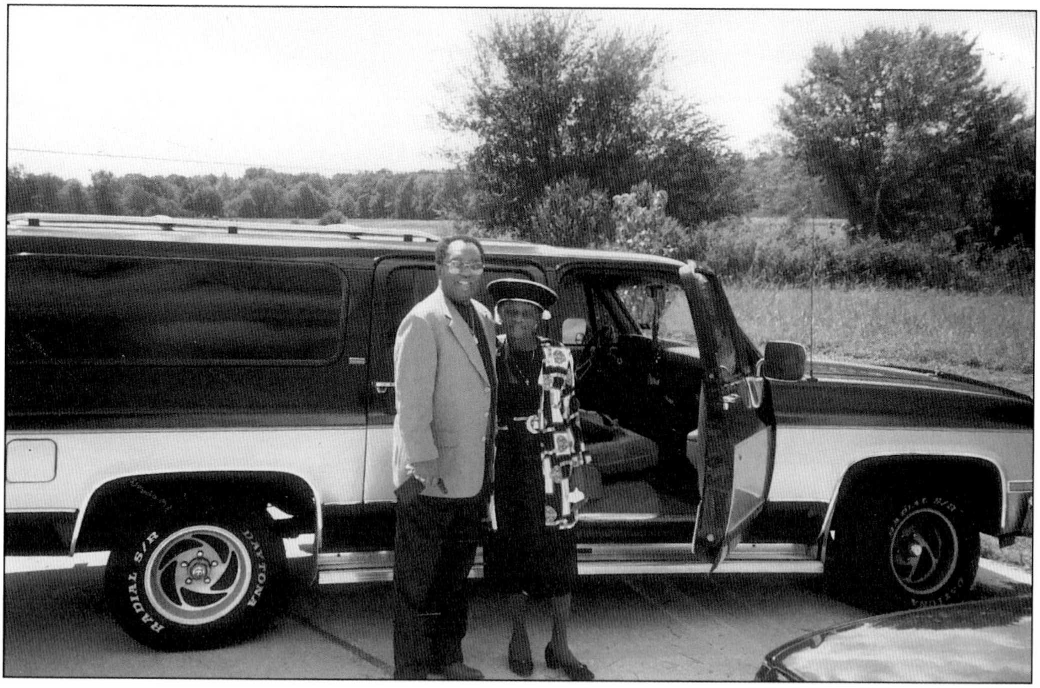

Jacob Hart poses with his mother Rosie Lee Hart at Harvey Chapel Missionary Baptist Church in 2000. Rosie Lee passed away in 2002. (Courtesy of L.V. Lipsey.)

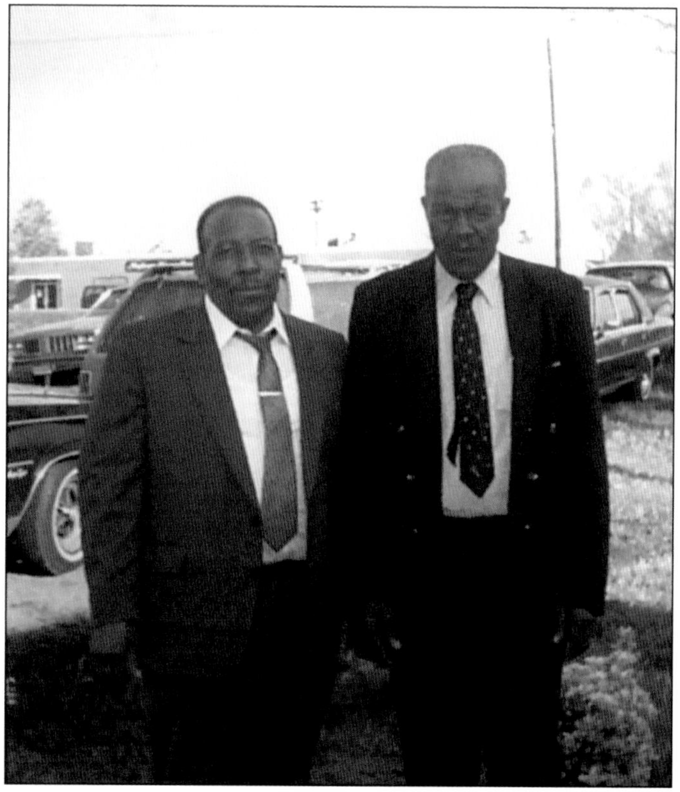

Bilbo Hart and Henry Kelly posed for this 1980s photograph taken at the family home of Mr. Hart. Both gentlemen were born and reared in Madison County. Mr. Kelly is deceased. (Courtesy of Mary L. Hart.)

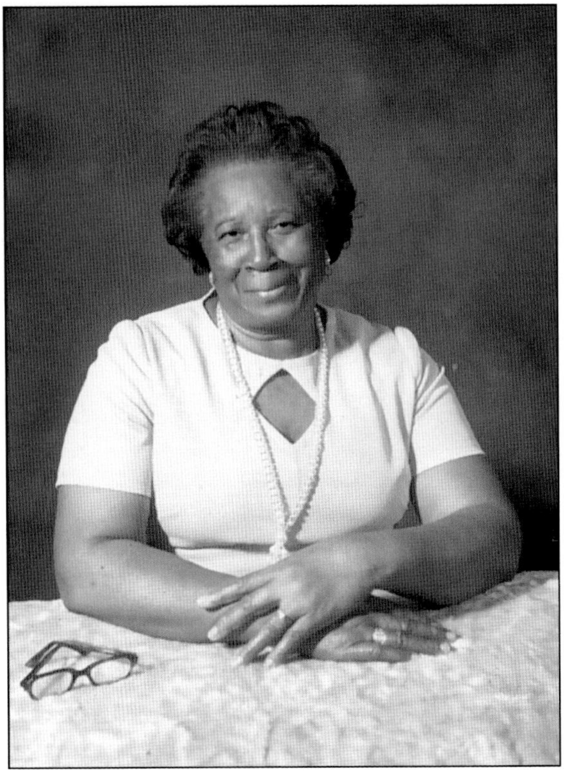

Varie Robinson is seen in this 1975 photograph. A lifelong resident of Madison County, she attended Pleasant Green Missionary Baptist Church. Her daughter Nancy is pictured below. (Courtesy of Umble Hawkins.)

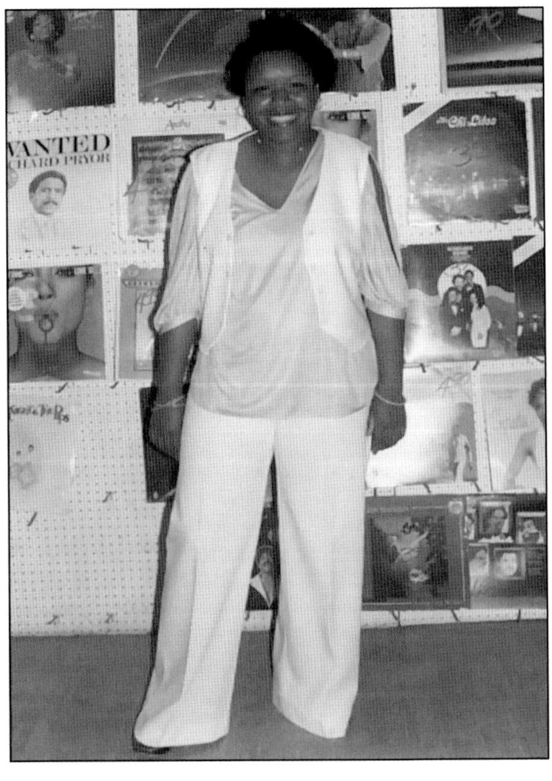

Nancy Caldwell, the daughter of Varie Robinson (pictured above), posed for this 1972 photograph. (Courtesy of Umble Hawkins.)

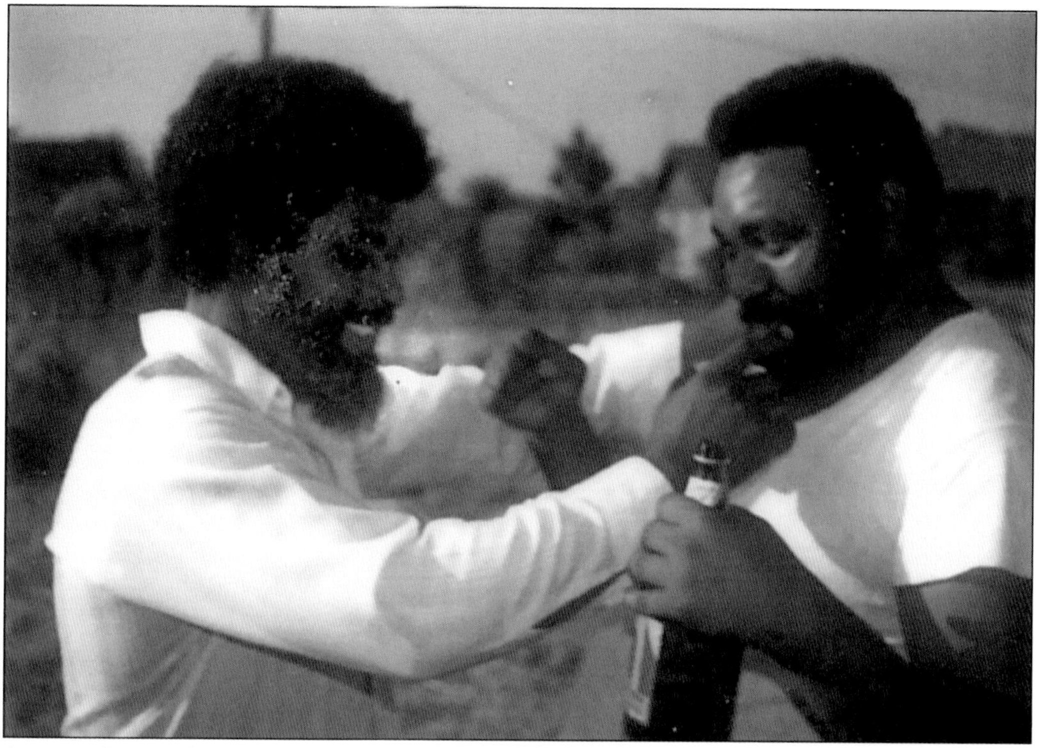

Sam Hawkins and Eugene Garner were caught by the camera in 1975. The two men grew up together in the same community. (Courtesy of Umble Hawkins.)

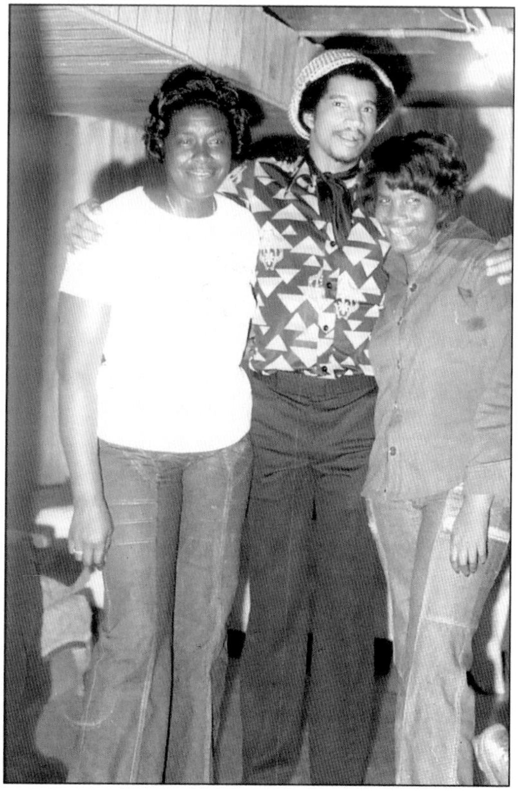

Bettie Cain, her son-in-law Billie Ray Bouldin, and her daughter Betty Jean Bouldin posed for this photo in 1974. (Courtesy of Bettie Cain.)

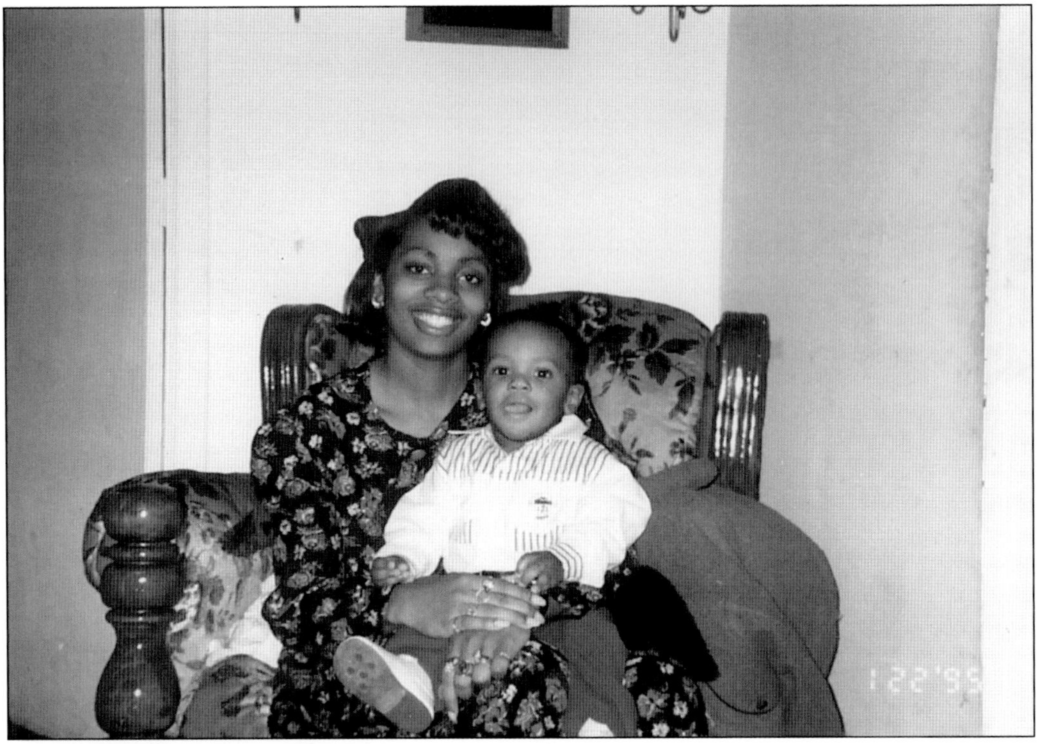

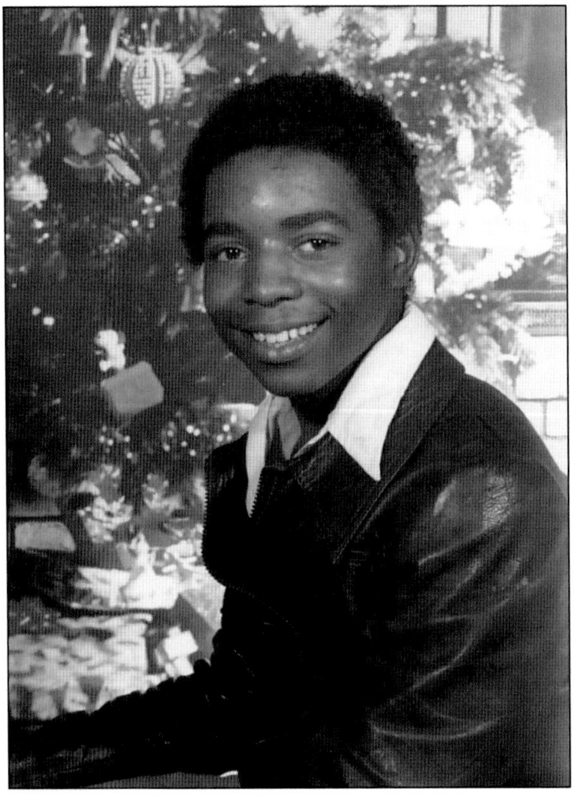

Latonyia Bess and son Kendarius Bess posed for this 1997 photograph. Latonyia was born and reared in Madison County. She was educated in Madison County and attended the Harvey Chapel Missionary Baptist Church. (Courtesy of Thelma Cain.)

Richard Rainy was 14 when this photo was taken. Richard grew up in Madison County and he attended Canton Public Schools. (Courtesy of Tommie Garner.)

Author Hayes and daughter Louise Hayes are seen in this 1963 photo. They are natives of Madison County. Louise was a graduate of the Rogers High School Class of 1959. (Courtesy of Louise Hayes.)

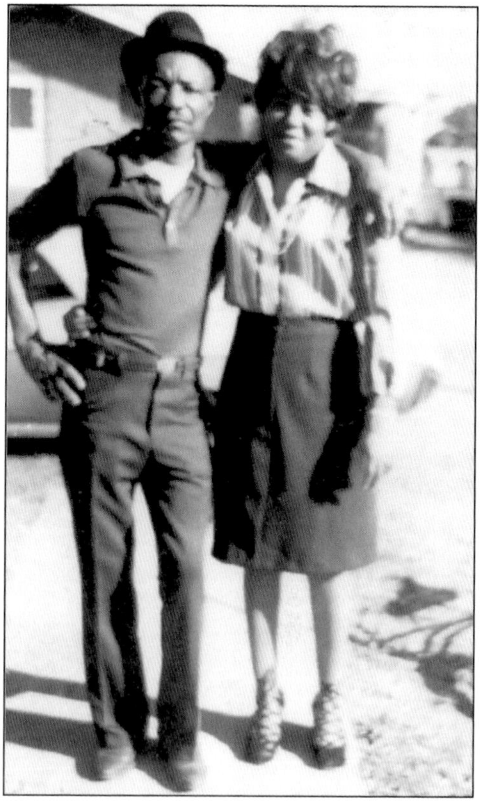

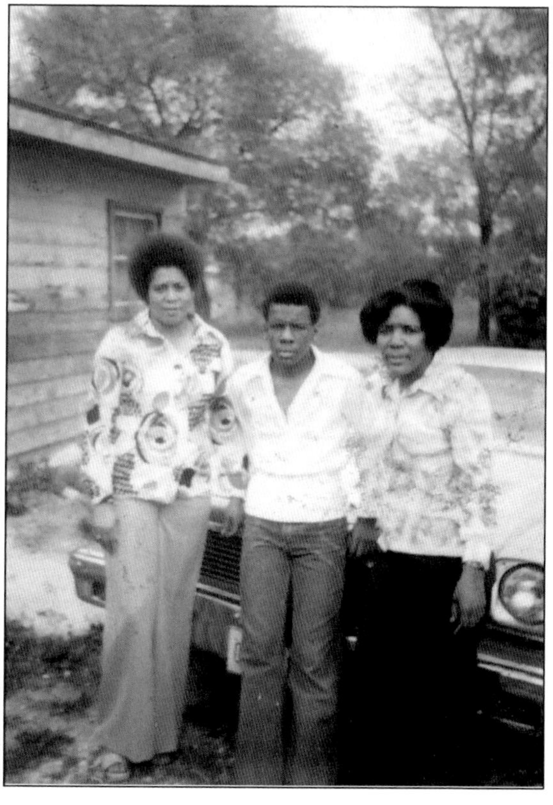

Seen in this 1970 photo are, from left to right, Louise Hayes, Don Waits, and Minnie Watts. (Courtesy of Louise Hayes.)

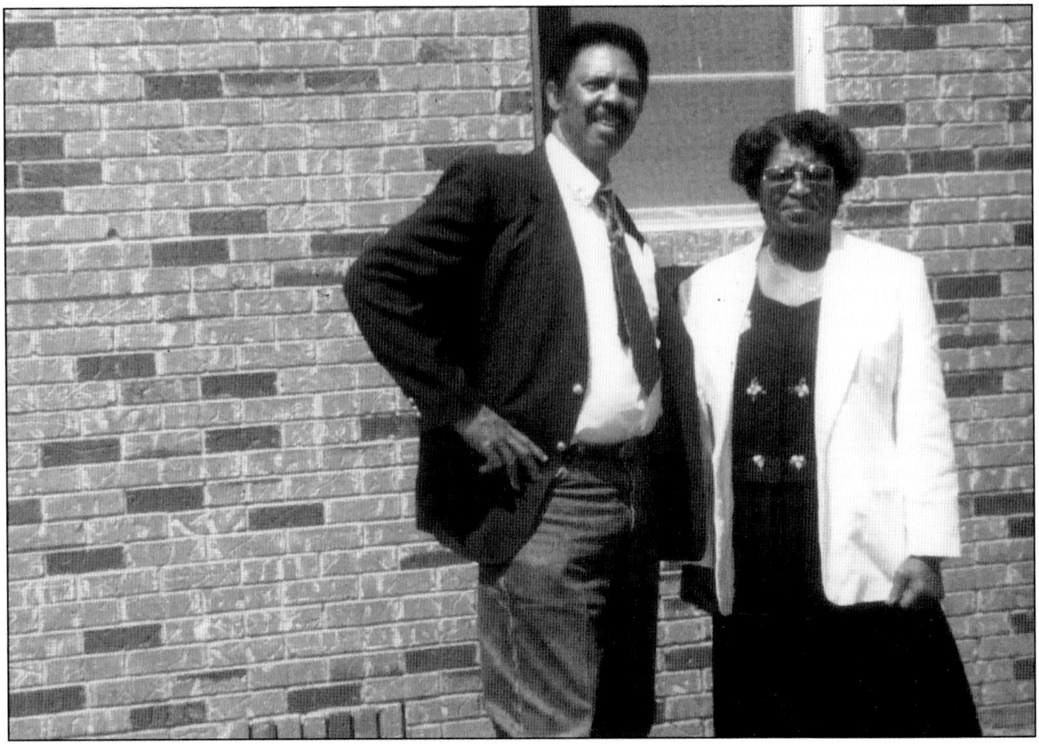

L.V. Lipsey and his wife Mary pose for this 1997 at Harvey Chapel Missionary Baptist Church. Lipsey is a deacon at the Harvey Chapel Missionary Baptist Church. He and his wife are the proud parents of five children; they have been married for 44 years. (Courtesy of L.V. Lipsey.)

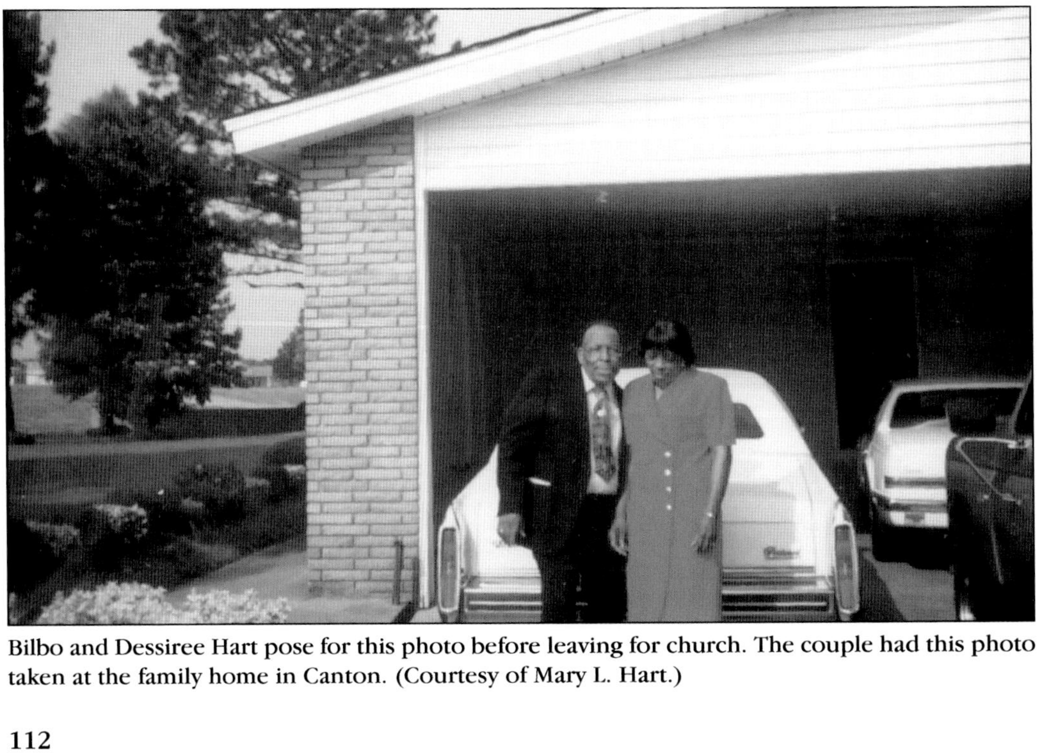

Bilbo and Dessiree Hart pose for this photo before leaving for church. The couple had this photo taken at the family home in Canton. (Courtesy of Mary L. Hart.)

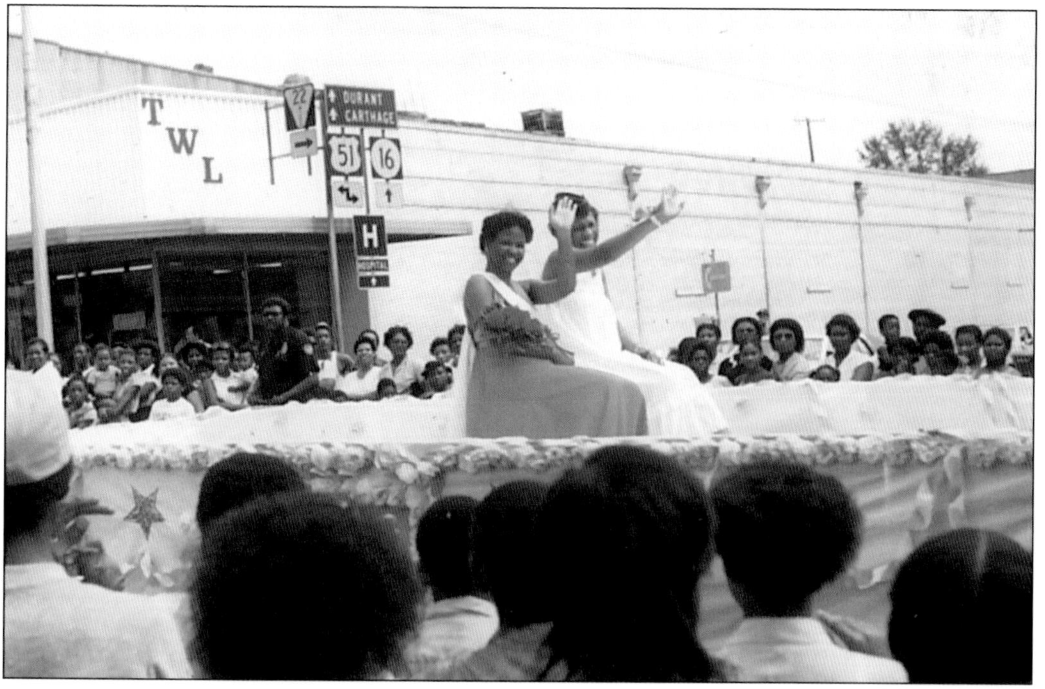

Maxine Sanders is seen on this parade float. She was given the key to the City of Canton in 1982. and was also crowned Miss Jackson State University. (Courtesy of James and Francis Sanders.)

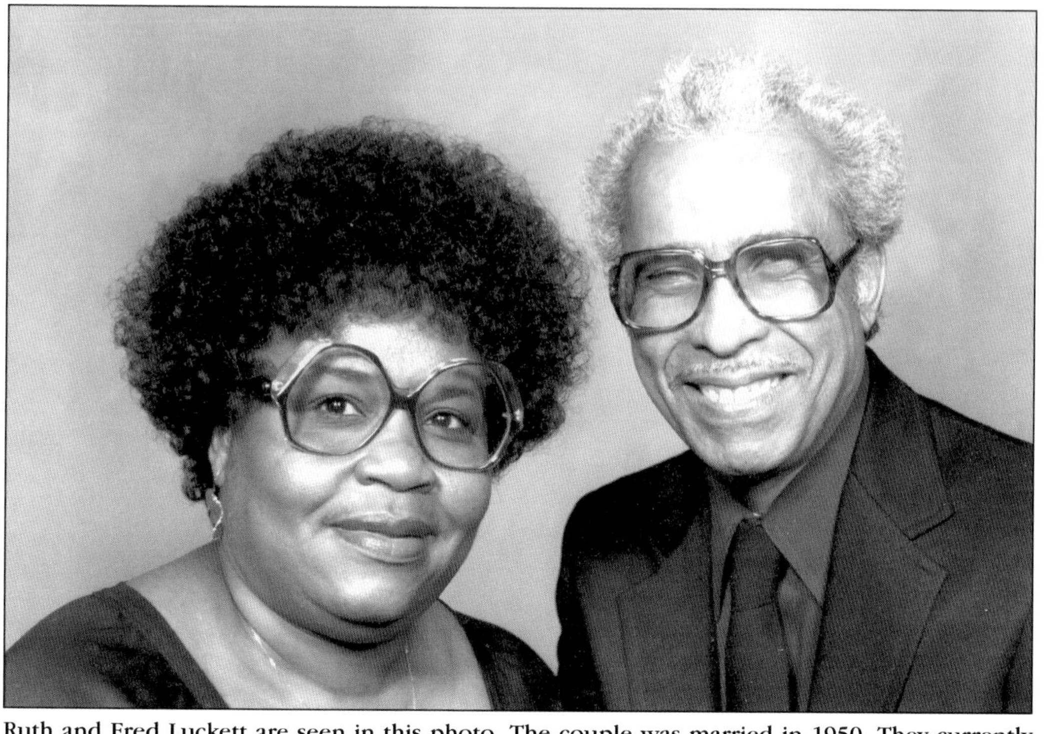

Ruth and Fred Luckett are seen in this photo. The couple was married in 1950. They currently reside in Canton. (Ruth Luckett.)

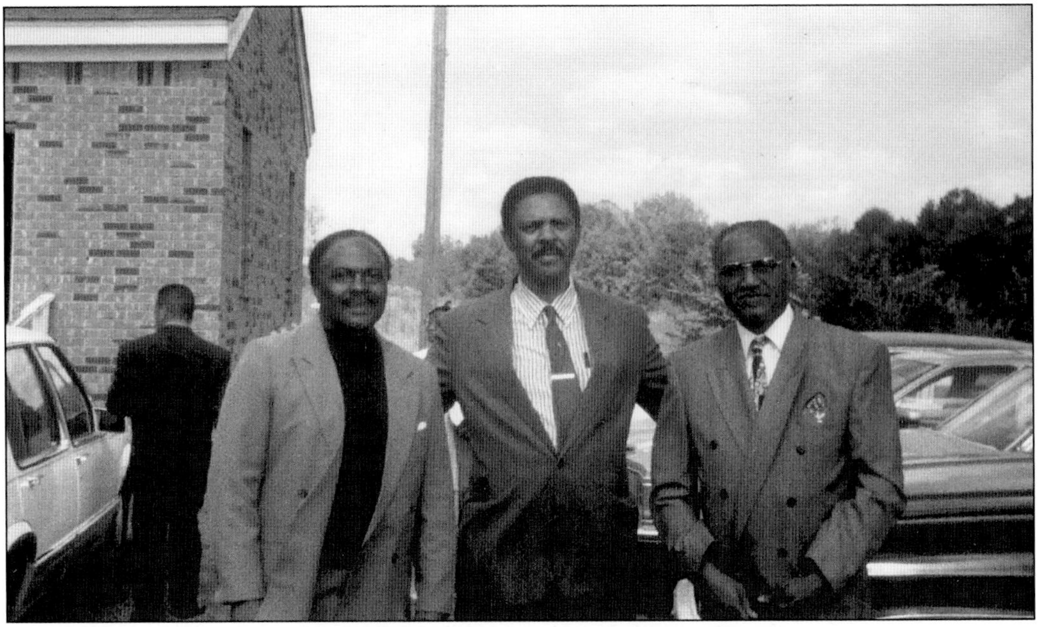

Curtis Cain, L.V. Lipsey, and Leonard Cain are pictured at church. (Courtesy of L.V. Lipsey.)

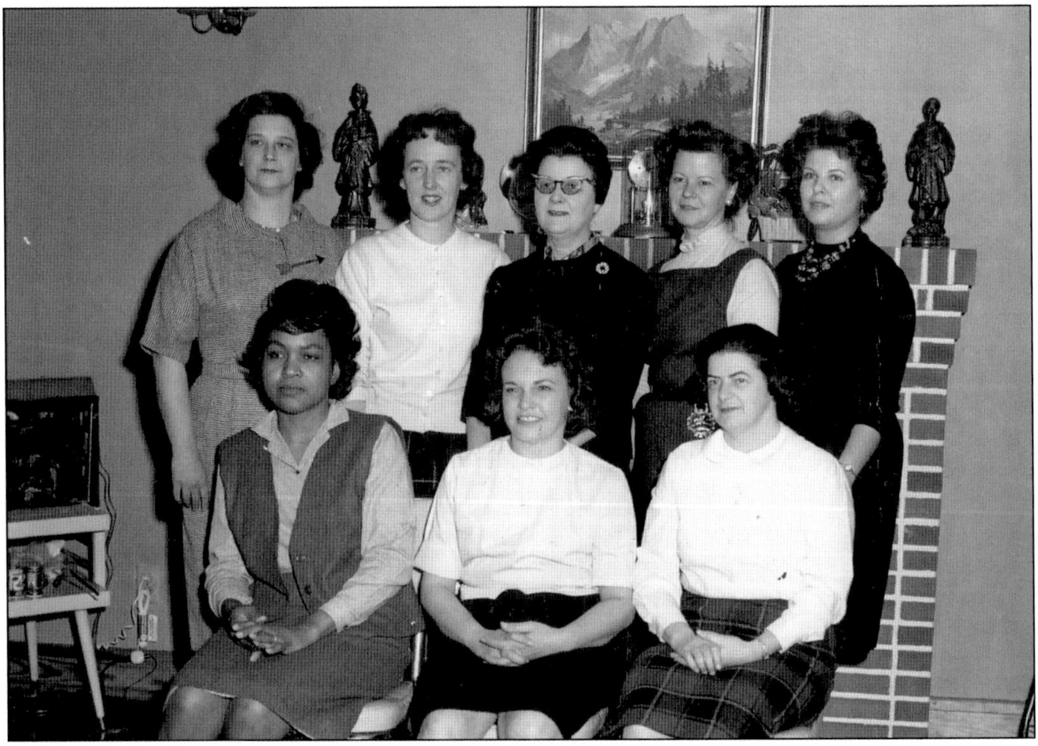

The members of the NCO Wives Club (noncommissioned officers), from left to right, are (front row) Mrs. Landres Cheeks, Mrs. Daniel Oglesby, and Mrs. Joseph R. Delong; (back row) Mrs. Elsie Nelson, Mrs. W.N. Sneed, Mrs. Franklin E. Altman, Mrs. Jerome N. Hughes, and Mrs. Frank D. Tibbitts. (Courtesy of Landres Cheeks.)

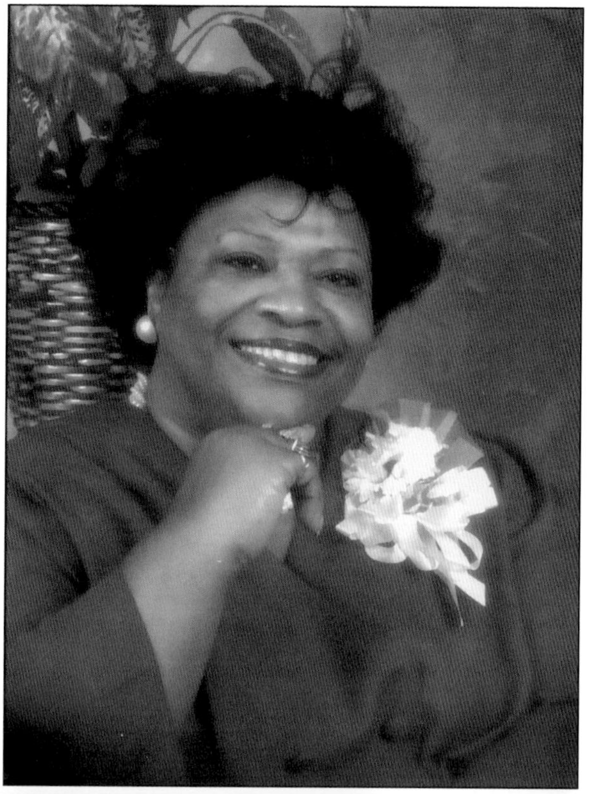

Evangelist Rosie Sutton, mother of three, was called to the ministry in 1992 at Harvey Chapel Missionary Baptist Church. She continues to sing gospel hymns and minister the word of God. (Courtesy of Thelma Cain.)

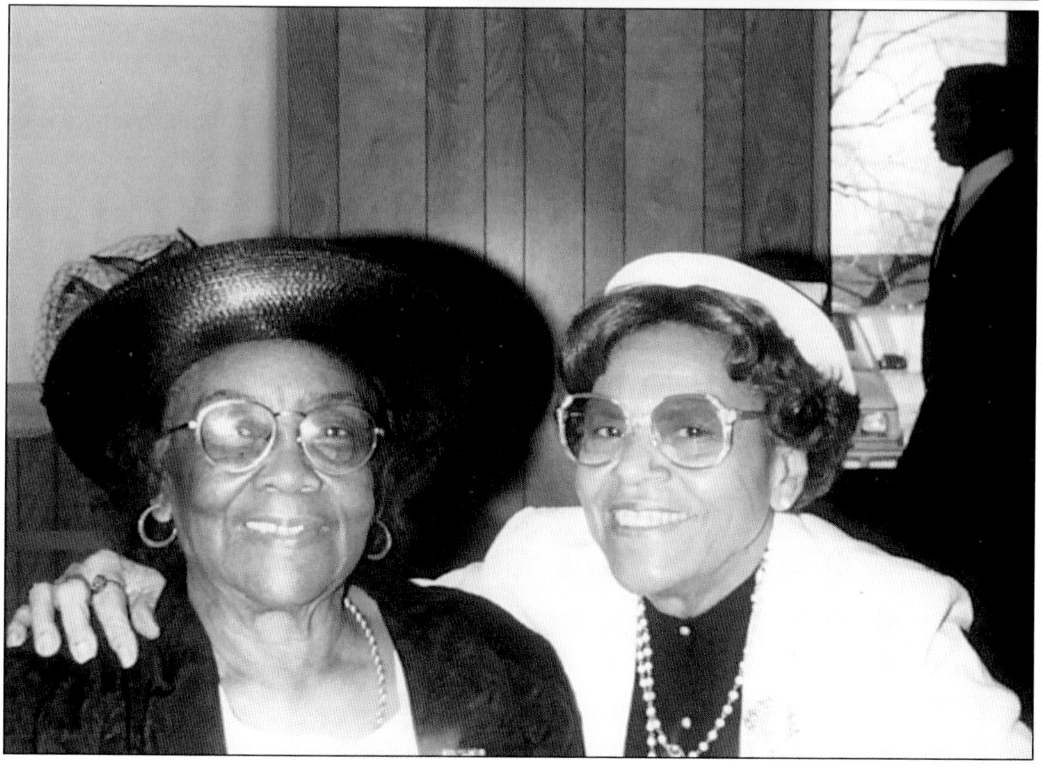

Alice Teen Berry (left) and Thelma Cain are seen in this 1980s photo. Both ladies were lifelong members of the Harvey Chapel Missionary Baptist Church. They served together on the mother's board at church. Alice Teen Berry is deceased and Thelma Cain resides in Canton, Mississippi. (Courtesy of Thelma Cain.)

From left to right are Kimberly Hunter, Doris Hunter (with hat on), Tina Hunter, Bobbie Joe Hunter Jr., and Rev. Bobbie Joe Hunter (sitting). Doris Hunter was a former member of Harvey Chapel and her husband, Rev. Bobbie Joe Hunter, grew up in the Ross Chapel Missionary Baptist Church. Reverend Hunter is the pastor of Greater Mt. Levi Full Gospel Church. (Courtesy of Thelma Cain.)

Mr. and Mrs. Bilbo Hart are shown in this 1960s photograph. The couple was dressed for a night out on the town. Mr. and Mrs. Hart continue to reside in Canton and are active members of the First Stokes Chapel in Madison County. (Courtesy of Mary L. Hart.)

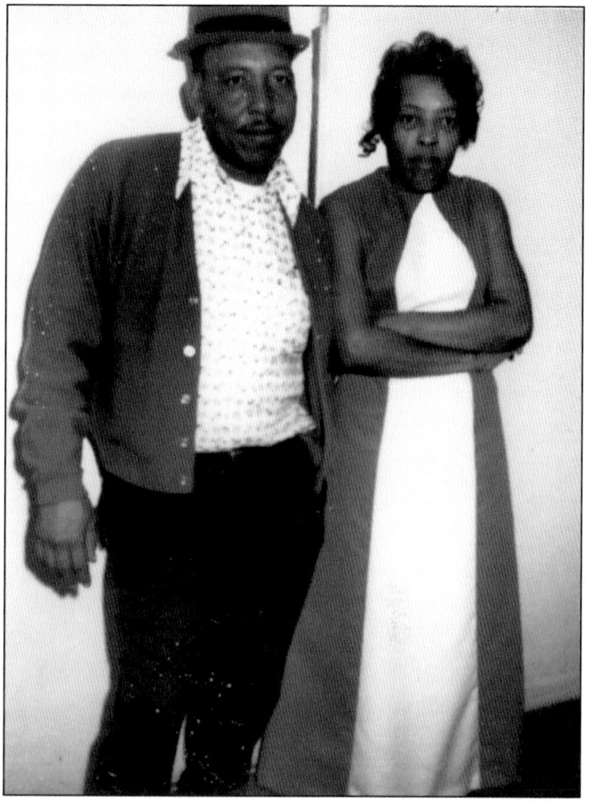

Mary L. Hart and her son, Frederick Hart, pose for this holiday photograph. Both mother and son are currently attending Jackson State University. Frederick is a Senior Airman in the Mississippi National Guard. (Courtesy of Mary L Hart.)

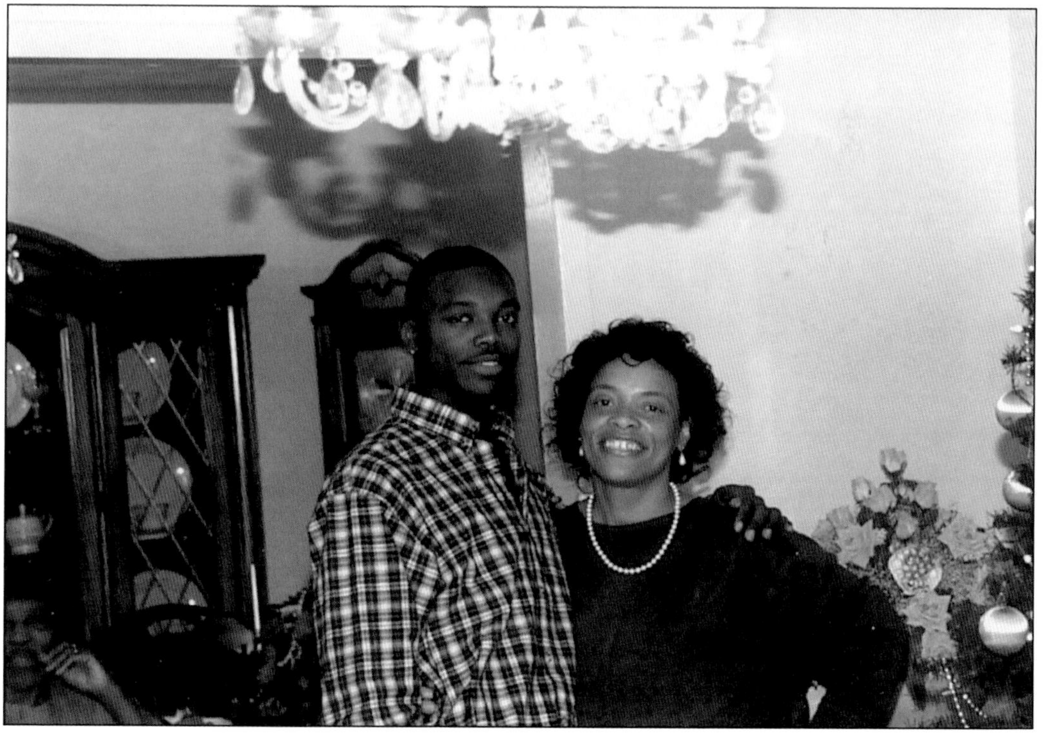

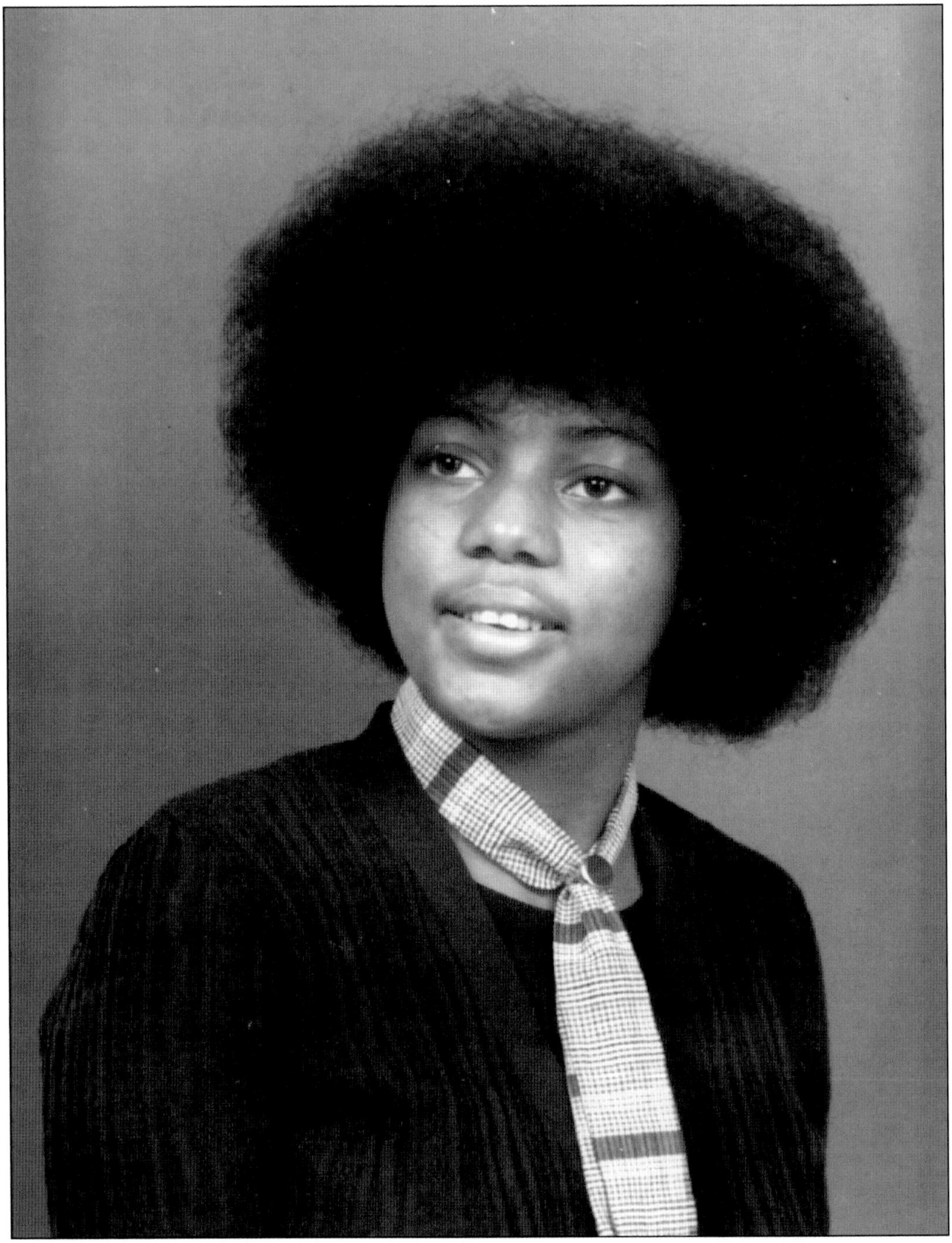

Attorney Eddye LuJean Coney Lane is the third daughter of Clarice Coney and the late Eddie E. Coney. She was educated in the Canton Public School system where she graduated high school at the age of 15. She became the youngest person to enroll at Jackson State University. While at Jackson State University, she was active with the nationally known band. She is currently practicing law in Columbia, South Carolina and is married to Dr. Henderson Michael Lane. They are the parents of Crystal Joy and Henderson Michael Lane. (Courtesy of Clarice Coney.)

Seven

MADISON COUNTY TODAY

"The world is before you and you need not take it or leave it as it was when you came in.."

James Baldwin, 1961

Madison County has experienced such tremendous change in the last 50 years. African Americans today live better than ever—in terms of economics, education, and social status. Cities in Madison County are revitalized and people of color hold prestigious positions within the community. Madison County and its African-American residents are moving in a forward direction in the 21st century. The people in this chapter are to be commended for the example they have set, as well as the gifts and talents they have shared with Madison County.

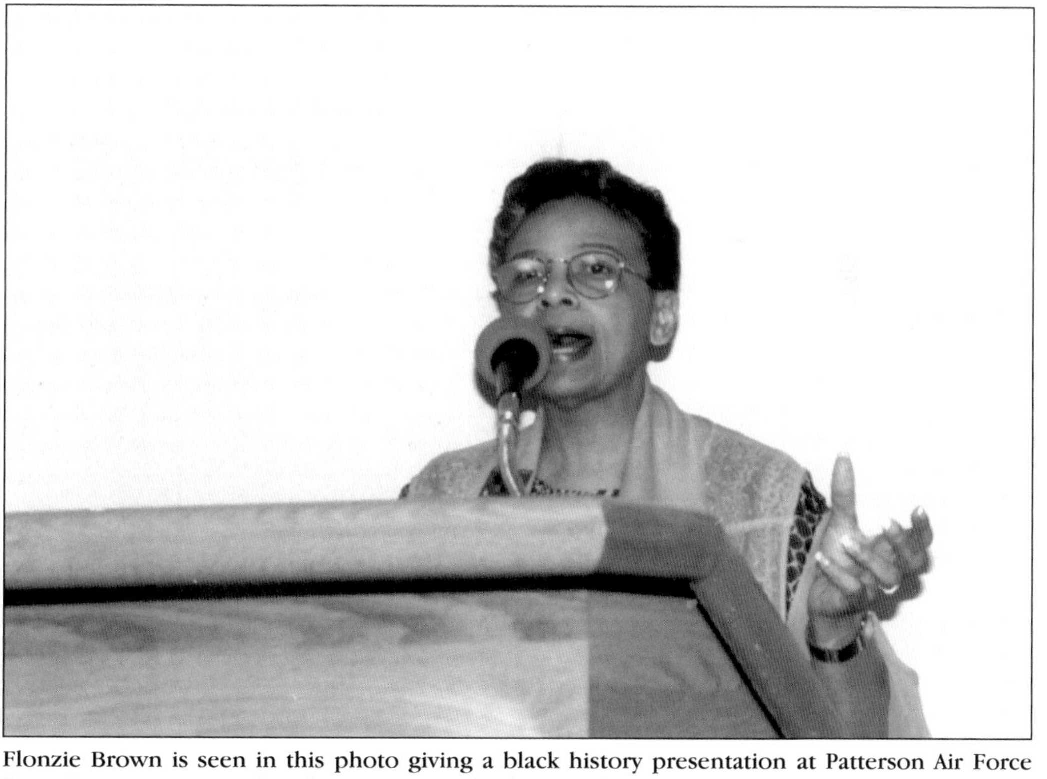

Flonzie Brown is seen in this photo giving a black history presentation at Patterson Air Force Base. Brown was one of Madison County's leading trailblazers for racial equality. She continues to serve Madison County as an example of excellence. She currently resides in Ohio, but she frequently travels to Madison County. (Courtesy of Flonzie Goodloe Brown.)

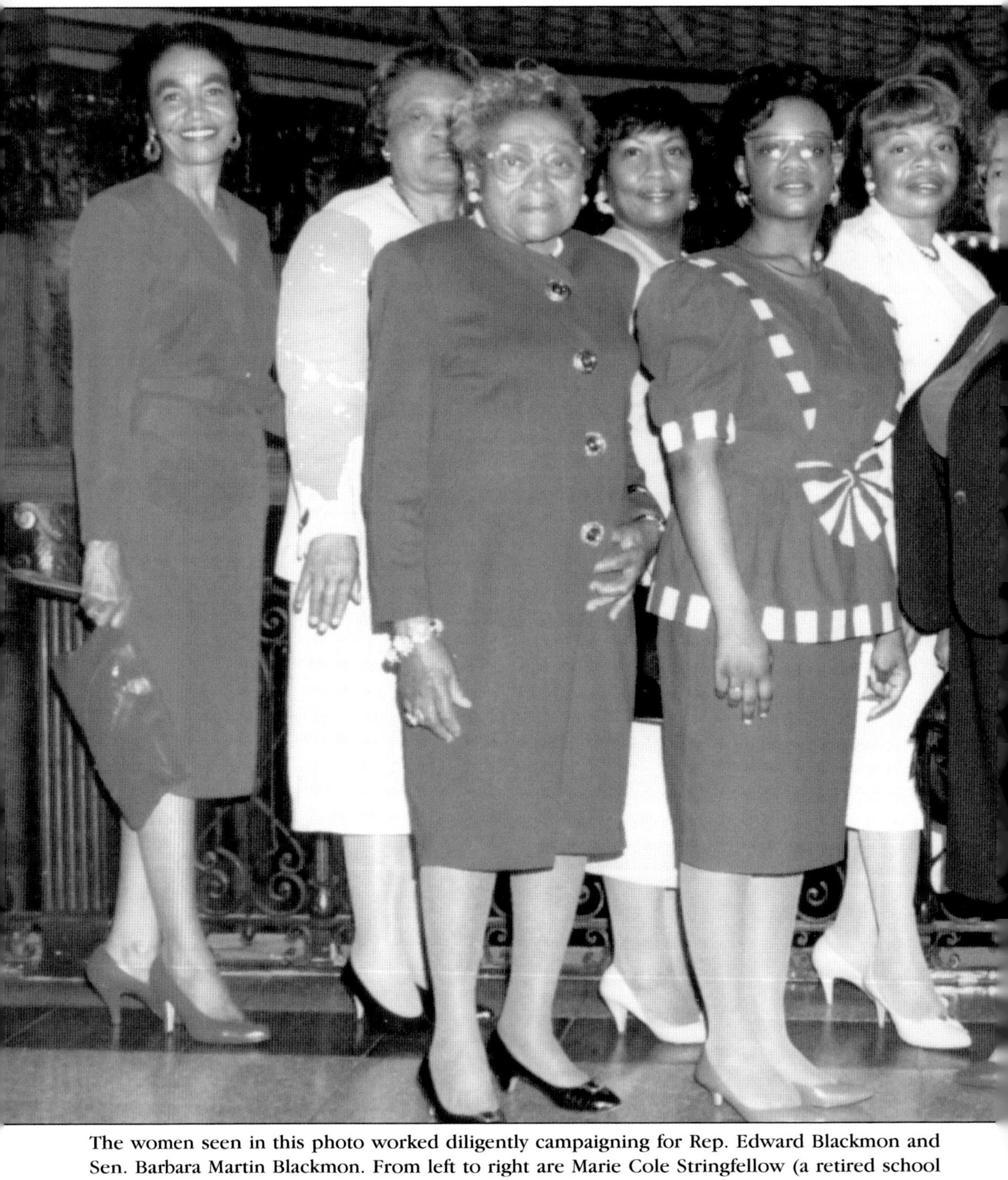

The women seen in this photo worked diligently campaigning for Rep. Edward Blackmon and Sen. Barbara Martin Blackmon. From left to right are Marie Cole Stringfellow (a retired school teacher), Margaret Jones (proprietor), Virgie Bartee (a retired school teacher), Charlie Mae Robinson (a Civil Rights activist and member of the Habitat for Humanity), LaShonda Johnson (MSPH Healthcare Executive), Hurstine Watts (a proprietor and member of the Planning Board Committee for Canton), Bertille Carmichael (the wife of Dr. G.A. Carmichael—Canton's first

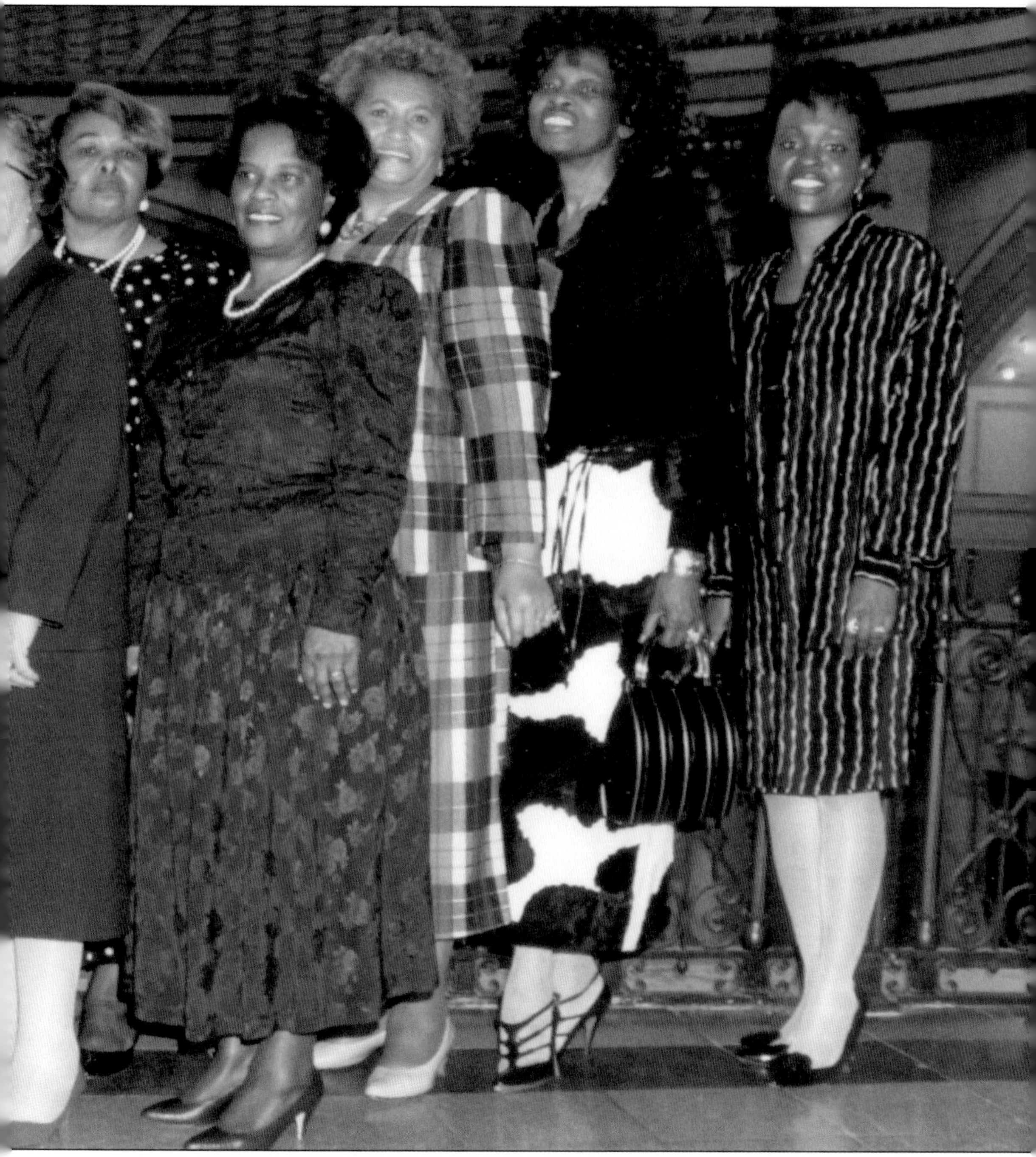

black doctor), Jewel Williams (a Civil Rights activist and Canton's first black female alderman and host of the radio talk show "Canton Cares"), Lena Mae Johnson (a retired school teacher and wife of Rev. Walter L. Johnson), Azzie Lee Jackson (Madison County election commissioner, community leader, and retired educator), Bessie T. Robinson (a retired educator), and Elaine McKenzie Harden (educator and musician). (Courtesy of Marie Stringfellow.)

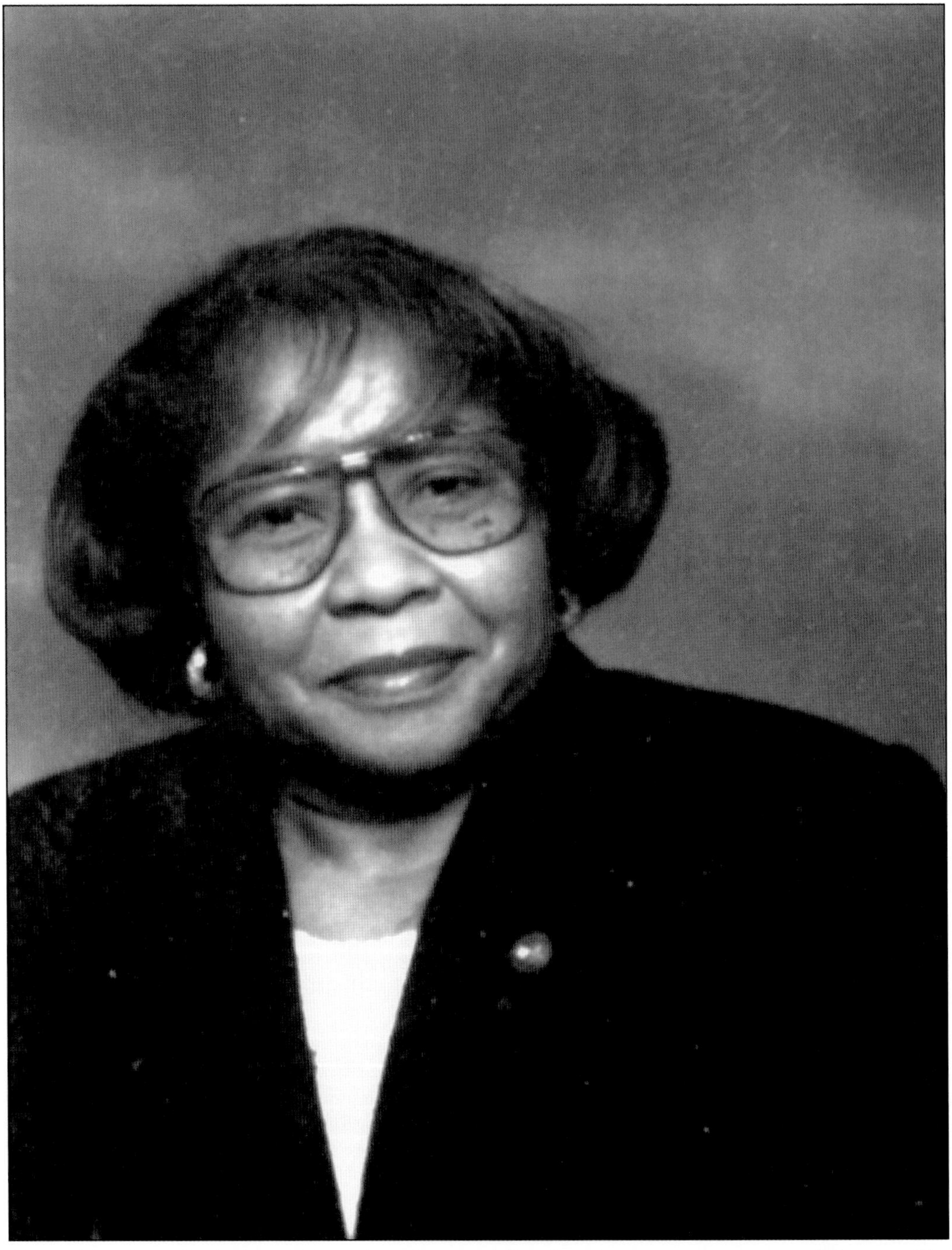

Mayor Alice Scott is the first African American and first female to serve as mayor of Canton. She has served in this capacity since 1994. Mayor Scott had been serving Madison County for many years before her mayoral duties. She was a former Madison County election commissioner, an assistant principal at Nichols Middle School, and a principal at McNeal Elementary School. Her dedication to service is to be commended. She has taken steps to revitalize the city and her door is always open to every citizen of Canton. (Courtesy of Mayor Alice Scott.)

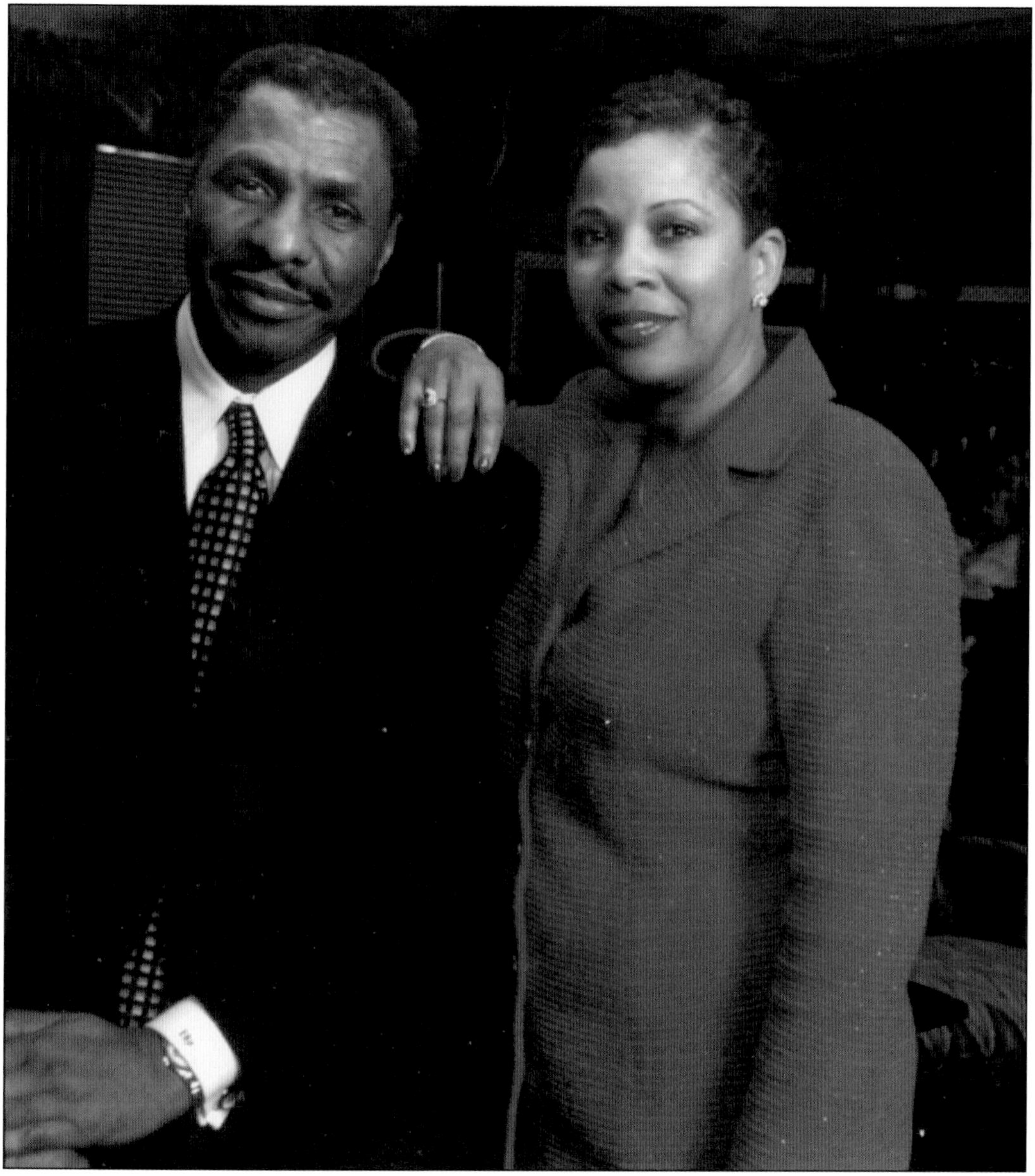

Edward Blackmon Jr. and his wife Barbara Martin Blackmon are pictured in this photo. Edward was a graduate of the Rogers High School class of 1967 and became a successful attorney. In his early years, he was active in the Civil Rights movement. Many changes can be contributed to his efforts and hard work at his law firm, Blackmon and Blackmon, which he established in 1989 with wife Barbara. An expert trial lawyer, he has obtained, on the behalf of clients, multimillion-dollar jury verdicts and settlements against some well-known and leading companies. He is a member of the Mississippi House of Representatives and is currently serving in his ninth year as chairman of the Judiciary B Committee. Barbara Martin Blackmon is a native of Hinds County and the managing partner at the firm of Blackmon and Blackmon. Mrs. Blackmon is an excellent tax attorney and has worked for leading companies. She has been a member of the Senate since 1992, where she represents District 21 (Humphreys, Madison, and Yazoo Counties). (Courtesy of Edward and Barbara Blackmon.)

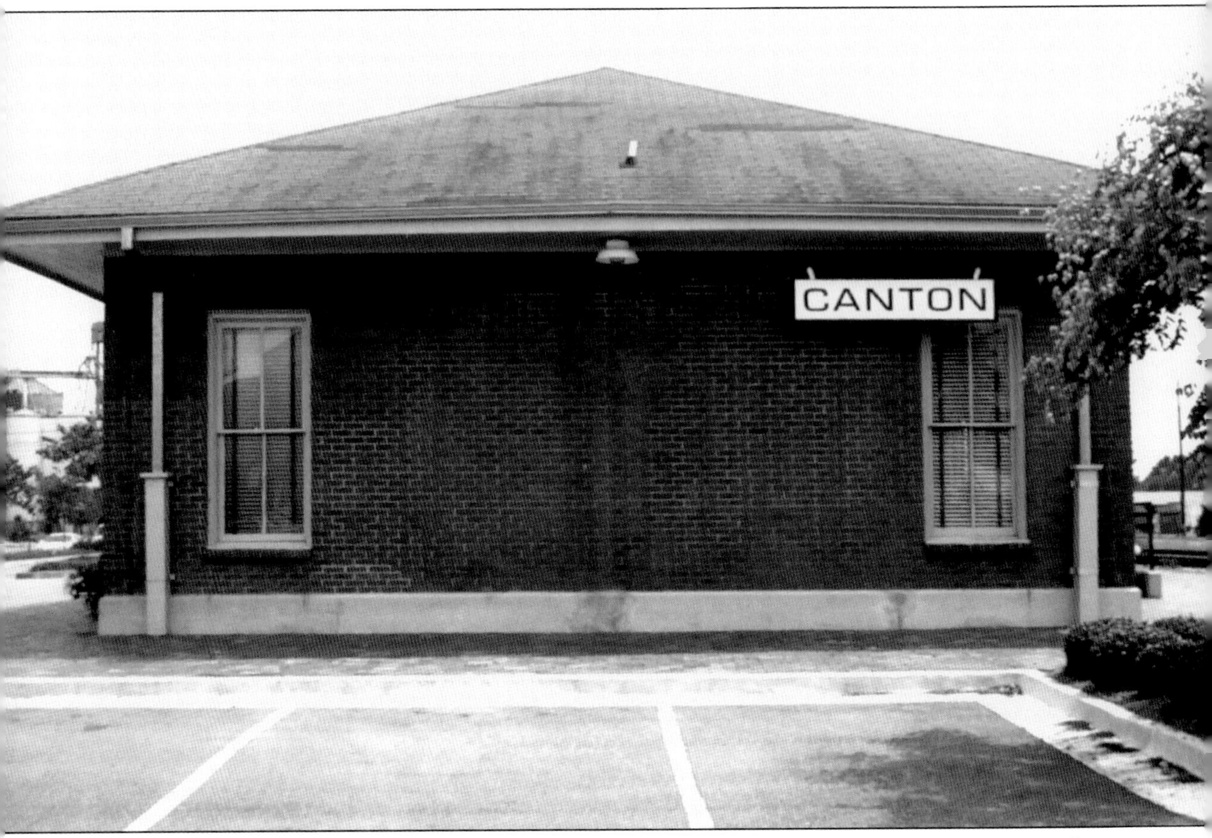

Pictured here is the city of Canton old train depot. The *Panama Limited* and the *City of New Orleans* were passenger trains that made daily stops at this depot. (Courtesy of the Author.)

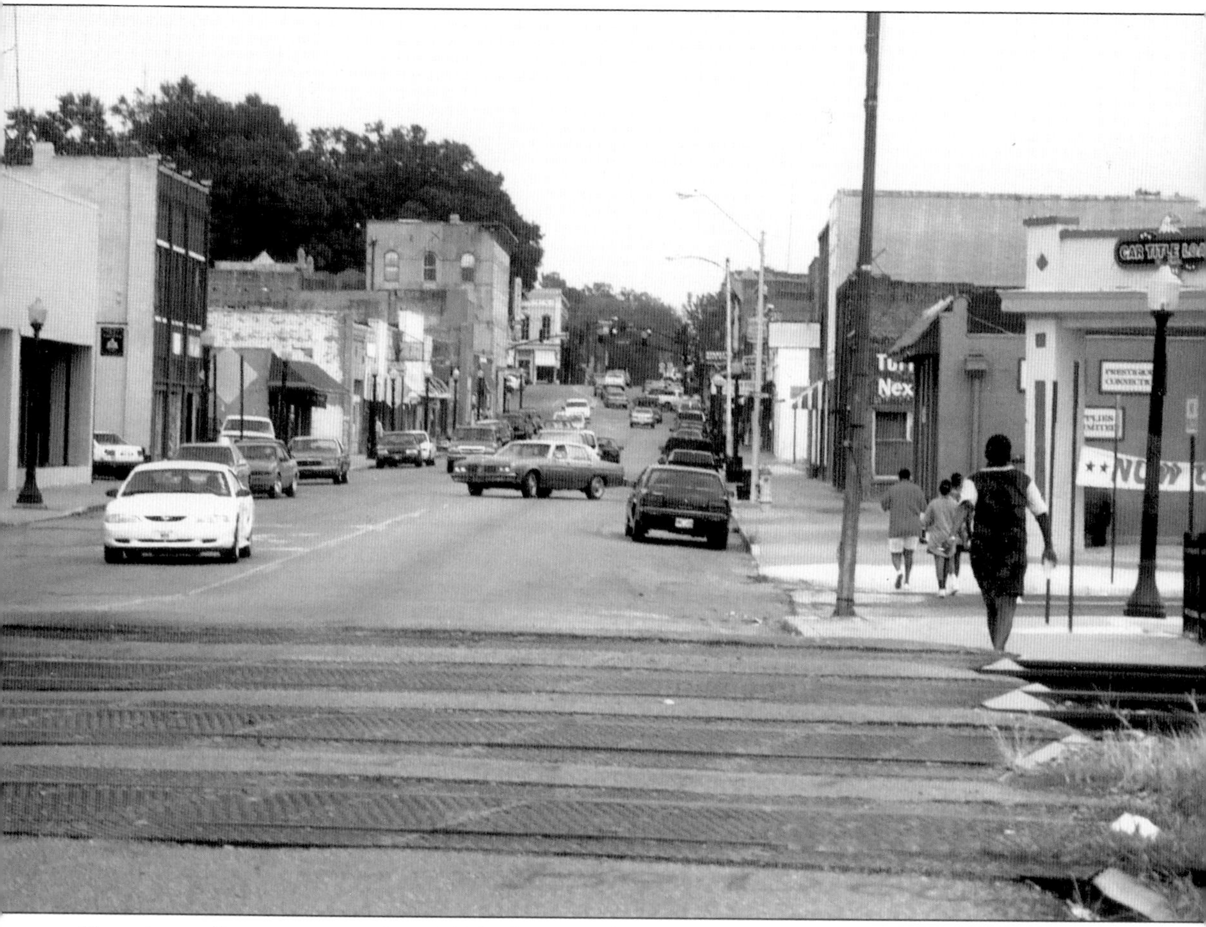

Downtown Canton is seen in a 1999 photograph. With a population of approximately 13,000 residents, Canton is located north of the state capital, Jackson, and is the county seat of Madison County. Nationally known for its bi-annual arts and crafts flea markets, Canton has recently become a popular site for major motion pictures (Courtesy of L.V. Lipsey.)

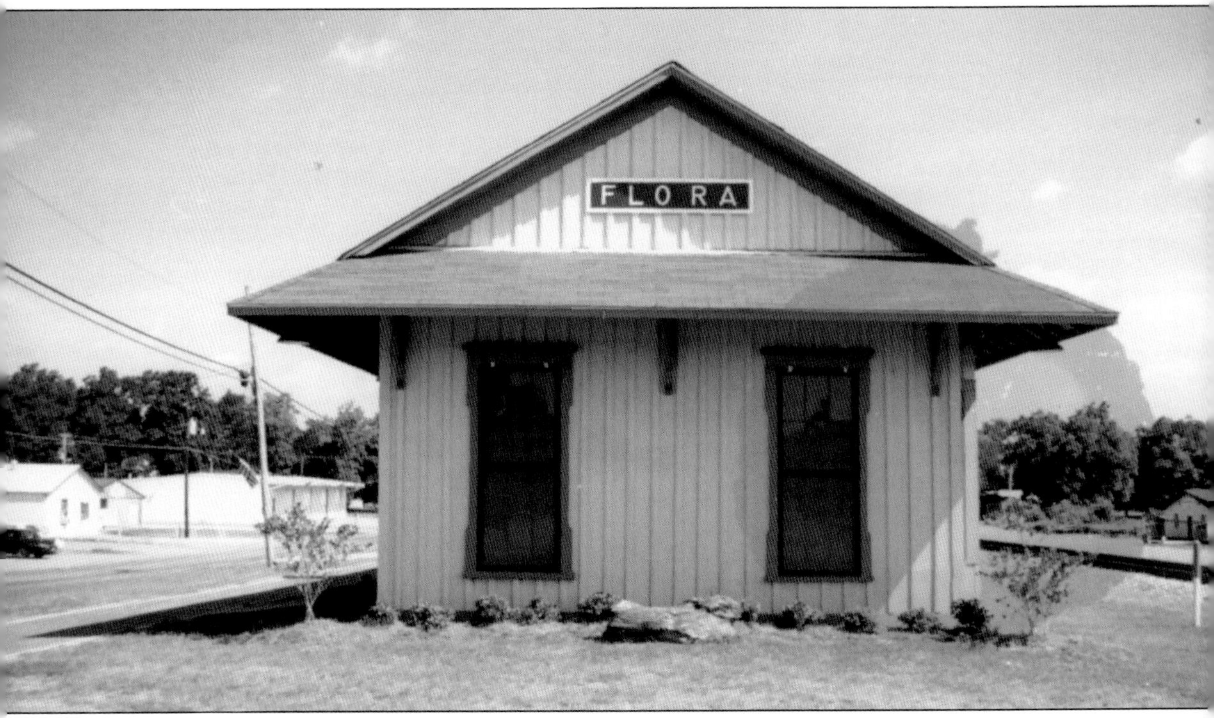

The city of Flora old train depot was home to the Illinois Central Railroad System. Both passenger and freight trains made stops here. (Courtesy of the Author.)

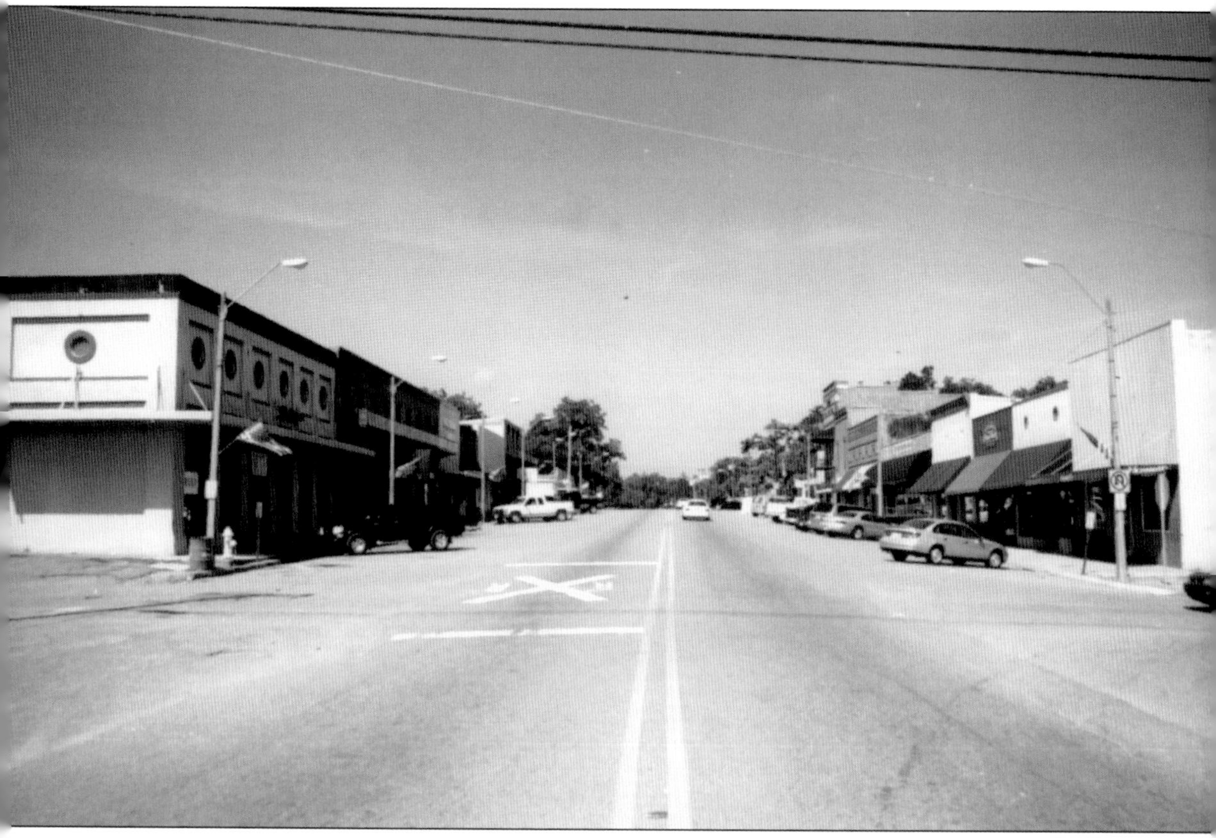

Downtown Flora is seen in this photo. Located 17 miles southwest of Canton, Flora was founded in 1882 and was named after Flora Banks Mann, the daughter of Daniel Mann. (Courtesy of the Author.)

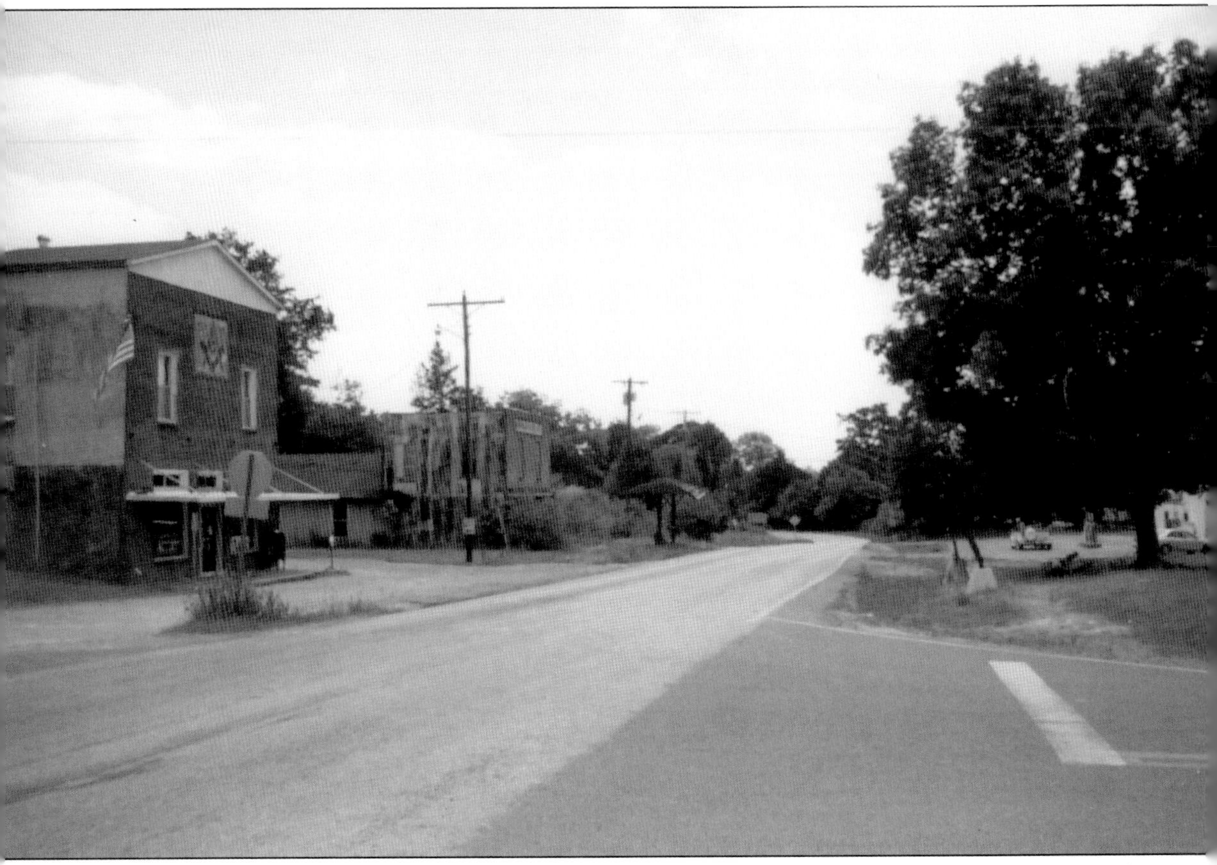

Located northeast of Canton, Camden was once a thriving town but the population decreased significantly in the mid-1900s as many people moved to larger cities in search of housing and employment. (Courtesy of the Author.)